MODERN SOUTH
ASIAN LITERATURE
IN ENGLISH

MODERN SOUTH ASIAN LITERATURE IN ENGLISH

Paul Brians

Literature as Windows to World Cultures

GREENWOOD PRESS
Westport, Connecticut • London

Library of Congress Cataloging-in-Publication Data

Brians, Paul.
    Modern South Asian Literature in English / by Paul Brians.
       p. cm. — (Literature as windows to world cultures)
    Includes bibliographical references and index.
    ISBN 0–313–32011–X (alk. paper)
    1. Indic literature (English)—History and criticism. 2. Indic literature
  (English)—South Asian Authors—History and criticism. I. Title II. Series.
    PR9484.6.B75   2003
    820.9'954—dc21   2003052842

British Library Cataloguing in Publication Data is available.

Library of Congress Catalog Card Number: 2003052842
ISBN: 0–313–32011–X
ISSN: 1543–9968

First published in 2003

Greenwood Press, 88 Post Road West, Westport, CT 06881
An imprint of Greenwood Publishing Group, Inc.
www.greenwood.com

Printed in the United States of America

The paper used in this book complies with the
Permanent Paper Standard issued by the National
Information Standards Organization (Z39.48–1984).

10 9 8 7 6 5 4 3 2 1

Contents

Acknowledgments

I owe a profound debt to the dozens of members of the SASIALIT Internet discussion list, more than it would be possible to name here, who generously answered queries. I am especially grateful for extraordinary assistance received from Sue Darlow, Uma Parameswaran, and Balaji Venkateswaran. Bapsi Sidhwa kindly provided definitions of various Parsi terms. Local readers whose advice I value include Azfar Hussain, Shila Baksi, and especially Fritz Blackwell, who worked on more parts of this study than anyone else. Finally, special thanks to my first reader, adviser, and editor: my wife, Paula Elliot.

MODERN SOUTH ASIAN LITERATURE IN ENGLISH

Introduction

South Asian culture has become highly popular around the world. Films like *Monsoon Wedding* and *Lagaan* have reached large audiences. The world of Indian popular films is the subject of a London musical called *Bombay Dreams,* and young women from New York to Los Angeles are having their hands decorated with intricate traditional henna designs. South Asia is now chic in the West in the way that Japan was a decade ago.

But preceding and expanding beyond these pop-culture influences is a profound and ever-growing international appetite for fiction by South Asian authors. Names like Rushdie, Mukherjee, and Roy are familiar to anyone with a passing interest in contemporary writing, appearing frequently as they do on bestseller lists and winning prestigious awards. This volume will assist readers who want to begin to explore the rich, varied, and fascinating worlds of modern South Asian fiction.

"South Asia" is a term that includes several nations, but for the purposes of this volume, it refers specifically to Pakistan, Sri Lanka, and India. These are the countries that have produced the internationally famed works under discussion. The great majority of the authors discussed here are Indian in origin.

Several different criteria were used to select the authors and works discussed. First, the coverage of this book was confined to authors who were at least born and raised in South Asia, excluding writers of South Asian descent born in Great Britain like Hanif Kureishi (responsible for several outstanding film scripts and novels) and Hari Kunzru (author of the wildly entertaining historical satire *The Impressionist*). All the books discussed in detail are set at least partly in South Asia, excluding works depicting only immigrant life, which fall more properly into the category of Asian American or Asian British literature. For a detailed survey of modern literature in other languages from India, see Nalini Natarajan, ed., *Handbook of Twentieth-Century Literatures of India* (Westport, CT: Greenwood Press, 1996).

The authors discussed also became internationally famous writing in English (an exception was made for Tagore, who—although he wrote primarily in Bengali—was the first South Asian author to become well known abroad for writing in English). This is to some degree a paradox, for—to give just one example—perhaps 3 percent of India's population can read English with enough fluency to enjoy these works in their original form, and relatively few of these books are translated into the national languages of India. They are more likely to be translated into German, French, or Spanish. The result is that such writing has a much larger audience abroad than at home.

Although many South Asians are proud of the international prominence of writers from their region, many also are resentful that talented authors writing in Hindi, Urdu, Bengali, Malayalam, Sinhala, and the other languages of the region remain mostly untranslated and unknown abroad. It is as if North American fiction were known around the world only through the works of French-speaking Canadians. South Asian critics often accuse English-language authors of "pandering to the West" by depicting typically exotic settings and stories or by providing excessive explanations of commonplace terms through footnotes, glossaries, and so on.

Discussions of the role of English in South Asia are endless and often heated. When the English brought their language to India and Sri Lanka, it was used as a tool to make the population easier to govern. English-language literature was taught in Indian schools before it was taught in British ones, to inculcate respect for the imperial power. People who speak primarily English in South Asia have often been criticized as rootless, inauthentic, and generally unfit to represent their cultures. But there is no consensus on what the national language of India should be. Hindi is the most widely used language in India, but not by people living in the South. The hostility between Sinhala speakers and Tamil speakers in Sri Lanka has been reinforced by decades of civil war. English has the great advantage of being politically neutral. The English occupiers are long gone, but their language remains a handy tool for writers who want to address a wide and varied audience within South Asia, even if that audience may not be very large. English functions in modern India like Latin in the European Renaissance, as a second language shared by enough people to make it a good vehicle of communication among various groups who share a certain level of linguistic skill.

It is often claimed that writers creating fiction in English are simply cashing in on a Western appetite for exotica, and perhaps the charge has an element of truth. But writers have always been stimulated by an eager audience.

When readers in the 1960s developed an appetite worldwide for Latin American fiction, many fine authors emerged to supply the demand. Commerce can create the desire to write a bestseller, but it cannot in itself create good books. The fact is that South Asia has produced an impressive crop of very talented authors who benefit by having an eager international audience for their work. In the long run, their books sell not just because readers abroad are interested in South Asia; those readers often became interested in South Asia in the first place because they liked the books its authors produced.

Of course South Asia has a lengthy history of great literary achievement stretching back millennia. Indians were writing masterpieces when most Europeans still lacked a written language. But modern fictional forms like the short story and novel came to South Asia through the British, during the colonial era; for that reason they are often seen as the products of an international culture rather than a national one.

The writers covered here have certain traits in common that make them unrepresentative of the populations they have sprung from besides speaking and writing fluently the foreign language of English. They tend to be well educated and from middle-class or well-to-do backgrounds in a region where huge populations are poor. They are urban, whereas most people still live in rural villages, and the majority make their homes abroad, in Canada, Britain, or the United States. And writers everywhere tend to be quite unlike ordinary people in their interests and talents. Getting to know their works is not the same as getting to know their cultures.

It is undeniable that one of the great appeals of South Asian English-language fiction is the access it gives Western readers to very different worlds from their own. But the views through the windows these works provide are not comprehensive. Fiction tends to concentrate on a handful of topics: family life, love, marriage, death, and war, in particular. Readers seeking information about Indian trade policies, environmental controversies, the green revolution in agriculture, or the burgeoning Indian computer programming industry have to look elsewhere. Although they cannot compete with nonfictional sources for factual information, novels and short stories are a wonderful way to begin an acquaintance with a country.

In fact, the essence of fiction is arguably that it is nonfactual. Even novels aiming at semidocumentary realism reshape the elements their authors draw from their lives and experience. The best fiction is not necessarily written by the writer who knows the material best, but by the one who can best shape it into a satisfying form. Some South Asian readers found John Irving's *Bombay in Son of the Circus*—based on his short visit to the city—more convincing than the pictures of Bombay painted by certain other writers who had been born and raised there. And the fantastic elements in writers like Rushdie and Suri cannot be judged by their accuracy. It is a mistake to expect documentary accuracy from novels and short stories. Fiction exists to reshape human experiences and feelings, to tell satisfying or disturbing stories, to amuse, excite, intrigue, challenge, and move the reader. In fact, what fiction does exceptionally well is to create an emotional connection between the reader and its subject. Fiction may not tell us the whole truth about people, but it may make us care about them.

The worlds visible through these fictional windows are wildly varied. Rohinton Mistry and Bapsi Sidhwa portray the tiny Parsi community, Khushwant Singh depicts Sikhs, and others concentrate on the dominant Muslim, Hindu, and (in Sri Lanka) Buddhist cultures. We meet street urchins, gangsters, prostitutes, peasants, small merchants, wealthy industrialists, and saints. Writers create satire, humor, tragedy, social criticism, and romance. Some write in experimental styles that require careful decoding; others are happy to lay out their tales in a traditional fashion that keeps the casual reader interested. Both men and women write movingly of the lives of South Asia's women and girls. Many write about the world of their childhood, others try to depict contemporary reality, and an increasing number are writing historical novels ranging back a century and more. It would be absurd to refer to "the South Asian reality." There is no such thing. South Asian literature is a colorful kaleidoscope of fragmented views, colored by the perceptions of its authors, reflecting myriad realities—and fantasies. One of the most inviting ways to overcome the biases in any particular work is to read more, and a growing audience seems eager to do just that.

The works selected here were chosen according to several other criteria. First, they were already well known. These are writers that people want to know more about. Interested readers can explore any number of anthologies of the stories of lesser-known South Asian writers, but the purpose of this book is a pragmatic one: to help readers with books they are likely to encounter on the bestseller lists, in the classroom, and in book groups.

Second, although the works date from as far back as 1915, this book concentrates on the recent blossoming of fiction in the past two decades. The books are presented here in chronological order. The works discussed had to be of a quality that make them worthy of close attention. A balance was sought between works with historical and modern settings, among stories set in various regions, and among works using various literary techniques. Six of the fifteen authors are women, but they were not included simply to represent women's writing. It so happens that a large number of the most talented and popular writers of South Asian fiction are female.

Each chapter begins with a brief biography of the author under discussion, emphasizing aspects of their lives that are relevant to understanding their fiction. Some argue that fiction should be read in ignorance of its creator's life, and it is quite true that any novel that cannot be appreciated on its own is a failure. But books exist in a social context, an important part of which is autobiographical. So long as the reader is careful not to view the author's life as providing an explanation for the fiction, a more sophisticated understanding of a literary career can emerge from taking biographical facts into account.

Next I provide an overview of the major works of the author under discussion. The bulk of each chapter is devoted to one work, selected because it is representative of the author's output and approachable by a beginning reader of such fiction. For this reason of accessibility, I concentrate on collections of short stories by Salman Rushdie and Anita Desai rather than their more famous novels. This is not a comprehensive survey of classic South Asian fiction, but an introduction to some of its most interesting authors.

The discussions provide historical and cultural background information that the Western reader may need to fully appreciate these works. Various aspects of novelistic style, structure, and characterization are commented on. I touch briefly on controversies over individual works, to convey a variety of alternative perspectives.

The individual chapters help untangle aspects of these works that may cause readers difficulty. A challenging book like Raja Rao's *Kanthapura* requires far more detailed discussion than one like Rohinton Mistry's much longer *A Fine Balance,* whose straightforward style can be understood easily by a relatively inexperienced reader.

At the end of each chapter is a very selective bibliography of sources for those seeking further information and insight. Except where no other sources are available, I have chosen essays, reviews, and interviews in general publications and on the Web rather than articles in scholarly journals. For advanced students, there is no substitute for such scholarship, but secondary-level students and general readers rarely have access to them in their local libraries, and they may lack the background to understand the technical language used in them. I consulted literally hundreds of scholarly books and articles in preparing this volume, but the format here makes citing most of them inappropriate. However, students working at the college level will want to pursue such sources in the standard MLA bibliography or may wish to try the informal bibliography of Anglophone literature I maintain at <http://www.wsu.edu/~brians/windowsbib.html>.

Those who pursue scholarship on South Asian fiction will soon discover that much of it falls into a loose category known as "postcolonial." The term is ill defined and much disputed, but an acquaintance with the major concepts within postcolonial studies is essential for advanced work in the field, and a couple of comprehensive introductions are listed in the selected bibliography later.

Finally, this book concludes with a glossary of non-English words and phrases used in the works specially featured within the chapters. The introduction to the glossary explains its limits and focus. In cases where authors have provided their own detailed notes, those notes are not duplicated in the glossary. To keep the list as simple as possible, the original language of each entry is not identified; but readers should keep in mind that the words here may come from Hindi, Malayalam, Urdu, Sanskrit, or any one of a number of other languages.

SELECTED BIBLIOGRAPHY

In addition to the specialized studies listed in the individual chapter bibliographies, the following resources provide more general background.

Allen, Richard, and Harish Trivedi, eds. *Literature & Nation: Britain and India 1800–1990.* London: Routledge, 2000.
  An interesting approach to studying Indian writing in relationship to British writing; contains many items useful for beginning students.

McLeod, John. *Beginning Postcolonialism.* Manchester: Manchester University Press, 2000.
  A balanced, well-written introduction to postcolonial literary criticism, including its most influential South Asian critics.

Miller, Barbara Stoler, ed. *Masterworks of Asian Literature in Comparative Perspective: A Guide for Teaching.* Armonk, NY: East Gate Books, 1994.
  Background on both ancient and modern masterpieces from India, China, and Japan. Texts discussed from South Asia include Anita Desai's *Fire on the Mountain* and *Games at Twilight*, R. K. Narayan's *The Financial Expert*, and Salman Rushdie's *Midnight's Children*. Useful background articles on the major influential ancient texts of India as well.

Mohanram, Radhika, and Gita Rajan, eds. *English Postcoloniality: Literatures from around the World.* Westport, CT: Greenwood Press, 1996.
  Useful articles with good bibliographies for more advanced students: Aparna Dharwadker and Vinay Dhardwadker's "Language, Identity, and Nation in Postcolonial Indian English Literature" (89–106) and Alamgir Hashmi's "Prolegomena to the Study of Pakistani English and Pakistani Literature in English" (107–17).

Niven, Alastair, ed. *The Commonwealth Writer Overseas: Themes of Exile and Expatriation.* Brussels: Librairie Marcel Didier, 1976.
  Contains two outstanding relevant essays: Kamala Markandaya's "One Pair of Eyes: Some Random Reflections" (23–32) and Uma Parameswaran's "What Price Expatriation" (41–52).

Philip, David Scott. *Perceiving India through the Works of Nirad C. Chaudhuri, R. K. Narayan, and Ved Mehta.* New Delhi: Sterling, 1986.
  Discussion of negative and positive portrayals of India by Indian writers.

Rege, Josna E. "Victim into Protagonist? *Midnight's Children* and the Post-Rushdie National Narratives of the Eighties." *Studies in the Novel* 29.3 (Fall 1997): 342–75.
  The influence of Salman Rushdie on recent South Asian fiction.

Rothstein, Mervyn. "Young Writers Leave Magic Realism and Look at Reality." *New York Times* 3 Jul. 2000: E1.
  An overview of younger Indian writers.

Sarma, Gobinda Prasad. *Nationalism in Indo-Anglican Fiction*. 2nd ed. New Delhi: Sterling, 1990.
  Detailed survey covering many lesser known works.

Walsh, William. *Indian Literature in English*. London and New York: Longman, 1990.
  A useful survey concentrating on older works. Includes some nonfiction and poetry.

OTHER RECOMMENDED FICTION

Many fine works of fiction had to be excluded from discussion in this volume for reasons of space. It would have been easy to double the number of interesting writers covered, and new ones are appearing all the time. The following is just a short list of a few outstanding works. Readers who enjoy the fiction covered in this book may well enjoy them as well.

Ali, Ahmed. *Twilight in Delhi*. London: Oxford University Press, 1966.
  First published in 1940, this brief novel is the best known by one of Pakistan's most famous authors. Its slight plot deals with love, marriage, loss, and death in a Muslim family; but the story serves mostly to knit together wonderfully evocative scenes of life in Delhi during the second decade of the twentieth century. It is also strikingly anti-British. Contains notes and a glossary.

Chaudhuri, Amit. *Freedom Song*. New York: Vintage, 2000.
  A collection of Chaudhuri's first three volumes of fiction. Less conventional novels than delicately impressionistic sketches and scenes (the first two, in particular, have almost no plot), but filled with insights and rich characters. *A Strange and Sublime Address* depicts the experiences of a young boy from Bombay visiting relatives in Calcutta, *Afternoon Raag* is set among Indian graduate students at Oxford, and *Freedom Song* depicts the lives of a large and varied cast of relatives in Calcutta in 1993.

Davidar, David. *The House of Blue Mangoes*. New York: HarperCollins, 2002.
  A multigenerational family epic set in the southernmost part of India, rich in old-fashioned scene descriptions, told at a leisurely pace. The plot focuses especially on the founder of an extended family settlement and on his son, who goes to work on a British-owned tea plantation. Caste conflict on the one hand and British-Indian conflict on the other are the mainsprings of the plot, which ends shortly before Partition.

Divakaruni, Chitra Banerjee. *The Unknown Errors of Our Lives*. New York: Random House, 2001.
  Short stories dealing mostly with Indian women, displaying considerably more sophisticated writing than her popular 1998 novel *The Mistress of Spices*.

Ghosh, Amitav. *The Glass Palace*. New York: Random House, 2001.
  Although overly ambitious (the plot rather falls apart at the end), this sweeping historical novel of life among Indians in Burma and Maharashtra from 1885 to the 1990s depicts colonial life from a refreshingly unsentimental but balanced point of view. A good corrective for those who romanticize the era of the British in India.

Nagarkar, Kiran. *Cuckold*. New Delhi: HarperCollins, 1997.

A colorful historical novel imagining the career of the husband of Mirabai, the sixteenth-century Hindu saint and poet-singer.

Seth, Vikram. *A Suitable Boy*. New York: HarperCollins, 1993.

This vast (1,500-page) family chronicle set during the first decade of India's independence is a favorite with many readers.

Chapter 1
The Fiction of Rabindranath Tagore: Quartet (1915)

Rabindranath Tagore may seem at first not to belong in the company of the other writers discussed in this book, all much younger than he and living in a very different world. In Tagore's day, India was still ruled by England, and the regions that now make up Pakistan and Bangladesh were part of that British India. His family belonged to the wealthy landowning *zamindar* class, which had been developed into intermediaries between the masses of laboring peasants and their British rulers.

But Tagore is important as the first modern Indian writer to become widely known around the world, beginning when he won the Nobel Prize for his poetry collection *Gitanjali* ("Song Offerings") in 1913. Although he wrote in Bengali, like the other writers, the language in which he acquired his worldwide fame was English. Also like many of them, he was eagerly sought after as a spokesman on Indian affairs. And like all of them, he drew both on the traditional culture of South Asia and that of Europe in creating his works. His works make a good starting point for the study of South Asian fiction in English because it is in his writing that Western readers begin to discover the literature of the region.

Tagore is also important in the history of modern literature in South Asia. He was not the first Indian writer to create novels and short stories, but he was by far the most influential early one, and he is the fountainhead of modern Bengali verse. Traditional poetry had been dominated by Sanskrit, a dead language that functioned like Latin in European culture; and he transformed Bengali into a vehicle for lyric poetry, experimenting influentially with styles and forms throughout his life. His short stories were the first in

South Asia to reflect the techniques of modern European short story writers, and his poetry continually evolved to become much more experimental as he grew older.

He also traveled widely, speaking on public affairs, on the arts, and on religion, all over Europe, in the Americas, in China and Japan. During the second and third decades of the twentieth century, he was one of the most famous people in the world, his bearded, long-robed image vivid in the mind of a wide public that might not have read any of his works but knew of him as a great Indian.

His background in several ways suited him to be an ambassador to the world. At a time when many Indians believed that travel abroad was forbidden by their religion, Tagore's grandfather Dwarkanath had not only entertained the British in India, he had traveled extensively in Europe and met many notables, including the pope, Queen Victoria, and Charles Dickens. Even the family name indicates their Westernization: "Thakur" was changed to the more easily pronounced "Tagore" for the purposes of dealing with the English.

But it is perhaps his religious background that was the most significant factor in opening Tagore to the outside world—at least, it needs the most explaining. Their traditional caste, the Pirali, belonged to the highest category in Indian society, the Brahmins; but they were considered inferior by other Brahmins because it was said that ancestors of theirs had smelled the breath of others who had been tricked into eating ritually unclean food.

In traditional Indian society, caste defined much of the individual's social existence. The caste of the parents determined the caste of their children, and they could marry only other individuals of the same caste. In addition, it was considered ritually defiling to eat with or eat food prepared by someone of a lower caste. These two restrictions divided Indian society into tight communities and greatly restricted social mobility. Those who suffered most were the "untouchables" at the bottom of the system who have been referred to by many labels: *sudra* (often spelled "Shudra"), *harijan* ("children of God"—a label invented by Gandhi to improve their image), "scheduled castes" (referring to their listing as protected groups in the law), and the preferred term today, *dalit*. Such discrimination was justified by the belief that people who had committed various offenses in a previous existence had been punished by being reincarnated in a lower caste. Although discrimination on account of caste is illegal under the modern constitution of India, the practice lingers on in many areas.

Even though the Tagores belonged to a relatively high caste, the fact that they were themselves the object of prejudice by higher-caste Brahmins helps explain why Rabindranath would share his family's sympathy for those of lower caste. Whatever the real cause of the Tagore's ambiguous social status, this wealthy, sophisticated family with a strained relationship to traditional Hinduism was drawn to the movement led by the great reformer Rammohun Roy, which evolved into the religion known as Brahmo Samaj.

Brahmos reject polytheism, the use of idols in worship, and many traditional Hindu rituals and restrictions. They are in some ways comparable to Unitarians and Reformed Jews in the West, rooted in an ancient faith, but seeking to simplify and rationalize it.

The rationalistic aspect of Brahmo beliefs clashed with a deep streak of passionate romanticism in Tagore. He rebelled against the family faith as a young man, finding inspiration instead in the mystical tradition of the millennia-old *Upanishads* and in the *bhakti* (devotional) poetry surrounding the worship of Krishna, eighth avatar (incarnation) of Vishnu. The latter sort of faith is often referred to by the term *Vaishnava* (worshipping Vishnu) (discussed later).

Although Tagore embraced certain aspects of traditional Hinduism, he shared his family's rejection of a host of caste restrictions and laws of ritual purity that characterized Indian life. In some ways he was ahead of his time, advocating, for instance, increased freedom for women. His older sister Swarnakumari was a writer, and he sympathetically portrayed women's struggles to express themselves creatively in his own works, especially in *The Broken Nest* (*Nastanirh*, 1901), made into a moving film entitled *The Lonely Wife* (*Charulata*, 1964) by his former student, Satyajit Ray. In fact, the sufferings and struggles of women are among his main subjects, which links him to more contemporary writers with many of the same concerns.

One of the traditions he spoke out against was child marriage, a custom rooted in a deep distrust of women. A girl raised in a family as a designated wife could be molded to be docile and obedient and was highly likely to have preserved her virginity—a quality strongly insisted upon in traditional marriages. Because many girls were married to men much older than they, it was not uncommon for a girl to find herself a widow before she had become a woman (child brides were treated and raised as children until they reached puberty). Because Indian tradition strongly discouraged remarriage, such a girl-widow faced a bleak life of loveless servitude in her late husband's extended family, forbidden to wear colorful clothing or jewelry or to enjoy most of the other pleasures available to married women.

Tagore himself was married reluctantly by his family to a bride of ten when he was twenty-two. He was never emotionally close to Mrinalini, often lived apart from her, and her death twenty years later did not seem to grieve him in the same way other family deaths did. He often expressed sympathy for women, but this sympathy was deeply personal, rooted in his affection for specific women, and not part of a systematic program of agitation for women's rights. In some ways he was a traditionalist, taking for granted that women's role is to do the housework, and he seldom delved into their inner lives in his writing. In his fiction we see women suffer, and often die wretchedly, but from outside: we rarely see the world through their eyes.

The most important woman in Tagore's early life after the death of his mother when he was still a teenager was his brother Jyotirindranath's wife Kadambari. At this distance in time we cannot know exactly the nature of their intimacy, but clearly he was deeply drawn to her and she to him. He dedicated several works to her and in *The Broken Nest* portrayed a relationship clearly based on theirs, although in the novel the woman is the more aggressive of the pair and the young man standing in for Tagore flees in horror when he realizes she has fallen in love with him.

Traditionally, well-off upper caste women were expected to remain sequestered in the house, visiting only occasionally at their parents' home or attending weddings of relatives. Most male visitors to a man's home were not allowed to see his wife; it was even considered indelicate for the visitor to ask such a question as "How is your wife?" Only close male relatives like brothers-in-law were exempted from these rules and could socialize with a wife. It is easy to understand how Kadambari could have been drawn to this handsome and sensitive young man who was given free run of the house. Although we will never know the details of their relationship, it is thought she may have loved him passionately. For whatever reason, at the age of twenty-five, four months after he married, she poisoned herself and died. For the rest of his life he was to return obsessively in his fiction to love triangles and other forbidden passions, usually ending in the premature deaths of the desired women. Rare is the Tagore hero who can settle down happily with the woman he loves.

The world that hailed Tagore as a Nobel laureate would have been very surprised indeed to learn of this passionate, earthy side of the Indian writer, because he was known in the West as a Hindu mystic, loosely grouped in with popular figures like Vivekananda (1863–1902) and Ramakrishna (1836–86). The fault was partly Tagore's. He had translated various of his poems into vague, dreamy English in a way that appealed to the mystical side of the great Irish poet William Butler Yeats (1865–1939). His endorsement of *Gitanjli* helped mightily to promote Tagore among Western readers, and the author, overwhelmed by his reception among people who had no knowledge of his very different Bengali originals, never made clear how poorly they had understood him.

Westerners tend to focus on the other worldly aspect of mysticism that seeks to distance itself from the here and now to enter a realm of pure spirit. But the Vaishnava tradition within which many of Tagore's poems and songs exist is very different. Hymns to Krishna often focus on his relationship with his female lovers, the *gopis* (cowherds' wives), of whom Radha is his most dearly beloved. Their courtship, quarrels, and love play are the subject of countless ecstatic poems by such important writers as the fifteenth-century Vidyapati and the sixteenth-century female poet Mirabai. The most influential work in this genre is the great twelfth-century poem cycle called the *Gita Govinda,* by Jayadeva. It has been widely sung, recited, danced to, and illustrated for all the centuries since.

Devotees of Krishna as lover feel that by enacting the role of Radha they are approaching true intimacy with the divine spirit. Although the imagery they use is often explicitly erotic, their thoughts are supposed to be spiritual. The union of the lovers is taken as a metaphor for spiritual union. It was this tradition in Hinduism that powerfully influenced Tagore.

As a poet also saturated with the spirit of Victorian English poetry and the even more restrained Indian sense of propriety, he avoids any shocking explicitness; but this yearning of the flesh is almost always at the heart of his works, and he repeatedly turns it in a direction away from the spiritual and into this world. Again and again human love is portrayed as the ultimate force that drives his characters, even to the point of destroying some of them. The combination of fierce desire and extreme restraint characterizes much of his fiction. Traditional Indian morals are very severe, and tourists who have learned about the culture from reading the popular *Kama Sutra* are surprised to learn that only in very recent years have lovers been shown kissing in Indian movies. Passion is portrayed in Tagore's fiction in accordance with nineteenth-century ideas of propriety through vague yearnings and subtle hints: never through explicit descriptions of sexual acts.

We should note that in South Asia Tagore is not known primarily for his fiction. It is his songs and poetry that still live today in his native Bengal (an area now divided between the Indian state of West Bengal and Bangladesh). Those who cannot approach Tagore through the original Bengali may find the *Selected Poems* translated by William Radice the best introduction. His collection ranges over the whole variety of Tagore's poetic works (except his some two thousand songs). Radice's translations, far more accurate and vivid than Tagore's own translations, are accompanied by voluminous explanatory notes. Tagore frankly admitted he was not an accomplished poet in English, although he was fluent enough to converse freely, deliver many speeches, and write essays in the language. He would probably have welcomed the efforts of Radice and other modern translators to bring his works to life in our own time.

He also wrote experimental plays, choreographed dances, wrote essays on literature, esthetics, history, politics, biology, medicine, mathematics, optics, and a vast array of other subjects, and poured much of his energy in later years into creating enormous numbers of drawings and paintings. His music remains very popular today and has frequently been used in films and other forms of popular entertainment. It would be difficult to find another twentieth-century writer anywhere in the world who could match the volume of his output and the range of the topics he treated.

Of his fictional works, the best known besides *The Broken Nest*, already touched on here, are *Gora* (1910; translated into English in 1924) and *The Home and the World* (originally *Ghaire-Bhaire*, 1916; translated in 1919). The title character in the first novel is a young man whose fanaticism for Hindu purity causes unhappiness all around him until he learns at the end of the book that he himself was not even born an Indian and is not a member of the caste to which he has so tenaciously clung. Some of the scenes are vividly realized, but the ending seems more than a little arbitrary.

The Home and the World deals with another subject also dear to Tagore's heart: the movement for Indian independence. He was a fierce opponent of colonialism; but because he also fiercely opposed nationalism, he was out of sympathy with much that went on in the name of breaking free from foreign domination. (It is one of the ironies of his life that this arch-antinationalist wrote the song that became independent India's national anthem.) *The Home and the World* concerns a young wife's fatal attraction to an unscrupulous and exploitative independence leader. Contemporary readers tend to find the characters overly simple and the politics of the novel baffling. Because it is an attack on one aspect of a cause he generally supported, it can mislead readers lacking the historical background about his politics. It is especially important to know that the villainous leader named Sandip, although loosely based on real independence leaders, has nothing to do with Mahatma Gandhi. Tagore disagreed with much in Gandhi's goals and methods, but he never believed him to be a villain.

Experts agree that the early translations of Tagore's fiction give only a pale reflection of his way with language, so we are choosing to focus here on a work that was well translated for the first time relatively recently by the Bangladeshi writer Kaiser Haq: *Quartet* (*Chaturanga*, 1915; translated 1993). It is a brief work—more a novella than a full-length novel—but it contains in an appealing narrative structure most of the representative themes of his longer works, many of which have been explored later by other authors we discuss.

The Bengali title of the novel, *Chaturanga*, refers to a four-handed board game a little like chess. The English title *Quartet* is a simplification, but both refer to a quartet of characters: two young friends and the two young women they become involved with. However, there is no neat pairing off in couples. This novel actually revolves around two "triangles."

The title also alludes to the four chapter titles, each named after a different character: "Uncle" (the uncle of one of the young men), "Sachish" (the young man himself), "Damani" (the second of the two women), and "Sribalash" (Sachish's friend, the narrator of the novel). In pronouncing these names, note that Bengali lacks an "S" sound, so the names of the two heroes begin with an "sh" sound. Haq provides an excellent glossary of terms and names at the end of his translation of the novel; his explanations are not repeated here, so the reader should consult it frequently.

The novel is set in Calcutta in the early part of the twentieth century, among upper-class, well-educated Indians. Sachish and Sribalash meet at school, and they soon strike up a fast friendship. Sribalash is drawn to the brilliant charisma of Sachish to the extent of idolizing him. When the narrator says in the second paragraph, "I loved him," nothing homosexual is to be implied: strong friendships among men are common in cultures where heterosexual friendships are rare.

It is a cliché to think of India as a land in which religion saturates the very air; but many highly educated Indians were skeptical of religion even in the nineteenth century. Remember that Tagore himself grew up in a religious atmosphere that criticized traditional pious practices and beliefs. The news that Sachish is an atheist is shocking to the other students, but not bizarre. Tagore's deep distrust of traditional popular religion is reflected in the way he recounts the good deeds of the atheist characters and the meanness and cruelty of the religious ones.

Sribalash's shock at discovering that the friend he regards as almost a god does not himself believe in gods is compounded by discovering that he belongs to a relatively lowly caste. The thousands of castes are broadly divided into four groupings called *varnas.* Sribalash belongs to the highest varna, the Brahmins, but his friend belongs to the much lower goldsmith's caste in the Vaisya varna.

If Sribalash were a traditional Hindu, he would have been expected to shun Sachish socially and especially to avoid eating with him. His mention that he was eventually to share a meal with him is a daring statement of his willingness to let his friendship override his upbringing.

Tagore also satirizes traditional beliefs by suggesting that as a boy he believed the eating of beef to be worse than murder. Traditional cow veneration has strongly prohibited the eating of beef by Hindus for millennia. Readers should note the clash of bigotries, with the boys scorning Sachish's disbelief while they condemn the racism of their teacher.

Like another famous Indian writer, R. K. Narayan, Tagore was notably unhappy and unsuccessful at school, and both often portrayed teachers in a negative light. Tagore tried to compensate for his own childhood experiences by setting up a sort of experimental school called Santiniketan, to the support of which he devoted much of his life and income. Among its students were two brilliant figures: the filmmaker Satyajit Ray and Indira Gandhi, future prime minister of India.

The contemptuous Prof. Wilkins is of course an Englishman who considers himself exiled to an ignorant, backward corner of the world. His treatment of the boys reminds us of the intimate ways in which the insults inflicted on India by colonialism were manifested in individual lives. Sachish battles Wilkins with weapons drawn from the teacher's own culture, the writings of English rationalist and positivist philosophers. Sachish would have read such British writers as John Stuart Mill (1806–73), Jeremy Bentham (1748–1832), and Herbert Spencer (1820–1903)—all mentioned by name in the novel. Positivists rejected traditional philosophy's obsession with the sort of abstract, spiritual issues traditionally called "metaphysics." They dismissed religious questions as meaningless and tried to create a rational, scientific basis for philosophy. The Englishman scorns his Indian students, failing to see that one of them has leaped beyond him by his insights into the teacher's own culture.

We then learn that Sachish has received his training in rationalism from the "Uncle" of the chapter title: Jagmohan. Thomas Malthus (1766–1834) is famous for having been the first to discuss in detail the possibility of humanity outgrowing its food supply, which explains how Jagmohan was influenced by reading him to avoid remarriage after his wife died: this is his contribution to population control. The irony is that this childless man acts very much like a father to Sachish, much more so than the boy's own father, Harimohan. (Whereas "Hari" is a name for the god Vishnu, "Jag" is short for "jagat"—which means "world"—obviously a suitable name for a worldly man.) Certainly they are emotionally closer, as the father lavishes all his affection on the less worthy of his sons, Purandar.

Harimohan is a pious Hindu, but it is established from the beginning that he is a self-indulgent, self-centered man. He and Jagmohan are natural enemies, and their contempt for each other's beliefs will shape most of their lives, leading eventually to a literally divided household. Keep in mind that the traditional Indian extended family often includes three generations living under one roof—as did the household Tagore grew up in. The religious differences explored in this novel tear asunder the usually supreme ties of family.

Jagmohan's learning leads him to be compared to two famous English scholars. Thomas Babington Macaulay (1800–59) was an eminent historian who shaped the policies that aimed at creating an English-influenced upper class in India to serve the empire; and the vastly erudite Dr. Samuel Johnson (1709–84) was the creator of the first dictionary in English. Kayastha who deal with the hides of dead animals, particularly cows, are among the most reviled of all in the traditional Hindu caste system; so it is not surprising that beef-eating Muslims would have taken to the trade of tanning. Jagmohan's friendship with them is an spectacular insult to his pious Hindu relatives.

When Jagmohan scornfully claims that the drummers he has hired to irritate his relatives are celebrating the dunking of his god, he is referring to a custom by which a religious festival is concluded by dumping the image of the deity into the river to be dissolved back into the clay and straw of which it was made—a reminder to pious Hindus that the image is not the god, but here suggestive of Jagmohan's impudent rejection of gods altogether.

Nanibala is typical of the young widows whose maltreatment was attacked by both his Brahmo relatives and Tagore himself. She is absolutely defenseless against Purindar, whose exploitation of her is only worsened by the fact that he has seduced rather than merely raped her. As we will see, she actually loves the man who has ruined her life and cannot finally accept rescue at the hands of anyone else. The first quartet of the novel is composed of Nanibala, Purindar (her seducer), Jagmohan (her rescuer), and Sribalash (who is accused of seducing her). It should be noted that, at the time, a maid impregnated by her master's son in Western countries would also have been summarily dismissed and abandoned to the streets. There is nothing exclusively Indian about Nanibala's fate.

Toward the end of this chapter we encounter a minor instance of Tagore's tendency to summarize briefly scenes that we would have expected to be more fully realized: Purandar, he writes, "put up money to hire the services of a woman who would pose as Noni's mother and plead with Jagmohan to give back her daughter. But Jagmohan drove the imposter away with such a terrible look on his face that she didn't dare go back" (17). A more important example occurs on p. 27, when Sribalash unexpectedly undergoes a conversion. Whether this sort of thing is caused by haste—Tagore was a very prolific writer—inattention, or deliberate choice, such leaps are characteristic of Tagore's plots. The unwary reader who skips a line or two in a story that otherwise unfolds at a leisurely pace may well find that the story has shifted puzzlingly in a very short space.

When Jagmohan decides to marry Nanibala, we must remember he is going against the custom that rejected marriage with a widow. Although he may have selfish motives (she is, after all, an attractive young woman), he is nevertheless behaving in a heroic, almost saintly manner.

Young women caught in the throes of passion usually die in Tagore's fiction. This conforms to the conventions of the time, which required that most female "fallen women," no matter how guiltless, had to die. It is a rare piece of Victorian or early-twentieth-century fiction in which a woman who commits adultery or has premarital sex, even against her will, is allowed to survive at the end of the story. But Nanibala's fate is also a reflection of the author's obsession with the suicide of his sister-in-law, Kadambari. In Tagore's world, good intentions and pious deeds cannot overcome the power of a fatal passion.

The opening of the second chapter, "Sachish," leaps from the death of Nanibala to that of Jagmohan, clearly a major turning point in the novel. Jagmohan's death results from an act of even more saintly generosity than his offer to marry Nanibala, and it confirms the pattern established early on of contrasting the nonbeliever's goodness with his sanctimonious brother's meanness. Haq says in his introduction that the novel ultimately rejects atheism. Tagore certainly did in his personal life; but I am not so sure that Jagmohan's faults are such as to make him less than admirable, although Sribalash clearly shares his glee in behaving in a way that is both impeccably virtuous and offensive to believers: "We became the scourge of those who had any kind of religious belief, and deliberately undertook charitable work of the sort that would not win the approval of our more respectable contemporaries" (23).

Haq's note on the term *sannyasi* in the glossary ("one who has renounced the world; a religious mendicant") may need some amplification for readers who are not familiar with the concept. In Hinduism, a Brahmin male should ideally go through four stages (*ashram*) in life: celibate religious student (*brahmachari*), married householder (*grihastha*), forest dweller (*vanaprastha*), and finally wandering ascetic (*sannyasi*). After having raised a family including at least one son, the devout Brahmin can choose to retire to a simple life of contemplation in the forest wilderness and eventually undertake the severe ascetic life of a beggar, ideally ultimately fasting to death.

There is no particular pressure for any one individual to actually take up such a lifestyle, because Hinduism envisions many rebirths for each person before he is ready to abandon the things of this life to achieve *moksha:* release from the cycle of rebirth and blending with the universal spiritual realm of *Brahman*. Women, for instance, need to be reborn as males before they can attempt it. Restrictions are put in the way of Brahmins seeking to shirk their family responsibilities by frivolously entering on the sannyasi path. However, it is naturally tempting for poverty-stricken men to become fake sannyasis for the sake of the alms they will collect. Hence supposed sannyasis of unknown character are commonly suspect.

Swami Lilananda, the guru who entrances Sachish and converts him (also called *guruji*), is a *sadhu* (holy man) devoted to the Vaishnava practices surrounding Krishna as lover of Radha that were discussed earlier. His name refers to the *rasa lila* (dance of love) that the god performs with his lovers. Countless pictures, songs and dances represent the religious ecstasy in which the worshippers seek to become one with the god they not only long for, but who equally longs for them. *Rasa lila* also refers to various erotic practices and arts that are reflected widely in South Asian poetry and fiction.

Although the metaphors of Vaishnavism are intensely erotic, their practice is supposed to be severely ascetic. The rest of the novel consists of the pull of these two opposite ways of life on the central characters, with eroticism embodied in the second of the young widows in this work: Damini. The second quartet is therefore formed of Sachish, Sribalash, the swami, and Damini, with all three of the men being drawn powerfully to this young woman who does not share the passivity and frailty of Nanibala (her name means literally "puppet made of cream," implying one who is too delicate for hard labor). Religion guides them to enact the role of Radha in relationship to Krishna, but their maleness betrays them as Damini guilelessly plays the role of Radha herself. It is not so much anything she does that is the problem; it is what she is: overwhelmingly attractive and charming.

The more serious object of Sachish's devotions is Brahman, here called "the Universal Soul that inheres in all beings." Hindus often believe that not only are all humans ultimately one, so are all living beings, including animals down to the lowliest insect. The loss of individuality in a blending with the spiritual reality of Brahman is the ultimate goal of the devout; but Sribalash is at first repelled by this idea. His Western-influenced education has led him to value his individuality far too much to find such a prospect attractive, and in this he is very like Tagore. The writer saw the divine spirit living within all things; but he remained attached to the particular, the individual, and resisted the Hindu impulse to shrug off the claims of this world for a larger nonphysical essence. In the context of his work, the conventional "sin" of attachment is really a sign of loving devotion.

Damini acts as a distraction from their meditations without even being seen: the clink of her keys, the call of her voice to a maidservant, are enough to disturb the would-be ascetics gathered around their guru. She is the victim of a husband besotted with religion, who sold her jewelry to give to Swami Lilananda. To appreciate what a shocking deed this is, one must understand that although a woman usually has to bring a large dowry into a marriage, the jewelry she is given as a bride becomes her personal property, the evidence of her status as a respectable married woman, her insurance against disaster, to be disposed of in only the most dire necessity, and never without her consent. Shibtosh's act in "liberating" her from the desire for gold is, as Tagore writes, "brigandage in the name of spiritual devotion" (32). His death has left her not only widowed and unprotected, but impoverished. She depends for her survival on the guru who had enriched himself at her expense, but at first she takes her vengeance by cooking tasteless food and allowing the milk to go sour.

Hindu widows are expected to shun all jewelry and makeup, dress in plain white garments, and generally project an air of asexuality. Damini defiantly remains an earthy, desirable woman. This is the more powerful side of her vengeance. Her abrupt conversion is most unexpected, and at first inexplicable, until we see she is drawn to join the Vaishnava worship sessions more by the magnetic charms of Sachish than by those of Krishna.

The mysterious rock carvings by the cave they visit illustrate the tendency in India for one religious tradition to blend into another, but the reference to possible Greek influence calls for a more detailed explanation. After Alexander the Great crossed the Indus River to defeat Puru ("Porus" in Western classical texts) in the fourth century BC, he left behind a Greek-speaking lieutenant who founded a dynasty of rulers on the northwestern fringes of India in Gandhara. Their striking sculptures of rulers and gods adopted the muscular male form of Greek classicism, with its thin, many-pleated draperies. The style spread from there east, so Greek sculpture finds a distant echo in the lightly clad Buddhas of lands as distant as Japan and Thailand. Sorting out the Greek Gandharan influences from native Indian ones is a job for experts, as Tagore suggests.

Sachish finds that he cannot escape the lure of Damini in this cave, for she enters his dreams as a fearsome serpent, then in reality kneeling at his feet, spreading her hair over him (a common religious symbol: the sources of the sacred Ganges River were said to have flowed through the locks of Shiva's outspread hair). She had earlier spread her hair over the Swami's feet, but we now understand where her true devotion is directed. Her failure to break through Sachish's resistance causes her to abruptly abandon her devotions. Even the simple act of sewing on buttons becomes a sign of defiance; but her essential goodness is illustrated by her rescue of the kite (a kind of hawk) and puppy. She can bring the most ill-assorted creatures together under her loving care. Having laid claim to her own will, she lays claim to her story as well: this third chapter of the novel is named for her.

When Guruji says of Damini that she must die as the result of Krishna's hunt, he is speaking metaphorically; but the sinister foreshadowing of his words is inescapable. Sachish remains seemingly invulnerable to her appeal, meditating on "the divine workings of Hladini [pleasure], Sandhini [eternity] and Jogmaya [a human form of Krishna]." ("Jogmaya" was also the name of Tagore's mother.) But the very objects of his devotion torment him by constantly reminding him of her.

When he tells Sribalash that Damani is a beguiling agent of nature designed to distract men from their devotions, he is drawing on the Hindu concept of *Maya:* the physical world of nature that we mistakenly believe to be the ultimate reality, but in fact conceals the higher reality of Brahman. Maya is often personified as a woman, so Sachish is being very conventional indeed. Sribalash is more in tune with Tagore's views in insisting, "We must row the boat of life in Nature's current" (47). Human beings live in the physical world, whether we believe in it or not, and we ultimately have to deal with it on its own terms.

Damini does not surrender easily. She cleverly begins to devote herself to Sribalash, who gradually comes to understand that she does not love him, but is only using him to make Sachish jealous. Anyone who has ever been caught in such game playing can understand the pain that the narrator must experience, fascinated by her nearness but unable to capture her heart; but he does not express it openly. We are expected to understand without him pouring out his heart.

Damini also rebels by claiming the right to read modern secular literature—perhaps books like the one we are reading. Literature is frequently a vehicle of liberation for women in Tagore's works, either as readers or as writers. Her eventual sacrifice of her reading is all the more poignant when we remember how fiercely she had fought for it.

Although Damini's quick switches of allegiance may seem at first bewildering, the key to the consistency in them is Sachish's attitude toward her. She can subject herself to the whims of Guruji, whom she despises, only because Sachish has asked her to. The result is that she is thrust again as a troubling force into the center of Sachish's devotions, but "he could no longer regard her as a metaphor for a transcendental mood. Damini didn't embellish the songs any more; the songs embellished her" (54). In fact, Guruji has been displaced from the center of his own cult by Damini: it is she whom everyone looks to.

As if it were not enough to feature two abused women in one slim volume, the narrative is punctuated by the sensational story of Nabin's first wife's suicide after having arranged his marriage to her sister. Westerners have often fantasized erotically about polygamy, describing or painting the delights of the harem. Women's own accounts of their experiences are often much more negative. The wife of a man who could afford more wives than one often had to suffer in silence while he sought out and devoted himself to a new bride. (One of the best ways to become acquainted with the sufferings caused by polygamy is to view the 1991 film *Raise the Red Lantern* by the Chinese director Yimou Zhang.) Tagore seems determined in this book to touch on a wide variety of issues relating to women's problems: arranged marriages, spousal abuse, rape, discrimination against widows, and polygamy.

The "Postscript" to "Damini" seems at first to be one of those abrupt leaps forward commented on earlier, but this turns out to be a sort of "flash forward," which will keep us intrigued until the end of the novel to find out how it will end.

Sribilash defiantly clings to the "householder" stage we have earlier spoken of as the mode of perfect fulfillment for him. He goes beyond even the typical young man in insisting that he and his bride go into marriage with their eyes wide open. It was traditionally considered unseemly for the bride-to-be to look boldly in the face of her proposed groom before marriage, and in ideal arranged weddings the first clear look the groom has of the bride is during the ceremony. (The plot of Tagore's melodramatic novel *The Wreck* turns on this fact: a pair of newly married people wind up with the wrong partners because they have not looked them in the face at the wedding.) Even couples who have not been so circumspect during the courtship, which amounts mostly to very public negotiation between the two families, enact this highly romantic moment at the ceremony.

The attitude expressed here is in contrast very Tagorean: fierce, open love of the world, embraced without reserve. Unfortunately for Sribalash, Damini does not feel the same toward him. It quickly becomes clear that he is second best in her heart—but Sachish, whom she prefers, will not embrace her in his quest for purity of spirit. His resistance to her is not entirely pure, however, as Damini clearly states when Sribilash unwarily says that those preoccupied with their spirits do not even notice women: "Don't they indeed! In fact they take notice in a way that's quite weird" (66). Daimini understands that the extreme lengths to which Sachish goes to resist her only reveal the strength of the fascination she exercises over him, but she also understands she will never have him.

In a sense, Sribilash can never really have her either, because her heart belongs to Sachish. Sachish can only embrace her by rejecting her embraces, turning her in his mind into a formless spirit into whose darkness he walks along the riverbank. In the end, Damini finds that the only loving thing she can do for him is to do as he asks and walk away from him.

Unfortunately, this proud woman has to sacrifice her own self-esteem and accept his image of her as a dangerously seductive force. It is not clear whether in choosing to join herself to Sribilash she is taking refuge from the world or committing emotional suicide. Her despair is interrupted by a brief premarriage "honeymoon" period in which she at last recognizes Sribilash's good qualities: but her anxiety to have Sachish at the ceremony and to keep him near afterward make clear that she has not gotten over him.

Her longing finally consumes her, and she yearns for the shore where Sachish so memorably rejected her, which now represents death. She makes the ritual gesture of "taking the dust" from her husband's feet (touching them respectfully) as she leaves this life, suggesting she will be his fully only in some future existence, an existence we know Sribilash does not believe in. Like so many of Tagore's love stories, this one has ended tragically.

The novel has no simple lessons to teach. No one forms an ideal marriage. No one attitude toward religion proves fully satisfactory. Friendship and love have been at their most intense among these characters, and the result has been heartache for all of them. A traditional Hindu conclusion would have stressed the need to move on, along the path of renunciation; but Tagore simply wants to show us the human heart, in all its fullness, and make us sympathize with the suffering that fills so many lives here on earth.

SELECTED BIBLIOGRAPHY

Chatterjee, Bhabatosh. *Rabindranath Tagore and Modern Sensibility.* Delhi: Oxford University Press, 1996.
　　A collection of sensitive essays written over three decades, including two that touch on *Quartet*: "The Knife's Edge" (82–106) and "Modern Sensibility" (167–79). The first of these puts the erotic tension we have discussed here in the context of a survey of his major works of fiction. Note that this was written before the publication of Kaiser Haq's translation, and the characters' names are rendered slightly differently.

Desai, Anita. "Re-Reading Tagore." *Journal of Commonwealth Literature* 29.1 (1994): 5–14.
　　An introduction to Tagore by one of India's finest modern writers.

Dutta, Krishna, and Andrew Robinson. *Rabindranath Tagore: The Myriad-Minded Man.* London: Bloomsbury, 1995.
　　The standard biography. Contains many photos of Tagore and his family and associates.

Gupta, Mahasweta. "Translation as Manipulation: The Power of Images and Images of Power." *Between Languages and Cultures: Translation and Cross-Cultural Texts.* Ed. Anuradha Dingwaney and Carol Maier. Pittsburgh: University of Pittsburgh Press, 1995. 159–73.
　　Overview of the ways in which Tagore's translations from Bengali into English concealed much that was culturally important. Contains two examples retranslated by Sengupta in striking contrast with Tagore's versions.

Lago, Mary M. *Rabindranath Tagore*. Boston: Twayne, 1976.
Basic introduction to and overview of Tagore's works by an expert on the subject.

"Rabindranath Tagore." <http://www.cs.brockport.edu/~smitra/tagore.html>.
A set of well-researched essays, including a substantial biographical essay and a few modern recordings of his songs in WAV format.

Radice, William. "Atheists, Gurus and Fanatics: Rabindranath Tagore's 'Chaturanga' (1916)." *Modern Asian Studies* 34:2 (May 2000): 407–24.
Examination of the religious themes in *Quartet*. Don't miss the concluding note in which Radice modifies some of his earlier statements in the article.

Sen Pandit, Lalita. "Caste, Race and Nation: History and Dialectic in Rabindranath Tagore's *Gora*." *Literary India: Comparative Studies in Aesthetics, Colonialism, and Culture*. Ed. Patrick Colm Hogan. Albany: State University of New York Press, 1995. 207–33.
Historical background and comparison with Kipling's *Kim*.

Tagore, Rabindranath. *The Housewarming and Other Selected Writings*. Ed. Amiya Chakravarty. Trans. Mary Lago, Tarun Gupta, and Amiya Chakravarty. 1965. Westport, CT: Greenwood, 1977.
A good sampler of his short writings in modern translations.

———. *My Reminiscences*. London: Macmillan, 1917.
Informal sketches of scenes from the author's youth.

———. *Quartet (Chaturanga)*. Trans. Kaiser Haq. Oxford: Heinemann, 1993.
This superior translation of a short novella is an excellent place to start in exploring Tagore's fiction.

———. *Selected Poems*. Ed. William Radice. Harmondsworth: Penguin, 1985.
Standard modern collection of Tagore's poetry in outstanding translations accompanied by voluminous notes. Contains a useful timeline of Tagore's life.

"What to Read in Tagore?" *Indian Literature* 29.3 (May–June 1986): 61–64.
Useful checklist of the most important Tagore works in translation; especially valuable for singling out recent translations by other hands.

Chapter 2
Raja Rao: Kanthapura *(1938)*

Raja Rao is cited in every survey of modern Indian fiction for his impressive contributions to literature in the form of five novels and a number of short stories scattered over a writing career that rivals in length his close contemporary R. K. Narayan. He was born on November 5, 1908, into a wealthy Brahmin Kannada-speaking family in Hassan, Mysore State, in southern India. A distinguished rajah was visiting the family at the time, and his mother decided to name him "Raja" in honor of this auspicious occasion. In 1915 his family moved some 400 miles to the north and sent him at the age of seven to a Muslim-run school in Hyderabad, the Madarasa-e-Aliya. He was the only Hindu student in the institution. After high school, his parents hoped a more northerly climate would help his ailing lungs, and he was sent to live with a cousin and study for a year at Aligarh Muslim University, in Uttar Pradesh, near Delhi. Thus from very early in his life Rao was placed in a situation that isolated him culturally and emphasized his difference from others, a pattern that was to be important in his later career.

Back in Hyderabad he earned his BA at Nizam's College, where his father taught, studying history and English, and won a scholarship that led him to study French at the University of Montpellier in 1929 at the age of nineteen. His antagonism toward the British had drawn him to France, whose language and literature were to influence him profoundly from then on. In 1929 he married Camille Mouly, a brilliant *lycée* (high school) teacher who was fascinated by India and Hinduism (she later wrote a book on the subject). She urged him to begin writing, at first in Kannada; but he soon switched to English, in which he felt he could better express his complex ideas. At this point he was a young man raised speaking Kannada, educated in Urdu, studying Sanskrit and English, further educated in and fascinated by French, destined for a career writing in English. But this cosmopolitan background did not only broaden his horizons; it emphasized his own uniqueness in these surroundings and led him to cling to his Indian and specifically Hindu roots more and more as he matured. He speculated about the possible influence of Hinduism on the Cathar heresy of medieval Provence (southern France) and studied for a time at the Sorbonne in Paris with the distinguished Professor Louis Cazamian, researching the impact of India on Irish literature.

The year 1933 marked an important turning point in Rao's life: he returned to India and began his search for a guru, a teacher of the Vendanta tradition who could help him find the particular path in Hinduism that would mean the most to him, visiting the first of several ashrams he was to explore. That year he also began publishing short stories in magazines, both in English and in French.

The 1930s were a period of tumult in India, as more and more people were swept up into the movement for independence (*swaraj*) from England. Although many forces were at work, the group that had emerged most prominently was the All-India Congress, led by Mohandas K. Gandhi, a lawyer who had fought a highly successful campaign for the rights of Indians living in South Africa and returned to his native country to take up the struggle against the British. Although Rao was no activist, he could not help being drawn to this cause. The result of his fascination with Gandhi was his first and still his most famous novel, *Kanthapura*, written in his early twenties and finally published in 1938. It was characteristic of Rao that he should write the story of this quintessentially Indian village while living in a thirteenth-century castle in the French Alps.

It is somewhat surprising that a novel sharply critical of the English should find a publisher in London at this time, but less surprising that it was not printed in India until later. After all, the government of India was still British and very concerned about potential troublemakers like Rao. The style of the novel baffled most English readers, and it was to emerge only gradually as a classic. Not that his work was completely unknown at home; English-published books were commonly sold in India, and he received some early reviews there.

More and more often he visited India. Only after the novel was published did he actually meet Gandhi, in 1941, spending some months with him. He eventually became actively involved in the independence movement, but not as a member of Congress. Instead he was involved with young socialists working underground, and in 1943–44 worked as the co-editor of a radical journal called *Tomorrow*. He also worked with groups promoting traditional Indian culture in opposition to the overwhelmingly English emphasis of official government-sanctioned education.

Simultaneously he was continuing his spiritual quest, and in 1943 in the sage Atmananda Guru felt he had found the inspiration he had been seeking throughout his adult life. From then on he was to think of himself more and more as a Hindu following the spiritual and philosophical path called Vedanta, and less and less as a political being.

In 1947 he published his first collection of short stories, *The Cow of the Barricades and Other Stories,* but most of the contents had appeared elsewhere years before. The title story is of particular interest because it reads almost as a preliminary sketch for his first novel, using the same sort of unsophisticated narrator, village setting, and Gandhian theme as *Kanthapura.* In 1949 Rao was divorced. He was to be remarried twice in later years, both times to American women.

His second novel, *Comrade Kirillov,* was written in the 1950s and published in 1966 in French. It did not appear in its original English form until 1976. Inspired partly by Fyodor Dostoyevsky's *The Possessed*—a critical portrait of the sort of radical socialist revolutionaries the Russian author had associated with in his youth—Rao's work similarly depicts an Indian initially fascinated by Gandhi, but becoming involved in communism and rejecting the Gandhian ideals. He becomes disillusioned with the Soviet Union when Stalin allies himself with the British in World War II, for Britain seems a far more threatening enemy to India than does Hitler. After visiting the USSR, he ultimately turns back to his homeland and its traditional values.

Because *Comrade Kirillov* was unprinted for such a long time, his third novel—*The Serpent and the Rope,* which appeared in 1960—seemed to mark the end of a very long silence. This lengthy, difficult work is obviously based on his own experiences, concerning a young Brahmin studying in France who marries a Frenchwoman from whom he later becomes estranged and eventually divorces. The protagonist has the same academic interests as Rao, but the author transfers his own fascination with Buddhism to the wife. The novel is highly intellectual, filled with long philosophical passages, and many readers find the protagonist rather unlikable. His treatment of women has been especially objected to by several critics. Yet in India, *The Serpent and the Rope* is widely considered a classic and has been much studied and commented on. For the advanced reader, it is full of stimulating ideas, but it often disappoints those looking for a lively story or vivid characterization, and it lacks the charms of *Kanthapura.*

The Serpent and the Rope has often been called the most Indian of novels because of its protagonist's quest for meaning in Vedanta, a lofty philosophical interpretation of Hindu ideas; yet some commentators have noted that his quest is profoundly shaped by European thought, and that he is less a typical South Asian than the sort of Indian a Westerner might imagine: unworldly, ascetic, interested ultimately only in matters that transcend ordinary life.

Throughout his career Rao has swung back and forth between literary pursuits and his interest in philosophy. He taught Indian philosophy at the

University of Texas (1963–67), but in the middle of that period brought out another novel, *The Cat and Shakespeare* (1965), comic in tone, but so difficult that it baffled most reviewers. Scholars sometimes praise it and several have tried to explain it, but no one has succeeded in making it popular.

In 1978 *The Policeman and the Rose,* a short story collection reprinting some of the earlier tales and adding some new ones, was published. This was followed in 1988 by the lengthy novel *The Chessmaster and His Moves,* exploring similar themes to those developed in *The Serpent and the Rope;* and in 1993 by *On the Ganga Ghat,* a collection of eleven sketches of characters and life in Varanasi, the sacred city by the Ganges that every pious Hindu hopes to visit and where many go to die (Rao uses the older British spelling "Benares"). These are not exactly short stories—do not have much of a plot—and they lack the unity that would make them into a novel, but they contain some of Rao's most charming writing. The style is not particularly difficult and wonderfully evokes a kaleidoscopic array of vivid scenes. However, despite a few footnotes and a glossary, Rao leaves much unexplained that will puzzle the novice reader of Indian fiction. For Indian readers and others willing to venture into the unfamiliar, this is a delightful little book.

In 1998, at the age of ninety, he returned to the subject that had figured so prominently in his first novel by publishing a 480-page biography, *The Great Indian Way: A Life of Mahatma Gandhi,* focusing especially on Gandhi's years in South Africa. He currently lives in Texas with his third wife, Susan, who has also adopted the path of Vedanta so important to her husband.

Outside of India, Rao remains almost exclusively known for his first novel, *Kanthapura,* which is often taught in courses on Indian or world literature. It guarantees his place in the list of influential writers in English from the 1930s, which also includes Narayan and Mulk Raj Anand. Together they marked the maturity of Indian writing in English internationally. Although *Kanthapura* is far simpler than his other novels, beginning readers often need some assistance in getting started with this experimental work, and in 1967 New Directions published an edition with very extensive notes explaining words and terms for the non-Indian reader. Only the first 182 pages of the American paperback consist of the text of the novel.

Although several Indian critics have complained about these annotations as overly detailed and pandering to Western ignorance, other readers are very grateful for them. Much that would otherwise be obscure is made clear if the reader consistently consults the notes while going through the novel, at least for the first time. Because Rao has so thoroughly annotated his own work, no entries have been added to the glossary of the present volume dealing with *Kanthapura.* Because Rao's notes are arranged in chronological order and not alphabetically, it is important to consult them the first time an unfamiliar Indian word or name occurs.

Rao explains more in his notes than he really needs to. Once the reader has caught on to a few basic patterns, the book is not terribly difficult to read and can be quite absorbing. Rao is attempting to tell the story of the independence movement from the ground up. After all, in the long run it was not Gandhi alone, but the masses of ordinary Indians that he helped inspire, who won independence. This is not a biography of Gandhi—he does not even appear in the novel—but is instead the story of how one small rural village becomes swept up in the *Satyagraha* (nonviolent resistance) campaign of the 1930s.

It is important to read the brief introductory "Author's Foreword," which explains what Rao is trying to accomplish. He wants to give the effect of an oral narrative, modeled on the style of the traditional Sanskrit *Puranas* that mix storytelling with religious doctrine. One of the simplest aspects of this style is the use of the simple connective "and" to string phrases together into very long sentences. Narratives influenced by spoken delivery often wander from topic to topic in this way, without building grammatical units that focus clearly on a single point. Whatever drifts into the mind of the speaker is uttered at that moment and explored at leisure until she drifts back to what the reader is liable to think of as the main thread of the story. This sort of technique is used in many places in the Hebrew Bible, and it has been suggested that the latter was actually a greater influence on Rao than the *Puranas.*

Resist the temptation to be impatient with the narrator; you are becoming acquainted with her character and with the life of the village as she slowly unravels her tale, and she will eventually make all clear. Toward the end, events build to a climax and the narrative flows in much more conventionally.

Rao's anonymous narrator also tells her story in an unusual syntax, somewhat influenced by Kannada, somewhat by Shakespearian English, and somewhat by Victorian poetry. Sometimes—notably, at the beginning of certain chapters—the narration leaps from simple gossip to transcendently beautiful scene painting in a way that some critics object to, but may be experienced as the flourishes of a practiced storyteller who knows how to impress her audience. The word order may be unusual, but the ideas they convey are seldom truly obscure. After a while the reader adapts and learns to follow the old woman's tale as it unfolds.

Another striking feature of the book is the way in which its narrator has a very limited understanding of her subject. She has never met Gandhi (no one in the book has), and she doesn't clearly grasp all the issues involved in the movement he leads; but she is inspired to take part, partly because the injustices inflicted by British imperialism are so obvious and partly because Gandhi's movement seems a natural adaptation of her accustomed ways of thinking.

Part of Gandhi's genius was presenting his ideas as grounded in tradition in a way that made them seem simultaneously revolutionary and conservative.

He said that although he was often mistaken for a saint trying to be a politician, he was actually a politician trying to be a saint. He was a sophisticated, highly educated, and articulate lawyer who explained to the British in no uncertain terms why they needed to "quit India." Yet he framed his ideas in a Hindu context that spoke powerfully to the broad masses of Indians. The image of the meditating, self-sacrificing, nonviolent ascetic who acquires great spiritual power and transforms the world is a familiar concept in Hinduism. Not infrequently ascetics of this kind are seen as potentially so powerful as to threaten the jealous gods, who seek ways to interrupt their meditations and austerities. The "hunger strike," as it has come to be known in the West, was not a really novel tool in India. Gandhi's fasts were so influential precisely because they were not novel. The power of humility was not a new idea in India; it was simply given a new form and focus by Gandhi.

He would certainly have objected to being worshiped as a god; yet it is understandable that some were tempted to do so. The distinction between the human and divine realms is much more permeable in Hinduism than in religions like Judaism, Christianity, and Islam. Gods are said to have been born and even die on occasion. Gods may worship other gods. Mortals famed for their deeds or piety may be commemorated by temples in their honor after their death and seen as incarnations (*avatars*) of more familiar gods like Vishnu or Shiva. Rao expects us to understand that the villagers in regarding Gandhi as a divinity are simply following a familiar pattern, although one that a sophisticated person like the author would not share.

Gandhi's use of religious terminology and ideas enabled him to frame revolutionary notions in a context that gave the appearance of being conservative, summoning Indians to return to their roots and reject the corrupting influence of the British on their culture. He did this in a quite sincere, subtle, and complex way, but few Indians ever read his writings. Instead, they received his message at many removes from its source, grasping the essence but missing the nuances. Rao is not blaming Gandhi for their misunderstandings; he is simply saying this is how the *Swaraj* movement under Gandhi worked at the grassroots level.

One aspect of the movement in Kanthapura that accurately reflects Gandhi's own practice is the use of religious worship services as protest meetings. The authorities were hesitant to prohibit what were after all traditional patterns of religious expression, although they had become vehicles for political organization.

What the novel does not make clear is that all this use of Hinduism contributed to the eventual alienation of Islamic groups from Gandhi. The only Muslims in this novel are oppressive tools of the British. The heroes and heroines are uniformly Hindu. Even by 1938 "communal" violence between Hindus and Muslims had repeatedly broken out; and of course at independence the new nation was to plunge into a Hindu-Muslim bloodbath of unprecedented proportions. But Rao has the advantage of writing before independence, before the agony of Partition. He idealizes the movement in a way that is realistic, but too limited to give a full picture.

Moorthy is the young man who, inflamed by a vision of Gandhi, brings the message back to his village; yet Moorthy is not the protagonist of the novel. Although he is largely responsible for getting his fellow citizens involved in the protests against the British, he himself disappears at the climax of the story, and in the end—like the young Rao himself—moves away from peaceful resistance toward revolutionary socialism. But interestingly, the novel doesn't take us along with him. This is not the story of Moorthy; it is the story of Kanthapura. The villagers are the focus of the plot, not their leader. In an even more radical move, the whole cast of village characters we have come to know throughout the early portion of the novel is replaced by a new array of names in the final chapters, conveying the feeling that this movement is larger and more significant than the specific individuals who make it up. Without these individuals, the movement would not exist, and yet any one of them can be removed and the movement goes on.

Rao has not tried and failed to write a conventional novel; he has rather succeeded in writing a collective novel, not unlike Emile Zola's *Germinal* (1885) in which a coal miners' uprising continues to inspire revolutionary sentiments among the workers even after its immediate goals have been frustrated and its leaders have been killed or have moved on. Zola was the inventor of the novel of social movement in which mobs could be come more vivid characters than individuals. Although Rao has never mentioned Zola as an influence, it would be surprising if the Indian author had not encountered *Germinal* while living in France. Or perhaps he is simply receiving the spirit of Zola through Ignazio Silone, whose novel *Fontamara*—published shortly before, in 1936—Rao has singled out as his immediate inspiration. It depicts a small Italian village struggling through troubled times in a way that clearly belongs to the same tradition, with the Fascists taking the role played by the British in *Kanthapura*.

The narrator begins by immersing us in the world of Kanthapura, a village we have never heard of, but which is the world for her. The British are the red-faced foreigners from somewhere far away who carry off the local produce, creating the traffic that groans along on carts through the lanes of the village. She may not understand the economics of agricultural exports, but she knows exactly how much Subha Chettee paid for his bulls.

The references to Kenchamma allude to a traditional pattern of religion in India, where it is sometimes jokingly said the gods outnumber the mortals. That each locale should have its own god is a widespread notion, made more comprehensible by the tendency to blend all divinities into one ultimate reality. The myriad manifestations of the divine are just vehicles for a larger truth, just like the locally important saints in various spots in Catholic countries. Kenchamma is the goddess of Kanthapura, she insists, not of villages like Talassana. Trade is embodied in Subha Chettee, worship in Kenchamma, but that does not mean the people of Kanthapura are incapable of understanding the larger issues about to sweep over them.

The coffee and cardamom estates are plantations owned by the British and worked with underpaid and abused labor imported from far away. American readers may be surprised at the term "coolie" being applied to these laborers, because they are more familiar with it in the context of China, yet the term is originally Indian. The two main social groups in the village are the traditional small farmers, craftsmen and merchants, on the one hand, and the impoverished coolies practically enslaved on the estates, on the other.

Although Rao is otherwise a very male-centered author, the focus of this book is largely feminine. Not only is the narrator a woman, but she is addressing other women (note the occasional use of the term "sister" applied to her audience). The villagers worship female gods, the most effective protests are carried out largely by women, the most vivid characters are women. Rao is engaging not so much in feminist protest as in an effort to show that the movement for Indian independence, although led by the middle classes, also involved those at the very bottom of society: the powerless, those maltreated even by their own culture.

Note the way in which the narrator slides back and forth between ordinary village life and the realm of the mythical. There is no separation between them in her mind. Everyday life does not need to be transcended to reach the divine; everyday life is saturated by the divine.

One of the more subtle bits of characterization in the book is the narrator's casual statement that there are only twenty-four houses in the village. This seems tiny indeed, until we realize pages later that she is counting only the houses of Brahmins; the hundreds of others from lesser castes are simply extras in the drama of her life until the crisis moves them to the forefront and unites all these formerly divided people into a single force. This was one of Gandhi's principal aims. He felt that traditional discrimination based on caste weakened Indian society and had to be rejected not only because it was humane and just to do so, but because it was politically necessary.

The word "quarter" is not to be understood in its mathematical sense, for there are five quarters in *Kanthapura*. Hindu castes are linked to traditional occupations like weaving or pottery making, but that does not mean everyone belonging a caste actually pursues its traditional way of making a living. The "potters," for instance, farm and make bricks. Near the bottom of society are the *sudras*, common laborers, who in many villages would make up the bulk of the population. The narrator ends her survey with them, not even mentioning the untouchables (*pariahs;* now more often referred to as *dalits*), who are also unmentionable in her world—invisible until they are thrust forcefully into her life.

Like the political movement that will soon capture her allegiance, religion is a grassroots matter in Kanthapura as well. The discovery of an abandoned *linga* (more commonly spelled *lingam*) leads naturally to the creation of a temple and a pattern of worship that will be a vehicle for the movement against the British. Worship for these people is a pleasure they seek out, not a duty imposed from above. And it is a highly social pleasure, a way of enjoying each other's company. A *Harikatha* is an absorbing form of entertainment as well as a religious exercise.

Moorthy begins to spread the message of the Mahatma ("Great Soul"— not Gandhi's name, but a traditional Hindu honorific title applied to him on account of his saintliness). But the narrator does not welcome it. Gandhi's rejection of caste discrimination and advocacy of the remarriage of widows is a sign of the collapse of values, so far as she is concerned. Her sense of charity extends to Brahmin orphans, not lesser beings.

Jayaramachar's myth of the birth of Gandhi as a reworking of the story of Shiva and Parvati from the *Ramayana* is meant to be amusing as well as inspiring. Rao does not expect his readers to believe one word of this fabulous tale, but we are meant to be impressed by the power the image of Gandhi exercises over the popular imagination, which digests the novelty he represents in the best way it can. Gandhi is compared to Krishna, an exceedingly popular god who is understood to be an avatar of the great god Vishnu in human form but with supernatural powers. Krishna is a demon slayer, a protector of the people against evil forces, just as Gandhi struggles to free the people from the oppression of the British. Gandhi is the Krishna of this age. If his charity toward untouchables and widows is offensively unorthodox, his message of nonattachment to worldly possessions and passions is tradition itself.

It is hinted that Jayaramachar's message antagonizes the police into arresting him or at least banishing him from the village, but the upshot is that increasing numbers of people are converted to the cause, which now has a life of its own. But the police hope to have the last word: they send Badè Khan, the Muslim (Rao uses the old-fashioned term "Mohammedan") agent of the plantation owners to keep an eye on things in Kanthapura.

In Chapter 2 Badè Khan is clearly revealed as weakened by his status as an outsider, although he represents the power of the government imposed on them from above. Rangè Gowda, the village head man (*Patel*), has more traditional legitimacy and respect; he can afford to be dismissive of this newcomer—at first. But when Badè Khan says that the Patel doesn't know who he's speaking to, he's telling the truth. It's only natural that the estate manager, Mr. Skeffington, should take Badè Khan under his wing; this move makes it crystal clear whom the policeman really serves. The ultimate power of the government is hidden, but will reveal itself when the soldiers who back the policeman up arrive on the scene.

Another village villain is Waterfall Kenchamma (the suffix *amma,* meaning "mother," is routinely tacked on to the names of married females in Kanthapura). Her malevolence springs from more personal sources than does Badè Khan's: envy. She hates Moorthy because he refused to marry her daughter who was quickly approaching an unmarriageable age by the standards of the time, and she is jealous of the neighbor whose house has become Moorthy's base of operations.

Moorthy launches into a detailed explanation of the economics of rice, which it may be tempting to skip, but it is vital to follow the discussion. This is the heart of the explanation of how imperialism works, extracting wealth for the British from these impoverished Indian peasants. So long as they remained enmeshed in this trade system whose rules work against them, they can never be truly free.

Intimately related to this theme is the best known aspect of Gandhi's economic strategy: the rejection of foreign cotton and the popular production of homespun (*khadi*) cloth. Gandhi made the spinning wheel his symbol, linking it to the old Buddhist image of the wheel as the cycle of life, death, and rebirth (a wheel remains a symbol of India today, appearing on the national flag). Some argue that he spent too much energy and too many resources on a narrow campaign that had in the end relatively little effect on the British; but its symbolic value was great. Nanjamma is dubious at first partly because her status as a Brahmin defines her as a person who should not have to do such work. In the end she spins not because she understands the point of it all, but because she is willing to imitate Gandhi, and Gandhi spins daily. The thread she produces may not be terribly useful, but the change of heart it takes to align her with her neighbors—all of them spinning in the cause of independence—is invaluable.

The most significant village villain is Bhatta, the moneylender, who is revealed in Chapter 3 to combine an air of piety with a taste for luxury. His economic interests are intimately entwined with those of the British. He began life modestly enough as an astrologer, but his rapacious ways have enabled him to buy and sell politicians and acquire power over much of the population. At the end of the novel Bhatta will survive unchanged, safely off to the holy city of Kashi (the sacred precinct in Varanasi) where he can practice his devotions and increase his income at the same time. He represents a way of using Hinduism for personal gain that contrasts strikingly with the path of the public-spirited Moorthy.

Bhatta has strong arguments on his side in objecting to Gandhi's campaign for rights for the pariahs because the other Brahmins really feel the same as he does. Much of their identity is tied up in the existence of castes who are emphatically not Brahmin, and the pariahs are the extreme case. Rangamma can only defend him by repeating what she has heard, that Gandhi wants to preserve caste distinctions involving intermarriage and dining together. These are not small points, for the prohibition against marrying someone not of your caste or against sharing a meal with a lower caste are the defining characteristics of caste, the bedrock on which the whole system rests.

In the 1930s Gandhi engaged in a vigorous debate with untouchable leader B. R. Ambedkar. Gandhi, the upper-caste Bania, did indeed advocate crossing traditional caste boundaries, himself adopting an untouchable girl, sharing food with untouchables, and performing the ultimate, defining untouchable task: cleaning latrines with his own hands and advocating that others do the same. But he refused to make caste in itself the main focus of his campaign, arguing that the traditional association of certain jobs with certain groups was sanctified by Hindu tradition and should be interpreted as a spur to duty rather than as an excuse for privilege. Ambedkar replied that Gandhi's subtle distinction would be never be grasped by ordinary people: any tolerance shown toward the institution of caste inevitably meant acceptance of the associated prohibitions in the mind of the average Hindu. Rangamma's confusion seems to illustrate Ambedkar's point.

Given what we know about Stalin's Soviet Union in the 1930s, Rangamma's idyllic portrait of life in the USSR seems intolerably naïve, but for many people around the world the ideal of Marxist liberation from capitalist oppression still held powerful appeal, and not only among simple folk. Jahawarlal Nehru, the country's sophisticated founding premier, admired a good deal about the Soviet system as well, and the policies of postindependence India were socialist for a very long time.

Bhatta's threat to have Moorthy outcasted is no idle gesture. A Brahmin who let himself be contaminated by contact with untouchables could lose his standing in the community in ways that were even worse than being an untouchable. Theoretically no one would feed him or marry him. He would be cast out not only of the society of Brahmins, but out of the society of all Hindus. Untouchables might have a wretched role to play in society, but they did have an assigned, secure role. An outcaste had none.

It is interesting to watch how Moorthy himself and his supporters move from tentative gestures toward the pariahs, to denial that he has broken the prohibition, and finally to frank recognition that although he has broken the taboo, they do not really want to treat him as an outcaste. These changes are the result of his personality and reputation, but they are powerful changes, helping transform the inhabitants of Kanthapura into the kind of Indian citizens Gandhi is trying to create.

We now meet Ratna, one of the most important figures in the novel, widowed as a young girl. Tradition dictated that she not remarry, shave her head, shun all personal decoration, and live a life of pious contemplation awaiting death, perhaps for many decades. A century earlier she might have been forced to burn herself alive on her husband's funeral pyre. Widows came very close to not having a right to live at all. Since the mid-nineteenth century, however, progressive Indians had been campaigning for widows' rights; and Ratna eagerly lays claim to those rights in defiance of her disapproving neighbors. Already beyond the pale of conservative society, she has literally nothing to lose by standing up for the rights of others. She is just the sort of Brahmin who can understand what life is like for pariahs. Because she is attractive in a way that violates the popular conception of an asexual widow, she is a destabilizing force, disturbing her distant relative Bhatta, whose desire for her makes him hate her all the more.

His mother Narsamma loves her son like a "holy bull" (remember that cows are sacred to Hindus), and Moorthy is so brilliant that other mothers are trying to match their daughters up with him by asking for his horoscope when he is only sixteen. A boy that young could marry, but he was much less likely to do so than a girl of the same age. Moorthy is presented as a sort of holy mystic, having been inspired to follow Gandhi in a vision. Gandhi did not impose an oath of celibacy on his followers, of course, although he did take one himself and generally favored sexual abstinence. A traditional Hindu mother longs above all for her son to marry and beget an heir; devotion to spiritual matters can wait until old age. Moorthy's choice is further a problem for her because rather than following a traditional guru, he has cast his lot with the Volunteers. It is only by framing this decision in a traditional setting of divine inspiration that she can understand his choice to be a "Gandhi's man."

The comparison of Moorthy with Hanuman is highly significant, for in the *Ramayana* the monkey king was a powerful and revered warrior who assisted the great god Rama and is one of the most popular figures in Hindu mythology. But the values Moorthy espouses are particularly Gandhian: truth, love of humankind, and love of God. The burning of his foreign books and clothing reflect campaigns that were fairly widespread to boycott British educational institutions and imports, although they inevitably remind the Western reader as well of Italy's St. Francis, who cast off his clothes and other possessions when he decided to devote himself entirely to God.

Given that he has set himself on a path that conflicts directly with the interests of the British plantation owners, his mother's dream of marrying him to the daughter of a coffee planter is of course doomed to be frustrated. Note that the story of Moorthy's conversion experience is submerged in the discussion of his marriage prospects, which are much more important to the narrator. These prospects are foregrounded to convey her attitudes, and the reader is expected to see past them to understand what is important to Moorthy and what in the long run will transform life for everyone in the village, including the narrator.

The brief episode in which Waterfall Venkamma repents having criticized Moorthy and apologizes is important, for it humanizes her. She is not a malevolent demonic being, but a frustrated, envious woman. Her momentary mellowing makes it all the easier to accept her as a realistic character.

The passage that opens Chapter 4 is one of Rao's wonderful bits of scene painting, this time of the Kanthapura fair. It is partly this sort of vivid evocation of specific times and places that makes this novel so much more memorable than his other works. But it is not just so much decoration; the casual mention that images of the Mahatma are being sold alongside the more traditional ones of Rama and Krishna tells us that Moorthy is far from being the only person swept up in the enthusiasm for Gandhi. Yet his own mother is still not ready to accept the new way of thinking and considers him as having lost caste entirely. Whereas in the West rebellion against parents and independence are expected of young people as a matter of course, in India this schism between mother and son is profoundly tragic. She is in anguish over having to drive her son from his home, but she believes it is her religious duty to do so. The villagers would undoubtedly have blamed her ensuing death on Moorthy, and he is temporarily exiled from the village. But times are changing, and when he returns to live at home while working with the Pariahs, few think anything of it.

The opening of Chapter 5 is set on the vast Skeffington coffee estate, which has only hovered in the background of the story so far. The narrator has a fairly detailed grasp of the ways in which the *maistri* recruits laborers for the fields. Although it is doubtful that such a woman would be privy to such details or even interested in them, the account is itself an accurate portrait of the ruthless exploitation of poor peasants on colonial estates. Note the contrast between the promises made them while they are being recruited and the reality of life in the coffee fields. Not only are they not given the rewards they had been promised for relocating, they are forced to repay the estate for their transportation to the site of their exploitation.

The English estate manager considers himself "not a bad man" while behaving with the utmost brutality toward the workers, finally descending even to rape and murder. This is another realistic touch, for only in melodramas do villains gleefully twirl their mustaches and rejoice in their villainy; cruelty and exploitation are normally carried out under the guise of duty, discipline, and order.

It has often been noted that the desperately poor rarely lead revolutions, being too hopeless and occupied with mere survival to engage in political agitation. It is from the middle classes that revolutionaries usually spring, and that is the case in Kanthapura. Once the movement is well underway and a degree of hope infiltrates the poverty-stricken workers, they will be moved to join in, but not before.

The long passage on the ways of snakes is not merely a digression; it illustrates how the poor pass the time and keep their spirits up by telling stories. Snakes in Hindu mythology are not only a menace; they can also offer powerful protection to those they honor (look for the passage in Chapter 7 in which Moorthy finds a cobra's sheltering hood spread over him), and Siddayya says that snakes never kill the innocent. Yet in the midst of these reassuring fables we see the reality: the coolies risk their very lives working in these fields, protected from deadly vipers only by their flimsy hats—and the coolies are beaten for wasting their time talking about such things.

Another passage of poetic description depicts the onset of the monsoon rains, which are at first welcomed as a break from work, a sort of vacation. It is traditional to greet the beginning of the monsoon with rejoicing in India, for it marks a break in the oppressive heat and is crucial for agriculture. A long tradition of classical poetry depicts this as a time of leisure and lovemaking. But its more lasting consequence is the arrival of the deadly scourge of malaria, which mows down many of the poor, especially children and the elderly. Their ignorance prevents them from accepting the one beneficial gift offered them by the sahib: the powerful but bitter-tasting drug quinine. This episode illustrates how British ignorance of the social fabric of the people who labor under them prevents the landowners from working effectively with the coolies; but it also makes the point that not all social reform can involve the reaffirmation of traditional Indian ideas and the rejection of European ones. Independent India will have to be forged out of a mixture of ideas, both old and new.

The defiance of Badè Khan by Gandhi's men is described at the end of the chapter in a way characteristic of Hinduism, which in theory at least always granted higher respect to learned religious scholars than to powerful secular authorities. It is for this reason that the narrator emphasizes the learnedness of these young men; doing so provides a traditional framework for justifying their rebellion.

Finally, in Chapter 6, the conflict between the anti-British forces in the village and the authorities takes a physical shape. From now on, the story develops in a much more straightforward fashion, with fewer digressions, and is relatively easy to follow. Moorthy, as a good follower of Gandhi, imitates the leader in Chapter 7 by fasting to deter further violence. From the narrator's point of view, he is engaging in a traditional mode of devotion that is vividly described here, but Rao also depicts the ongoing struggle from now on as compounded of both peaceful resistance and explosions of violence. He is not interested in portraying these people as perfect *satyagrahis;* for the independence of India was won by ordinary people, not saints. The power of nonviolence as used in the demonstrations against the British is undeniable; but it is also undeniable that outbursts of violence showed the British what they could expect if they failed to respond in the long run to Gandhi's campaign. But for now, Moorthy's fasting is far more powerful than any military action could be in attracting supporters to the cause, even if they are incapable of loving their enemies, as the Mahatma has urged them to do.

Moorthy's fear of Ratna's attractiveness echoes Gandhi's fear of his own sexuality, but it is not necessarily endorsed by Rao. Together they could have made a powerful team, and as we shall see, the life-affirming Ratna will eventually replace the ascetic Moorthy as leader of the local movement. Moorthy is far from perfect. It is moving that his Brahmin instincts still cause him to recoil from the threshold of a pariah household when he must first enter one, and that sipping coffee from a cup offered him by a pariah takes a degree of determination and courage lacking in most higher-caste Brahmins of his time. His outer struggle with the British is complicated by this inner struggle with his own upbringing. We can guess that he may even feel somewhat relieved that Rangamma pushes him into enacting a purification ritual afterward.

For all the emphasis in this novel on the power of the common people, it takes a familiar tyrant, old Rangè Gowda, to intimidate them into swearing their devotion to the cause, and the influence of old patterns is illustrated by the fact that the pariahs are still not allowed into the temple but must swear their allegiance from outside on the temple steps. It is now that Moorthy explains that women must be included in the leadership of the new organization (referred to by a familiar term for a village council as a *panchayat*), for by definition they represent the "weak and lowly" on whose behalf the struggle is being waged. This is an important moment, for from this point on the story will gradually shift to become the story of the women's resistance to the authorities.

Moorthy's arrest in the next chapter is portrayed from the point of view of the women as they slowly discover what has happened. When the focus shifts back to the young man himself, Rao subtly alludes to the arrest of Christ by alluding to a famous biblical incident in which Jesus is betrayed by Peter before the cock has crowed three times (Mark 14:66–72). In the ensuing reaction, Rangè Gowda's attack on the policeman represents an important escalation of the conflict. He is a respected local leader, no upstart youth; but he has irrevocably allied himself with Moorthy now. Moorthy's final excommunication is carried out by a swami demonstrably indebted to the British and who voices sentiments about the inability of the Indians to rule themselves that were not uncommon among upper-class Indians who worked closely with the colonial government.

The "don't-touch-the-government" campaign is an ingenious device that somewhat inconsistently but effectively appeals to Hindu ideas about ritual pollution. The English are declared to be defiling, whereas the formerly defiling pariahs are slowly becoming more accepted. That the role of the popular press is spreading such resistance is noted here. The reading of articles from the pro-Gandhi papers is mingled with readings from the sutras in a way that continues the pattern of secular protest in a sacred setting. When the peasants praise the mother goddess Kenchamma, it is in her role as demon slayer, and the "Red-demon" is clearly meant to represent the "red men": the British.

This pattern undergoes a significant development in Chapter 11 when Moorthy has vanished into prison and Ratna has become reader of the sacred texts, with Rangamma supplying anti-British interpretations. The workshops they conduct in nonviolent resistance among the women are models of what took place all over India during this period. In a later episode Ratna alludes to the fact that women have been beaten by their husbands for centuries without resisting; perhaps they can turn this experience with abuse into an advantage by stoically enduring the attacks of the police.

More inspiringly, women also cleverly go back in history to find a role model for militant women in the Rani Lakshmi Bai, who was certainly not a nonviolent person but who showed what a woman could accomplish in the 1857–58 uprising, which the British derogatorily called the "Sepoy Mutiny" and is sometimes proudly referred to by Indians themselves as "the First War of Independence." How successful they are in evoking this role model is suggested by the eagerness of a small boy to have his turn at pretending to be the Rani, despite the fact that she was a woman.

Chapter 12 begins with a prose poem on the season of planting. However, this crop, unlike those of most years, will be harvested amid blood and fire. The narrator shows her fascination with traditional ritual by giving us a detailed account of the blessing of the bulls and plows in a way that shows she is still the same person who began the tale of Kanthapura a hundred pages earlier, focusing on whatever catches her attention; but her account slides gradually into talk of Moorthy's return. The rituals of the village, no matter how traditional and important, cannot be sealed off from current events.

At the beginning of Chapter 13, the famous "salt march" to the sea at Dandi by Gandhi and his followers took place in 1930, so that gives us a date for the events depicted in the novel. Although Rao could not have known it, independence lay another seventeen long and bitter years in the future. The British outlawed Indian-manufactured salt to preserve the heavily taxed British monopoly on a commodity everyone needed. Gandhi's choice of this everyday item for his protest had an even more effective appeal than did the campaign to switch to homespun cloth, and it made the British look exceedingly mean-spirited and tyrannical.

Although Gandhi never appears in person in *Kanthapura,* he is no longer just a distant mythical character. First the salt march, then his arrest, make a powerful impact on the villagers; and they protest, as did Indians all over the subcontinent. His message comes through especially clearly when Moorthy declares that the movement will be suspended for six months if violence erupts on the side of the protesters—a tactic indeed used by Gandhi himself to try to rein in the passions of his followers.

The drinking of alcohol was traditionally discouraged by Hindus and Muslims alike, but the British are here depicted as using a palm wine "toddy" to exploit and degrade their subjects much as they had used opium against the Chinese. It has been argued that it is implausible for a group of impoverished coolies to fling themselves enthusiastically into a campaign against the one source of consolation they have in their lives, but this is the sort of intense moment in which people can be moved to do unusual things. There is no implication that the consumption of alcohol has been abruptly eradicated forever; but the coolies now clearly see and understand the role it is being made to play in keeping them down. However, the most important event in Chapter 15 is not the attack on the toddy shops, but the departure of thirty-three coolies from the estate. The British relied on poorly paid Indian labor to extract wealth from India for them, and when people as desperate as this are no longer willing to be instruments of their own exploitation, it is a great sign of hope.

From this point on, the uprising spreads, with more and more villages joining in. The British resort to mass arrests and torture, but the momentum created by the protesters from Kanthapura seems unstoppable. We are also reminded in Chapter 16 that not all heroic resisters are Gandhians, as Chandrayya tells the story of the Marxist Brahmin he met in prison.

Boycotting toddy and manufactured cloth is one thing, but the villagers strike at the heart of the system when they decide to boycott taxes. The whole imperial system rests on the collection of these taxes, mostly paid by the local farmers in kind, as a portion of their crops. From the time the tax-resistance strategy is embarked on, the final confrontation is inevitable. The ideology of imperialism spoke loftily of the civilizing burden born by the English, but at bottom it was a tool for extracting wealth from Indian labor, and nothing could be allowed to interfere with its smooth functioning.

Ratna leads the women in the siege of the temple, at first scolding those who want to leave by saying "don't be a woman," meaning they should not be weak and fearful; but Rangamma's example earlier then inspires her to provide a new model of what it means to be a woman by telling tales of heroic deeds accomplished by women, this time not princesses but contemporary women like themselves who are joining the struggle all over India. How drastically the village has changed is illustrated when a pariah frees them from the temple that in former times she would not have even been allowed to enter.

The use of rape as weapon against women in conflicts like this is all too familiar a phenomenon, exacerbated by the tendency of the victims to regard themselves as disgraced, like Puttamma. It is partly this traditional shifting of blame from rapist to victim that motivates the rapist: he violates not only his victim's body but deliberately robs her of her dignity. The acute sense of shame attached to a woman who has lost her virtue also undermines Ratna's leadership in the eyes of traditionalists like Satamma in Chapter 18. She sees the young widow's brazen behavior as ushering in an age of dishonor for all women who follow her.

Because the villagers have refused to pay their taxes, their property is seized and sold, effectively destroying the village culture. Their resistance leads to the worst attack yet, ending in a massive slaughter that would not be considered incredible by anyone who remembered the infamous 1919 Jallianwala Bagh massacre in Amritsar just a decade earlier in which hundreds of unarmed Indians were shot down by British-led troops. In the ensuing melee the villagers are not depicted as perfect *satyagrahis;* there are instances of violence on their side as well, but they are unarmed and pathetically vulnerable to troops armed with guns.

Ultimately the women respond by a "scorched-earth" tactic, burning down their crops and former homes to keep them out of the hands of the British. This may seem like a catastrophic conclusion to their heroic efforts, but it is important to note that though the villagers have been separated from the village, they have been transformed by their experiences. Scattered across the countryside, some of them are the kernels of the next wave of resistance. Even though Moorthy himself has turned his back on Gandhi, the cause he advocated will continue to spread.

The discouraging note struck in the novel's final paragraph as we learn of the continued prosperity of some of Kanthapura's most prominent evildoers is met by a curse on the part of the narrator. However, her final statement is "But to tell you the truth, mother, my heart it beat like a drum." That "but" implies she is feeling something different from mere anger or cynicism. The drumbeat she feels in her breast signals a determination to continue the struggle for whose sake they have paid so dearly, despite the betrayal of countrymen and the ruthlessness of their imperial rulers. It is a cry of determination uttered in the very midst of the conflict, urging Indians to press on to the end.

SELECTED BIBLIOGRAPHY

Dey, Esha. *The Novels of Raja Rao: The Theme of Quest.* New Delhi: Prestige, 1992.
    This sharply critical survey of Rao's fiction through *On the Ganga Ghat* explores the non-Indian influences on him in a sophisticated and stimulating manner. It also contains the best recent bibliography of scholarship on Rao.

Naik, M. K. *Raja Rao.* New York: Twayne, 1972.
    This early study still provides beginners an accessible and useful introduction to Rao's most famous works.

Rao, Raja. *The Cat and Shakespeare. A Tale of India.* New York: Macmillan, 1965.
———. *The Chessmaster and His Moves.* New Delhi: Vision Books, 1988.
———. *Comrade Kirillov.* New Delhi: Orient Paperbacks, 1976.
    Originally published in a French translation by Georges Fradier as half of a volume entitled *La Chatte et Shakespeare, Camarade Kirillov* (Paris: Calmann-Lévy, 1966).

———. *The Cow of the Barricades and Other Stories.* Bombay: Oxford University Press, 1947.
    Contains the stories "Javni," "The True Story of Kanakapala," "Protector of God," and "Companions," "Khandesh," "Cow of the Barricades," "The Little Gram Shop," "Narsiga," and "A Client."

————. *The Great Indian Way: A Life of Mahatma Gandhi.* Delhi: Vision Books, 1998.

Biography of Mahatma Gandhi, focusing on his years in South Africa.

————. *Kanthapura.* New York: New Directions, 1963.

The annotated American edition of the author's 1938 novel, originally published in London by George Allen and Unwin.

————. *On the Ganga Ghat.* New Delhi: Vision Books, 1989.

Eleven untitled stories arranged to be read as a novel.

————. *The Policeman and the Rose.* Delhi: Oxford University Press, 1978.

Contains the stories "The True Story of Kanakapala: Protector of Gold," "In Khandesh," "Companions," "The Cow of the Barricades," "Akkayya," "The Little Gram Shop," "Javni," "Nimka," "India—A Fable," "The Policeman and the Rose," plus an essay on the author by pioneer critic C. D. Narasimhaiah, a brief glossary, and a valuable autobiographical sketch by Rao giving details of the author's early life.

————. *The Serpent and the Rope.* 1960. New York: Pantheon, 1963.

Shashikumar, V. K. "The Truth of It All." *The Week* 13 Dec. 1998. <http://www.the-week.com/98dec13/life7.htm>.

An interesting look at the author just after his ninetieth birthday; reflecting his intense interest in spiritual matters, but of limited use for understanding *Kanthapura.*

Chapter 3
Khushwant Singh: Train to Pakistan *(1956)*

Khushwant Singh is indisputably South Asia's best known English-language journalist. Over his very long career, he has written, edited, or translated over eighty volumes, a substantial number of short stories, and countless articles for magazines and newspapers.

Singh was born, he guesses, on August 15, 1915, in what was then the tiny Indian town of Hadali, a desert village in the Punjab, in an area now incorporated into Pakistan. Although as a journalist he has been one of India's hardest-working writers, like some of the other authors discussed in this volume he was not a particularly diligent student. But he was sent to good schools because he belonged to a wealthy family, going from St. Stephens College in Delhi to Lahore Government College (where one of his schoolmates was Faiz Ahmed Faiz, later to become a famed Urdu poet), and he left India in 1934 to study law at King's College.

While in England he encountered Kaval Malik, a girl he had actually gone to school with years before, and they fell in love. With the agreement of their parents, this love match was turned into a marriage that has lasted over sixty-five years. The couple settled in Lahore, where he struggled to establish a law practice for the next several years.

The next major turning point in his life was also the greatest event in the history of modern India and inspired his masterpiece, *Train to Pakistan:* the separation of India from British rule in 1947 and the splitting of the country into the Muslim-dominated country of Pakistan and the Hindu-dominated country of modern India. What should have been the joyful culmination of decades of anti-British struggle became a shameful debacle as Muslims,

Hindus, and Sikhs turned on each other in a fury of religious bigotry. The violence surrounding Partition is the main subject of *Train to Pakistan,* discussed in more detail later.

Singh was eager to get out of India in the wake of this calamity, and he took the opportunity to serve as a diplomat representing the new nation in England and Canada. While in Canada he tried his hand as a writer, achieving his first publication there. He began writing *Train to Pakistan* in London, but finished it after resigning from the diplomatic service in 1951, in the Indian city of Bhopal. He did not immediately become a full-time writer, however. At first Singh was in charge of English-language programming on All-India Radio, and then he became head of mass communications for UNESCO in Paris. Throughout his life he has been associated with broadcasting, appearing frequently in radio and television interviews.

Although he was already known in India as a short story writer, it was the publication of *Train to Pakistan* (originally titled *Mano Majra*) in 1956 by Grove Press in New York that brought Singh international fame. It was quickly translated into German and French, and later into many other languages as well, and became by far the best known fictional account of Partition.

From that point on, Singh considered himself primarily a writer, holding various editing jobs, writing a two-volume history of the Sikhs, and publishing his second novel, *I Shall Not Hear the Nightingale,* in 1959. It concerns a Sikh family in the Punjab during World War II, focusing on the ineffectual and eventually disastrous efforts of a teenaged boy to take up arms against the British and the sexual adventures of his highly passionate wife. Although it is a minor work, it contains several vivid scenes. Typically for Singh, the British are presented not unsympathetically, and nationalist terrorism is satirized. It is not that Singh doesn't love his country; he just insists that his fellow citizens should not allow affection and pride to color their understanding of the past.

His ambiguous attitudes toward the English are manifested in many ways in the novel. The protagonist has a dog he has contemptuously named Dyer, after the general responsible for one of the worst massacres carried out in India by the British (the Jallianwalla Bagh Massacre in Amritsar, 1919), but it is pointed out that he dearly loves that dog. His small band of would-be terrorists kills an informer, but almost by accident. The local British deputy commissioner is depicted not unsympathetically as a fair-minded, tolerant person who supports the general idea of Indian independence while insisting it must be postponed until after the war to prevent a Japanese takeover. The young man's father is torn between his support for the independence movement and his sympathy for the British.

The sensational figure of the wife seems more like an erotic fantasy than a thoughtful portrait. It can be said that both partners in this marriage are driven by their emotions in highly self-destructive ways. Throughout much of the book, the coming disaster of Partition is foreshadowed, and these small disasters may be seen as premonitions of the larger disaster to come.

Besides writing for a living, Singh taught at Princeton, the University of Hawaii, and at Swarthmore College in the United States, where he was in 1969 when he received an invitation to return home to become editor of the *Illustrated Weekly of India,* a rather stodgy English-language cultural journal. Over the next decade he turned it into a racy popular magazine, running a series on minority communities, suspenseful fiction, nude pinups, and his own breezy and often controversial columns, many of which are collected in *Khushwant Singh's Editor's Page* (1981). His outspoken enjoyment of sex and whiskey, his sympathy with Pakistan, and his praise of the British administrative system during the Raj created a sensation, and since then he has been viewed as an outrageous but highly entertaining iconoclast.

Although he was generally a strong supporter of Prime Minister Indira Gandhi and her son Sanjay—especially during the period of the Emergency (1975–77) when she was at her least popular as virtual dictator of India—he eventually offended her and was essentially removed from his editorship at the request of the government in 1978. It was at this time, according to Singh, that he began work on the novel that was to become his third major work of fiction: *Delhi.*

Singh served as a member of Parliament (1980–86), often providing a dissident if unpredictable voice in national debates, but his main work continued to be journalism and editing. He is especially well known as a columnist to the *Hindustan Times,* which he also edited (1980–83), and for his work for many other newspapers and magazines. He has long served as an editor for Penguin India and acknowledges that he recommended against their publishing Salman Rushdie's controversial novel *The Satanic Verses* in India in the 1980s, even though his own writings are at least as cheerfully irreligious and bawdy as Rushdie's.

Despite the fact that work on *Delhi* had begun much earlier, the influence of Rushdie's *Midnight's Children* (1981) was apparent in the structure, themes, and narrative technique of Singh's novel when it finally appeared in 1990. It is less a novel than a collection of fictional sketches depicting figures from Delhi's past, emphasizing sex and violence in large doses. Readers desiring more background to the stories told in *Delhi* should consult his lively history of the city: *Delhi: A Portrait* (1983). Colorful but uneven, the novel sold extremely well in India but was little noticed abroad, where he continued to be thought of exclusively as author of *Train to Pakistan.*

As the fiftieth anniversary of Partition approached, the national state television network Doordarshan commissioned a remarkably faithful film version of *Train to Pakistan* (directed by Pamela Rooks, 1996, in Hindi). The national celebrations in 1997 were muted by the awareness that Indians were also observing the anniversary of a holocaust, and Singh's novel continued to embody that holocaust in the minds of many.

He returned to fiction once more with *In the Company of Women* (1999), essentially a set of wild erotic fantasies with a curiously abrupt moralizing conclusion that sold wildly in India but has been generally ignored elsewhere.

Among Singh's nonfiction works, it is especially worth seeking out the charming *Nature Watch,* a set of essays with illustrative watercolors by Suddhasattwa Basu, one per month, tracing the varied bird life and the shifting appearance of flowers and trees throughout the year in Delhi. His sensitive descriptions of birds and trees echo those in *Train to Pakistan. Nature Watch* resembles a children's book in format, but is clearly aimed at the adult birdwatcher and nature lover. His *India: An Introduction* (1974; reprinted under varying titles) is still widely read as a general introduction to the culture, although it is now rather dated.

To understand *Train to Pakistan,* the Western reader needs some essential background. Khushwant Singh was born and raised a Sikh, although not a pious one. The Sikh religion originated in the sixteenth century when its founder, the Guru Nanak Dev, blended features of Islam and Hinduism to create a faith that rejected idolatry, polytheism, discrimination based on caste, and *sati*. Although it began as a pacifist religion, the tenth guru, Gobind Singh, converted the Sikhs in the late seventeenth century into a military sect. Both the British and Indian national governments have taken advantage of Sikh fighting skills, although only a minority of Sikhs have ever actually served as soldiers.

The men almost universally adopt the surname "Singh" and wear the distinctive Sikh turban. Sikh men are also supposed to grow their hair and beards long and wear an ornamental sword called a *kirpan* at all times. They tend to be taller than the average Indian and have an undeserved reputation among other Indians for being conservative and dimwitted: a stereotype the brilliant Khushwant Singh delights in smashing with his carousing, free-spirited ways. The outsider is most likely to encounter them as taxi drivers, from Delhi to New York.

Although Sikhs constitute less than 2 percent of the Indian population, their military history and striking appearance make them familiar everywhere in South Asia. They were in the majority only in the northern region called the Punjab until Partition divided their land between Pakistan and India, a decision that has left them deeply embittered ever since. In the region described in *Train to Pakistan,* they are the prosperous landowners who employ numbers of impoverished Muslims to work on their plots. Relationships are basically friendly, but an underlying tension is caused by the difference in religion and in class.

What South Asians call "communal" (interfaith) violence usually has some kind of economic as well as spiritual basis, a pattern observable as well in places like Northern Ireland, Israel, and Macedonia. Religion may be the excuse that inflames the passions of these villagers, but Singh makes clear that their conflict is ultimately over money and power.

Islam had been introduced into Northern India over many centuries, first by merchants and then by conquering hordes from Central Asia, who sometimes ruthlessly sought to suppress what they viewed as the impious practices of the Hindu faith, but more often followers of the two religions have lived peacefully side by side. Sikhism may be viewed as an attempt to bridge the gap between the two faiths, but in fact the Sikhs wound up largely isolated and by the mid-1940s saw themselves losing not only their property but their status as guardians of the British presence in India.

The main violence during Partition took place between Hindus and Muslims. Pakistan was created during the negotiations for independence partly as the result of the intransigence of Muhammad Ali Jinnah, militant leader of the Muslim minority in British-ruled India and adversary of Mohandas K. Gandhi, who in contrast advocated a united secular state welcoming followers of all religions. Fighting between the two groups had already erupted repeatedly before midnight, August 14, 1947, when England granted India its independence, simultaneously splitting the country in two.

The British had done much to foster enmity between Hindus and Muslims, setting one group against the other, and they might have prevented some of the worst rioting by not withdrawing their troops so hastily from the region after Partition. But they were eager to exit the land and leave the Indians to battle it out, and the result was appalling. Their staunchest allies, the Sikhs, felt particularly betrayed and enraged.

Fearing further violence and domination, some seven million Muslims migrated north to the newly created Islamic territory of Pakistan while an almost equal number of Hindus and Sikhs moved south into Hindu-dominated India. Along the way, mobs raped, pillaged, and massacred on an unprecedented scale, despite the pleas of the deeply chagrined nonviolent leader Gandhi, who tried especially to restrain the violence of his fellow Hindus and was assassinated for those attempts by a Hindu fanatic. Hundreds of thousands of women were ravished, often in public. The total of number of deaths will never be known, but estimates run as high as two million.

Khushwant Singh was living and working in Lahore when Partition came, and he had to abandon his home and property and flee for Delhi, where his parents lived. In an interview with Pavan K. Varma (5–6), Singh recalled a harrowing trip from back home from a trial in which he passed through seemingly deserted villages where the remaining inhabitants where cowering in their homes. A passing Sikh captain warned him that Sikhs had been slaughtered all along this road, and picked him up in his truck and took him to the deserted railway station at Taxila.

Then the train came along. it pulled up near the railway signal on the other side. I heard some shouts and screams or something. I didn't know what it was. When I got into the train, I was in a first class compartment and I sensed danger. They had apparently picked up all the Sikhs near the signal and butchered them. I got into my train and locked up the door and came up to Lahore through absolutely deserted railway stations. I came to Lahore late in the afternoon. Not a soul could be seen around or on the railway station. My friend Manzoor Qadir had come to pick me up. So he took me home. Then I heard next day about the massacre of Sikhs near Taxila, and Manzoo Qadir of course saw much more of it because he was travelling, and he being a Muslim was safe. But the victims were largely Sikhs because they were easily identified. The Hindus you couldn't make out till you examined them more closely [laughs]. I saw a few people being murdered, Biharis at a Petrol pump. One was killed by young boys, boys of about fourteen or fifteen. One got in front of him, the other just plunged his dagger into his breast from the rear. He just came and stabbed him. That kind of things. They had a favourite game. Boys would sit on either side of the road with a rope and if a cyclist came along and it happened to be a Sikh, they would pull up the rope, and so he fell. They went and killed him and ran away. This was becoming a daily occurrence in Lahore.

Surrounded by butchery, he took the train south, not to return to his old home even for a visit for many years thereafter. A friendly Muslim occupied his house and guarded it against anti-Sikh mobs and later sent him his possessions, including partially drunk bottles of whiskey, forbidden to Muslims—a kindness that Singh has never forgotten. Throughout his later career Singh has insisted on reminding his fellow Indians that the Pakistani people include many individuals who can be decent, kind, and generous.

Singh chooses to set his story among these people, the Sikhs, who initiated some of the worst violence. Clearly he wants his own community to face its past unblinkingly; but clearly he also believes they were manipulated by cynical Hindu and Muslim officials who sought power and wealth by inflaming religious passions. Although Singh makes clear elsewhere that he believes the British played a role in inflaming "communal" tensions, he insists that interreligious conflict is a profoundly Indian problem that must be solved on Indian terms. The beginning of a solution is to face unblinkingly the crimes of the past in all their bloody irrationality, which is what he tries to accomplish in *Train to Pakistan*.

The beautifully written opening of the novel—clearly aimed at foreign readers unfamiliar with the realities of rural Punjab—introduces us to the agricultural village of Mano Majra, where prosperous Sikhs and impoverished Muslims live side by side, very much the sort of place Singh grew up in. Theoretically both Sikhs and Muslims reject caste, but in fact caste still pervades their lives, especially in the shape of untouchable "sweepers," who are disdained for their very necessary work of cleaning latrines.

As in Narayan's *The Guide,* the train station is the focus of life in the town. Evening prayers for Muslims and Sikhs alike are timed by the railroad schedule. The train is in a way an alien intrusion, introduced by the British; but it is also neutral territory, the focus of coming and going, the route by which news travels, and the path history takes to erupt in the village.

Singh shows how the various communities of the village are intimately intertwined, especially by the power of desire. The *budmash* (criminal) Juggut Singh ("Jugga") loves Nooro, the daughter of a blind Muslim weaver who is also the leader (*Imam*) of the mosque, much respected as a wise elder even by the Sikh population. The Hindu government magistrate Hukum Chand desires the young Muslim singer and dancer who entertains at his home (although it takes a long time for him to bother learning her name). When Jugga questions Iqbal in prison about foreign women, he expresses common stereotypes about them, but he also continues the theme of erotic attraction binding diverse peoples together—a subject Singh has explored at length in his other writings. (For more about the difficulties Jugga mentions that are involved in attaining marital bliss in traditional Indian extended families, see the essays in Singh's *Uncertain Liaisons*.)

In the opening scenes a band of Sikh bandits (*dacoits*) led by Malli robs and murders the local Sikh moneylender, tossing some bracelets in the Jugga's yard in hopes of framing him for the crime; the well-known criminal Jugga is off making love in the fields on this particular night with Nooro. The brutality with which he possesses her is typical of this sort of relationship, but we are supposed to understand that she genuinely cares for him. As we see eventually, he actually cares deeply for her as well. Their affair paradoxically keeps the village at peace, because the local Sikhs are terrified of him, and the girl he loves is the daughter of the local Muslim leader for whom, at any rate, they have a good deal of sympathy. Their potentially dangerous relationship functions to keep Mano Majra at peace until the outside world intervenes.

The purely criminal mayhem of the opening sets the stage for rumors of the wider social violence that has broken out in Amritsar, the traditional home city of the Sikh religion, where the famed Golden Temple is located. Amritsar is rich in the history of violence, having been the locale of the infamous Jallianwalla Bagh Massacre in 1919 and locus of much of the Sikh-Muslim violence in the Punjab in 1947. Unfortunately, this was not to be the end of Amritsar's sorrows, for in 1984 heavily armed Sikh separatists occupied the Golden Temple, and Indira Gandhi sent troops against them, killing many and grievously damaging the Sikhs' most sacred temple, leading five months later to her assassination by her own Sikh bodyguards.

A trainload of Muslims has been massacred by Sikhs and sent across the border, labeled "a gift to Pakistan." This incident, modeled on an actual occurrence at the time, becomes emblematic of the vengeance being wreaked by the communities on each other that bloody August. It is Hindu "outside agitators" who urge the peaceful Sikhs of Mano Majra to turn in vengeance on their Muslim neighbors, but the local people—far from being eager to plunge into the melee—hardly know that independence and

Partition have occurred; "Jinnah" is an unfamiliar name to them. Life goes on as it has for centuries, with little concern for the affairs of the outside world.

But violence looms. The fighting geckos that fall off Hukum Chand's wall are more than a simple symbol of animosity; traditionally the fall of a lizard off a wall is considered a bad omen. The magistrate's motives are not always clear; but although he is a not entirely unsympathetic character, he is clearly an opportunist who seeks tranquility rather than justice. He wants to rid the village of its Muslim population quietly, without undue violence, and to place the blame for the attack on the moneylender on a convenient scape-goat: Jugga. But as a result of the blunder of his assistant in also arresting Iqbal, he is stuck with one bogus suspect too many. Perhaps he releases them later hoping that these two men of action will do what he cannot: prevent the looming tragedy. But his role throughout much of the novel is one of a self-indulgent coward ready to go with the tide of madness around him not because he is himself a fanatic but because that is the path of least resistance. He personifies everything Singh detests about civil servants: corruption, laziness, and indifference to the suffering of others.

The crude popular test for a man's status as a Muslim is a quick check to see whether he has been circumcised. Normally, a Sikh would not have been; but for some reason Iqbal, who has lived for a long time in Europe, has been. In the film version of the novel, it is implied that his circumcision was a by-product of some surgery. The scenes in which men are assaulted and hacked apart are all too accurately portrayed. Sexual violence against both men and women was meant to be deeply humiliating in this culture where shame is deeply felt and modesty is a supreme virtue.

At first it seems that Hukum Chand will also commit sexual violence against Haseena, the young singer who has been brought to entertain him. Clearly there is nothing mutual or balanced about their relationship: she is bored while singing a passionate love song on the traditional theme of the moth fatally drawn to the flame. She is not really drawn to him, except for money, and she poses no threat to him.

Hukum Chand has been haunted since childhood by the prospect of death, but he has managed to put it into perspective, and even managed to put the rest of life into perspective because of his awareness of death—until the trainload of corpses arrives in Mano Majra. His loneliness becomes over-whelming in the face of such massive annihilation, and he reaches out for whiskey and sex to fend off the horror looming around him. But what moves him about Haseena eventually is not so much her sexuality as her vul-nerability: she reminds him of his dead daughter, and he winds up wanting her by him not as a lover, but as a companion to stave off loneliness, until he finally thrusts her out into the horror he so fears for himself. She is a pros-titute, and a Muslim, and he cannot bring himself to keep her with him no matter how much he is drawn to her.

Iqbal is an activist, a traveling organizer for the Communist People's League in India, but his politics mix sympathy for the people's sufferings with disdain for the people themselves. The overpopulation of India especially depresses him. He blames it partly on the sexual elements in Indian mythology, but in fact ordinary Hindus rarely make a connection between the erotic imagery in sacred texts and their own private lives. More accurate is the blame he places on "the son cult": the desire to have sons rather than daughters that keeps many couples trying desperately to have as many sons as possible. In traditional Hindu belief, one's funeral pyre must be lit by a surviving son, and this belief is a major obstacle to birth control.

Although the author shares many of his views, Singh is also determined to portray Iqbal as an ineffective social organizer, too distanced from the people he wants to organize to move them, and too hesitant to grasp opportunities when they occur. Although many of Singh's friends were Communists when they were in school together, he always rejected Marxist politics. Iqbal is a not unaffectionate portrait of the kind of idealistic but ineffectual young men Singh associates with the Communist movement.

Iqbal's nationalism also leads him to idealize the Indian National Army organized by Netaji Subhas Chandra Bose, which was organized in 1941 to fight against the British while they were being besieged by the Japanese during World War II. He is trying to move Meet Singh, the village leader, to feel solidarity with these militant rebels against England. Yet Meet Singh thinks of himself as a loyal subject of the Crown who fought for Britain in World War I—like many Sikhs—and preferred English to Indian officers. Their dual roles as maintainers of one sort of Indian tradition and as supporters of the British imperial government have created great ambiguities among the Sikhs, ambiguities to which Singh returns in his writings again and again. He himself has expressed resentment against the British exploitation and manipulation of his people while also expressing admiration for their administration and educational institutions during the period of the Raj.

As Iqbal argues vainly with Meet Singh, the Muslim Imam Baksh (referred to here by the affectionate title *chacha*—"uncle") points out one reason that Gandhi was much more popular among the common people than the Communists: he respected religion while they disdained it. Although he was basically a Hindu, Gandhi did indeed draw on a variety of faiths, including Buddhism, Islam, and even Christianity, in expressing his ideas. The Imam has heard that he reads the holy texts of Islam (the *Koran Sharif*), Sikhism (the *Unjeel*), and of Hinduism (the Vedas and Shastras). Singh repeatedly stresses the theme of peaceful, harmonious coexistence of the rival faiths in some aspects of Indian society that contrasts so strikingly with the fanatical violence erupting all around. Iqbal has been sent by the League to try to avert sectarian conflict, but his basic irreligiosity separates him from people like the Imam who might theoretically be responsive to his message.

In prison he finds himself given privileges denied to the lowly Jugga and meditates on the divisiveness of Indian society, although he also notes that caste is beginning to be disregarded by some in their matrimonial ads. Note that throughout the novel people are arrested on account of their religious affiliations, not because they are true suspects. This systematic profiling by faith is the legal equivalent of the faith-based massacres spreading across the land.

The reality of the outside world arrives in the form of the "ghost train" full of corpses that the authorities cordon off so they may dispose privately of the massacred dead. The cremation they carry out is no act of devotion (the victims are Muslims who would normally be buried rather than Hindus, who are traditionally cremated), but an attempt to conceal a crime and avert further violence. Yet the secret inevitably leaks out, and the second "ghost train," which arrives during the rains, must be dealt with differently.

Singh has been criticized by some for depicting the violence of Partition sporadically and distantly. No one in the village actually commits a killing based on religious hatred. Some of the briefly described scenes of mutilation and rape are undeniably vivid, but they are quite short.

However, when these moments of violence arrive, they have all the more impact for being surrounded by relatively peaceful scenes. The gore is much more jolting in this context than it would be in a long, numbing catalog of atrocities. It is precisely Singh's point that interreligious violence erupts with irrational suddenness among people who just days before have been living peacefully side by side. He shows how simple, basically decent people can be swept up by mob frenzy into committing terrible crimes. By isolating his vivid depictions of violence he points out that they are both insane and avoidable. Singh the outspoken individualist is a great believer in the power of dissent, and in his novel it will take the courage of a single man who is opposed to the mob to thwart the threatened slaughter at Mano Majra.

The coming of the monsoon is at first depicted as welcome to the parched villagers in a passage of extraordinary beauty that reflects Singh's lifelong fascination with the phenomena of nature. In India these cooling storms have exhilarating and even romantic associations. But this particular monsoon will bring with it a floodtide of death. Again, Singh demonstrates how horror can emerge out of ordinary everyday life.

We can see in the scene following the constable's visit the corruption stirring, which is caused by the prejudice that divides Mano Majra—as Singh writes—"into two halves as neatly as a knife cuts through a pat of butter." The interreligious tensions have always been there, but it is this particular intrusion by the outside world that precipitates the village into a state of undeclared civil war. Muslims and Sikhs suddenly view each other with fear and suspicion. Most important, they begin to generalize about each other, to lose sight of the individuality of those in the other group. When Meet Singh tries to inject a note of reasonableness into the gathering of Sikhs who begin accusing their local Muslim peasants of betrayal, although they have in fact done nothing to deserve hatred, the reply of a bigoted young man is simply, "They are Muslims."

The rest of the novel is about the way groups create images of each other as monsters and villains, with only a few able to hang on to a sense of the individual worth of people in the opposing group. Officials connive with the freed Sikh bandits to rob the departing Muslims under the guise of safeguarding their property. Hukum Chand knows better, but he goes with the tide of history that decrees banishment or worse for the Muslims. Iqbal knows better, but is too cowardly and unconnected with the people around him to do anything: he retreats into drink.

Only Jugga, the acknowledged villain of the town, acts heroically. Singh places his faith not in government bureaucrats or in radical ideologues, but in the simple passion of a young man who does not care that the woman he loves is a Muslim. It is ironic that the only real violence Jugga perpetrates in the novel is against her and against Malli; in the first instance he acts as a crude but passionate lover and in the second as avenger of a real crime. It is true that in both cases he acts from selfish motives—sexual desire and personal vengeance—but his honest, spontaneous act of heroism at the end of the novel singles him out as the sort of person all too rare in the world: someone willing to sacrifice his own safety for the benefit of someone else.

Notice that Jugga does not know for certain that Nooro will be on the top of the train speeding north, but he does know that if the Sikhs' plot succeeds, the death of the Muslims above will be followed by a massacre of those below. He can save Nooro only by saving the whole trainload of refugees.

His final act is highly dramatic—even melodramatic—and has been compared to the far-fetched acrobatic stunts common in popular Indian movies; but its imagery is so striking that it makes a perfect ending to the novel. His self-sacrifice is a model of what is needed at this particular moment. Others were ready to risk their lives to kill; only he was ready to risk his life to prevent killing.

Despite its portrayal of the failures of both government officials and political activists, the novel does not ultimately counsel despair. Singh depicts his characters as individuals capable of moral choice. Although most of them fail to make humane choices in this story, Jugga provides a reminder that even the worst individual can choose the good. The ultimate effect of the book's conclusion is not to soften the horror of Partition or shift the blame to the inevitable tides of history: it is to remind his readers that each of them is responsible for preventing recurrences of that horror in the future, whether through work in the streets or activities carried out within government. Singh is bitter, even cynical, about the failures of the government of India following independence; but he is never despairing. *Train to Pakistan* is an impassioned cry for tolerance, one that still has powerful resonance today.

SELECTED BIBLIOGRAPHY

Dhawan, R. K., ed. *Khushwant Singh: The Man and the Writer.* New Delhi: Prestige, 2001.
  Thirty-three essays by Indian scholars discuss all Singh's major fiction from multiple points of view.

Singh, Khushwant. *The Collected Short Stories of Khushwant Singh.* Delhi: Ravi Dayal, 1989.

———. *Delhi: A Portrait.* Delhi: Delhi Tourism Development Corp., 1983.

———. *I Shall Not Hear the Nightingale.* New York: Grove Press, 1959.

———. *Kushwant Singh's Editor's Page.* Bombay: IBH Publishing Company, 1981.

———. "On Myself." *Sex, Scotch & Scholarship: Khushwant Singh: Selected Writings.* Ed. Rohini Singh. New Delhi: VBS Publishers' Distributors, 1992. 7–39.
  Frank and detailed autobiographical sketch by the author.

———. *Train to Pakistan.* New York: Grove Press, 1956.

———. *Uncertain Liaisons: Sex, Strife & Togetherness in Urban India.* New Delhi: Viking Penguin, India, 1993.

———, ed. *Nature Watch.* Illus. Suddhasattwa Basu. Delhi: Lustre Press, 1990.

Varma, Pavan K. "Face to Face: Khushwant Singh speaks to Pavan K. Varma." *Khushwant Singh: An Icon of Our Age.* Ed. Kaamna Prasad. New Delhi: Jiya Prakashan, 2000. 2–21.
  One of the best sources for details on Singh's life, especially for the period of Partition.

Chapter 4
R. K. Narayan:
The Guide *(1958)*

R. K. [born Rasipuram Krishnaswami in 1907] Narayan died in 2001 after a distinguished writing career that spanned seven decades of the twentieth century, from 1935 (*Swami and Friends*) to 1993 (*The Grandmother's Tale*). He was the first Indian novelist to seize and hold the attention of large numbers of readers outside of India. Works by him have been translated into some fourteen different languages.

Like Tagore, Narayan was introduced to the West by a famous writer, in his case, Graham Greene, who suggested the title of his first novel and facilitated its publication in England. Greene remained a close friend and supporter of Narayan's all his life; but after the first few novels had appeared, Narayan's career was self-sustaining. People who enjoyed reading one of his humorous sketches of life in the fictional town of Malgudi were likely to continue reading his work.

Despite his popularity, he has received relatively little detailed scholarly attention. Narayan belongs to a category of recognized classic twentieth-century writers who resist classification as "modern" (Isaac Bashevis Singer and Robertson Davies are other good examples). His prose is simple and his storytelling mostly straightforward. No one would ever call him "experimental" or "cutting edge." Yet any survey of South Asian literature that ignored him would be slighting one of its acknowledged masters.

Narayan was born in the Tamil-speaking city of Madras in southern India, but spent most of his life in the city of Mysore, where Kannada is the dominant language. He was fluent in both languages, but he preferred to do his writing in English, the language in which he had been educated and which he defended, arguing that by then English had become a fully naturalized "citizen" of India. As a South Indian, he strongly resisted the drive to substitute the northern language of Hindi for English as the official unifying language of India. Like Tagore, he was an indifferent student; but unlike Tagore, he became extremely fluent in English, creating a style widely praised as transparent and natural.

As a young man he fell in love with a young woman named Rajam and managed to have his marriage to her "arranged" by both sets of parents in a way that was quite unconventional for the time, when love matches were actively discouraged. So determined was he to wed Rajam that he overrode the objections of the professional astrologer consulted by the parents who predicted doom for the match. He simply bribed another astrologer to offer a more favorable view, and the wedding took place. When Rajam died of typhoid five years later, in 1939, he was heartbroken and refused even to consider remarriage for the rest of his very long life. He claimed that he did not want to expose another woman to his unlucky destiny; but Narayan was not a superstitious man, and it seems probable that in reality he simply did not believe he could ever love another woman as deeply as he had Rajam. His devotion to her is movingly depicted in the partly autobiographical novel *The English Teacher* (1945). Narayan was a devoted father to their only child, their daughter Hema.

He wrote for various magazines and newspapers throughout his life, including some he founded, and his essays reveal a keen interest in contemporary events that is famously lacking in the timeless world of his major fiction. Some of his best informal essays are collected in *Next Sunday* (1960) and *Reluctant Guru* (1974), and the best of those in *A Writer's Nightmare* (1988). Aside from one novel dealing incidentally with Gandhi (*Waiting for the Mahatma*), the struggle for independence from Britain and the creation of the modern state of India finds few echoes in his novels and stories. Only in *Swami and Friends* does he satirize briefly the British-dominated education he received at a Christian mission school where the teachers felt free to ridicule Hindu gods. Although he has been criticized for his focus on private life, it can be argued that by dismissing the British almost entirely from his own fictional world, he declared his own independence from their transient influence. The theory that he ignored the British deliberately is supported by his comments on the opposite tendency in his 1984 *New York Times* article, "When India Was a Colony," reacting to the tendency of films to focus on the British "Raj":

Anglo-India apparently has a market, while a purely Indian subject has none, perhaps too drab for a commercial film maker. India is interesting only in relation to the "Anglo" part of it, although that relevance lasted less than 200 years in the timeless history of India.

I suspect that a film maker values, rather childishly, the glamour of the feudal trappings of the British Raj, with Indians in the background as liveried menials or for comic relief. (222)

The Englishman preferred to leave the Indian alone, carrying his home on his back like a snail. He was content to isolate himself as a ruler, keeper of law and order and collector of revenue, leaving Indians alone to their religion and ancient activities. He maintained his distance from the native all through. Indeed, the theme of E. M. Forster's "A Passage to India" was that an unbridgeable racial chasm existed between colonial India and imperial England. (223)

His India is not the India of the British-dominated Raj nor "postcolonial" India: it is just India, a land rich and complex enough to be worth exploring on its own terms.

And in some ways, Narayan is the most Indian of writers. It is typical for South Asian authors of works in English to emigrate to the West, yet Narayan stayed close to home throughout most of his life. Only in his fifties did he venture abroad, and despite many later business trips, especially to the United States and residencies at American universities, he always returned home to Mysore.

His works are set in the fictional town of Malgudi, partly based on Mysore, but with its own characteristics. His fictional setting has often been compared to Thomas Hardy's Wessex or William Faulkner's Yoknapatawpha County, but Narayan claimed that he simply invented a town he could mold to the needs of his stories without needing to do research. It is a quintessential small South Indian city, big enough to have a variety of petty industries and a wide variety of characters, but small enough for people to know each other.

After his first three Malgudi novels, Narayan turned away from autobiographically based fiction. *The Dark Room* (1938) was an early attempt to explore the plight of a woman trapped in an unhappy marriage. It has been generally considered a failure and is far grimmer than most of his generally lighthearted work, but it is significant as a harbinger of the work to come, when he was to return to portraits of women striking out for independence in *The Guide* (1958) and *The Painter of Signs* (1976). No one has ever called Narayan a feminist, and in fact he has been criticized for relegating women to marginal, often stereotyped, roles; yet in this he was a product of his times. But like Tagore, he was also clearly fascinated by creative, individualistic, rebellious women who rejected the restrictions of traditional social roles.

His main characters are men, many of them fitting a certain pattern: imaginative but unsophisticated, impulsive, excitable, easily influenced, and ultimately self-destructive. Margayya, the title character of *The Financial Expert* (1952), is a classic example, half con man and half fool, tangled up in his own schemes for making a fortune off the unwary. His characters' common failing is a comic shortsightedness that leads them to postpone the day of reckoning, which the reader sees all too clearly looming in the future.

A quite different aspect of Narayan's talent is manifested in his three volumes of Hindu tales: *Gods, Demons and Others* (1964), *The Ramayana* (1972), and *The Mahabharata* (1978). These brief prose retellings of classic works provide a useful introduction for readers seeking to become acquainted with the traditional background of much Indian fiction. *My Days: A Memoir* (1974) is an entertaining introduction to his early life and should be read by anyone interested in becoming better acquainted with Narayan. He also published many short stories and two travel guides to his local region: *Mysore: A Travel Record* (1946) and *The Emerald Route* (1978).

While at the University of California, Berkeley, in 1957, Narayan wrote his most famous and widely discussed novel, *The Guide*. In *My Days* he tells about his inspiration for the story that climaxes the work:

At this time I had been thinking of a subject for a novel: a novel about someone suffering enforced sainthood. A recent situation in Mysore offered a setting for such a story. A severe drought had dried up all the rivers and tanks; Krishnaraja Sagar, an enormous reservoir feeding channels that irrigated thousands of acres, had also become dry, and its bed, a hundred and fifty feet deep, was now exposed to the sky with fissures and cracks, revealing an ancient submerged temple, coconut stumps, and dehydrated crocodiles. As a desperate measure, the municipal council organized a prayer for rains. A group of Brahmins stood knee-deep in water (procured at great cost) on the dry bed of Kaveri, fasted, prayed, and chanted certain mantras continuously for eleven days. On the twelfth day it rained, and brought relief to the country side. (106)

Although Narayan was a practicing Hindu throughout his life, meditating daily and with belief in the supernatural, he was far from being fanatical or even devout. "Holy men" in his works are almost invariably rascals, and this news story probably attracted him more as an incongruity than as a demonstration of the efficacy of prayer. After all, if you pray long enough, the rains are bound to come some time or other—eventually.

The novel is unique among his works in its narrative structure. The tale begins near its ending, as the protagonist, Raju, tells a simple villager named Velan the story of his life. The narrative shifts back and forth between this biographical account and the development of the predicament in which he becomes trapped by peasants who treat him like the Brahmins in the story that inspired Narayan. Some first-time readers may find the work's construction confusing, but the plot is actually fairly straightforward: childhood, career as shopkeeper and tour guide, association with Rosie (a classical dancer), jail, and his role as a reluctant spiritual guide and miracle worker. If the reader pauses a moment when the scene shifts to note when the next section of narrative is set, it should give little trouble.

The novel, generally recognized as one of his finest, has been widely translated, including into the Indian languages of Hindi, Kannada, Tamil, Malayalam, and Marathi. It was also made into a film and a stage play, both considered unsuccessful (see his article on the making of the film, "Misguided 'Guide'").

He kept an interesting journal of his reactions to America while he was writing *The Guide,* published as *My Dateless Diary: A Journal of a Trip to the United States in October 1956* (1960). It is amusing to see him satirize Westerners in this book in the same way that he satirizes Indians in his fictional works. There is very little about the substance of the novel he was writing in this volume, reinforcing the impression that despite his frequent travels abroad, his interior homeland was always India. No one would ever guess from reading *The Guide* that it was written in a hotel near the University of California, Berkeley, and edited in New York, his favorite foreign city.

The central character, Raju, has more than a few characteristics in common with his creator. Like Narayan, he is a poor student at school. Narayan's first book was a guide to his local city, and Raju's main career is as a tourist guide. Both tend to view the behavior of others through a comic lens. Both are self-deprecating. Both are storytellers who prefer invention to research. In a bizarre twist, Narayan found himself cast unwillingly in the role of a Hindu mystic when he visited the United States in the 1960s (see "Reluctant Guru"), and he noted sardonically that he seemed fated to relive Raju's dilemma, although in an admittedly milder form. He was able to escape this stereotyping far more successfully than had Tagore, for it was confined primarily to those who had not read his books.

The Guide, although filled with comic incidents, is somewhat more serious in tone than many of his works, and sometimes it has been treated either as social criticism or theology. We consider the evidence for and against these interpretations as we go through the story.

The narrative begins intriguingly: "Raju welcomed the intrusion—something to relieve the loneliness of the place" (3). Intrusion into what? Where are we? Who are these people? It will take half the book's length to deliver the answers to all these questions, but meanwhile the reader is drawn in to listen to Raju's narrative along with Velan, to whom he is trying to explain himself. This is his first encounter with Velan—the one that earns him his reputation as a guru—but much of the rest of the story will be told at a later date, when Raju is trying to convince the peasant he is not a holy man worthy of veneration.

But the first section of his story only compounds the mysteries, as we see Raju explaining himself to someone else: the barber who shaved him some time ago upon his release from jail. Naturally, we want to know what his crime was, and we happily settle in to join the audience that seems to be gathering.

On page 6 a break in the narrative is marked by a space in the text to ease us back into the "present." Note these scene-shifting markers as they occur.

Although Rosie does not actually appear until far later in the novel, we get a brief, intriguing glimpse of her here, and we learn the most important thing about her: she is an orthodox dancer, a term with a rich set of associations for an Indian reader. In the chapter on Tagore, we discussed the Vaishnava tradition of celebrating Krishna's and Radha's love as a reflection of the mutual yearning of the human and the divine for each other. One of the most important ways in which this theological idea was expressed was performances in temples where young women called *devadasis* traditionally danced the story of their romance, enacting the role of Radha with flirtatious, sensual movements. The ancient Indian tradition of dance called *Bharata Natyam* to which this type of dance belongs demands extreme dedication from the performer involving years of rigorous training, but it can also have a strong erotic appeal.

Ideally, the dancers should perform as an act of devotion, and in fact some of them performed late at night before the image of the god, without any human audience. Yet such performances were also greatly enjoyed by audiences at the temples. It was the misfortune of the dancers that like most female musicians and dancers in most cultures before the twentieth century, they were considered morally little better than prostitutes and in fact supported themselves by sleeping with men who came to the temple, giving a fleshly form to the mating of divine and human. Men have been all too ready over the centuries to simultaneously adore the women's skills as performers and condemn them as private individuals, and temple dancers were traditionally treated as pariahs. The British endeavored to shut down this practice, and few traditional temple dancers were still performing by the beginning of the twentieth century. For some time there had been a tradition of secular entertainment alongside the tradition of temple dancing, and that continued to thrive. After independence, Indians eager to revive their cultural heritage brought together both secular and sacred dance on the concert stage, giving it the high status of classical art, although deprived of its temple setting. Today young women of highly respectable families often take Bharata Natyam lessons, just as Western young women often study ballet, neither aware of the abysmal social status to which earlier performers in both traditions were condemned. This novel is set during the transitional period, in which sophisticated audiences were eagerly seeking out stage performances of traditional dance but everyone was still aware of the unsavory earlier reputation of dancers. Thus Rosie, despite her incongruous name, suggests something very Indian and very sexy.

To explain how he met Rosie and her husband "Marco," he begins at the beginning, with his childhood, and the rest of his life story follows. He begins with the railway station. Trains play an important role even today in

India as a reasonably priced way to move around a very large country. Narayan said that when he first envisioned Malgudi, he imagined a scene on a railway platform. In this novel, the station represents travel, tourism, money, and excitement, so it is introduced right at the beginning, even though his father doesn't open a shop there until much later.

Raju displays his irresponsibility and rashness in the way he sells pepper-mints. This pattern of always seeking the easy route, "minimizing complications," will lead him instead into serious complications throughout his life. All the characteristics of the adult Raju are already present in this section: laziness, impulsiveness, and irresponsibility.

This portrait of his childhood is interrupted by the incident that sets him on the path to becoming a reluctant guru: the problem of the reluctant bride. It is commonplace to observe that the most successful "wise men" are sometimes the vaguest, so people can read into their generalizations whatever they wish. Often Raju is reminiscent of Chance, the half-witted hero of Jerzy Kosinski's *Being There:* what he has to say is generally useless in itself, but it provides an empty field to be filled in by his audience. Unlike Chance, however, Raju is taciturn more out of caution than lack of imagination. We will see he can be quite loquacious when he scents no danger.

It is ironic that it should be the prospect of an unending supply of free food that should trap him into his role as adviser and holy man. The philosophy of passivity he expresses at the end of this chapter is of course very convenient. What could be better than getting fed for telling people to let well enough alone?

Having done a decent job of repeating the familiar story about the Buddha, which reminds the listener that death and suffering are universal, he does not do so well when he launches into the story of Devaka, but he discovers that lapsing into silence actually works better than speaking. (Devaka was in fact the grandfather of the god Krishna on his mother's side.) This lapse in his memory takes him back to his childhood again and memories of his ambitious, gregarious, but self-centered father. Raju has inherited all of these qualities, but he lacks the dedication and self-discipline to fulfill his ambitions. In a strictly traditional household, no one could eat—especially not the wife—until the father did; so Raju's more casual father is actually being tolerant in allowing them to proceed with their own dinner, although oblivious to their needs.

Chapter 2 resumes the story of his childhood. His father's complaint that mission teachers insult Hindu gods recalls Narayan's own boyhood experience as retold in *Swami and Friends,* but it is almost dismissed as a joke here. Recent stories of attacks on Christian missionaries by fanatical Hindu nationalists may mislead some readers into exaggerating the antipathy between these two religions in India. For most of the second half of the twentieth century, Hindu parents were happy to send their children to mission schools to receive superior educations, and in fact they ran little risk of being "turned into Christians." After the British left, the missionaries learned to be more circumspect in their proselytizing.

As we return to the story of the reluctant bride, it is good to remember that arranged marriages were very much the norm, and fourteen was not an unusual age to marry. The girl's change of mind does not put her into an extraordinary situation, but brings her back into line with normal behavior. The result is undue credit for Raju, who is now regarded as a *Mahatma* ("great soul").

On page 28 Narayan plants a clue to the conclusion of the novel: "Raju was filled with gratitude and prayed that Velan might never come to the stage of thinking that he was too good for food and that he subsisted on atoms from the air." Ironically, every step in his development as a guru is motivated by the desire for food.

Some critics see the arrival of the railroad in Malgudi in Chapter 3 as a reflection of the British presence, and in fact it was the British who organized and commissioned the building of the railroads; but Narayan is perfectly justified in treating the station as an Indian creation: after all, it was built and run by Indians. It is a sign of Narayan's own modest form of nationalism that he doesn't single out any of the "important folk" in town as British, although the piper is undoubtedly a bagpiper. This Scots instrument was imported into India with the British army, as were brass bands. Breaking a coconut on the rail line is similar to the Western practice of smashing a bottle of champagne on the prow of a newly launched ship.

The story of how the wily taxi driver tricked his father out of his carriage sets a pattern of underhanded dealings that will run through the book, with Raju more often than not on the short end of the deal.

At the end of this chapter he tells us that he was happy to drop out of school, underscoring the irony of the fact that in the beginning of the next chapter this reluctant scholar is maneuvered into becoming a teacher. We begin to understand the irony of the novel's title: this "guide" who seems irresistibly to attract followers is himself guided only by whim and external circumstances. What prevents Raju from being a despicable fraud is the enthusiastic way in which he becomes impressed by his own abilities. Note how the narrator's comment, "No one was more impressed with the grandeur of the whole thing than Raju himself," leads directly into his first-person conclusion: "Now that I reflect upon it, I am convinced I was not such a dud after all" (40). His ego swells and collapses with his fortune, always driven by external events. The new school he has founded naturally leads him to discuss his old bookselling business.

When we return to the "present," his message that the villagers should learn to think for themselves is an easy way to escape responsibility for teaching them anything worthwhile; but it is also strikingly in contrast with his own passive mode of drifting through life, swept up by random enthusiasms.

Raju's observation, "the essence of sainthood seemed to lie in one's ability to utter mystifying statements" (44), reflects Narayan's own cynicism about professional gurus.

It is also the homebody Narayan whose voice pokes fun at the tourists who "forgo food and comfort and jolt a hundred-odd miles to see some place. . . . It seemed to me silly to go a hundred miles to see the source of Sarayu when it had taken the trouble to tumble down the mountain and come to our door" (49). Note how Raju's education as a guide is provided by his customers.

Just when we have almost forgotten about Rosie, she abruptly appears, associated—as she is throughout the novel—with the cobra. Raju strives to categorize her as not a stereotypical film beauty in a much-quoted bit of description: "She was not very glamorous, if that is what you expect, but she did have a figure, a slight and slender one, beautifully fashioned, eyes that sparkled, a complexion not white, but dusky, which made her only half visible—as if you saw her through a film of tender coconut juice" (56). She is not described in any detail: it is her powerful effect on Raju that convinces us she is truly beautiful. His first reaction to her is to feel ill clad and unattractive.

Rosie's devotion to her art is made clear by her request to study a cobra up close. It is somewhat disillusioning to learn that the famous snake charmers of India are not quite what they seem. The snakes have their fangs pulled, are drugged heavily, and are deaf to the music of the *been* (a simple piercing reed instrument effective in gathering a crowd in a noisy setting). It is the weaving of the instrument back and forth in front of the snake that attracts the attention of the cobra and makes it sway. Watch a snake charmer closely, and you may even see him clout his drowsy snake with the been to stir it up.

But neither Rosie nor Raju knows any of this: the snake exists in this story only to teach Raju how great a dancer Rosie is. Narayan does not mean us to take literally his statement that she was "the greatest dancer of the century" (58)—Raju is hardly in a position to know that—but the words clearly convey her overwhelming impact on him. The contrast with his mother's conventional reaction is striking and forecasts conflicts to come.

Raju charms Rosie by flattering her on the one quality that matters to her: her dancing. And he does so at just the right moment, when she is fighting with her husband. Typical of him, he dashes impetuously into pursuit of this married woman in a culture where adultery is viewed very seriously and the consequences can easily be fatal. Not that Raju is unaware of the danger. He comments that his "conscience" said, "He may shoot you." That this is fear speaking rather than any deep moral sense is made clear by the fact that another part of his mind asks, "Has he a gun?" (67).

Some critics argue that the story of their relationship is a sort of moral tale, warning against the hazards of illicit affairs. It certainly eventually turns into a disaster. But this is no exemplary model of the inevitable suffering brought on by adultery, like Leo Tolstoy's *Anna Karenina,* but more like Gustave Flaubert's more cynical novel on the topic, *Madame Bovary;* for so long as Raju behaves as a lover, things go well. It is when he begins to take a husbandly proprietary interest in Rosie that their romance deteriorates. Just as Emma Bovary was destroyed by her spendthrift ways, Raju will be ruined by his greed for the wealth Rosie's dancing can generate.

But in the early days of their relationship, it is Raju's enthusiasm for her artistry that, in contrast to her husband's outright contempt, draws the two together. Their first time together takes place while they are watching in the dark for wild animals. Raju is so rattled by her nearness that he mindlessly suggests they might see a lion—an animal not native to India. He is on the point of confessing his desire for her when her husband suddenly appears and interrupts their intimacy, asking what they have seen. Raju's reply might as well describe what has just occurred between Rosie and himself: "Something came, but it's gone" (69).

Narayan's satire might have been directed more against the husband, the traditional target of humor in such stories, and there are some instances in which he is the butt of jokes, as when he tells Raju as they are entering the cave, "Lead us . . . kindly light" (70), mindlessly echoing the title of John Cardinal Newman's famous Christian hymn "Lead, Kindly Light." Raju is being anything but kind and enlightening to Marco. Yet generally, it is the antics of the misguided guide that are the source of the novel's humor.

This scene in the cave suggests a sly parody of the famous Marabar Caves scene in *A Passage to India,* with the real action taking place outside and "Marco" cast in the role of the clueless foreigner. Raju is at his sharpest as he courts Rosie while her husband explores the art in the cave. He wisely draws out her bitterness toward her husband, emphasizes his admiration for her art, and displays his liberal views on caste when she explains she was raised as a traditional temple dancer. It may seem incongruous that she has an MA in economics, but parents wealthy enough to do so often send their daughters to graduate school in India, more to enhance their attractiveness as potential brides than to prepare them for careers.

But an MA alone is usually not enough to attract a husband. Although the importance of caste has diminished in India, it can still function as a serious barrier for young people seeking partners. A well-to-do young man who is willing to overlook low caste status like Marco would have been a rarity, so it is not surprising that Rosie's relatives were able to persuade her to accept him. Raju's thrill at hearing her say that dancers are regarded as "public women" (prostitutes) is of course the result of a reminder that she may be available, but he is smart enough not to say so.

When Raju exclaims at her good luck in not having a mother-in-law, the implications are much stronger than the traditional ones in the West. In the extended family structure, a new bride moves into the same house as her husband's parents, and the mother-in-law becomes her overseer and often her most severe critic. We can guess that had Marco's mother still been alive, he might not have been able to enter so freely into this unconventional match.

We are sensitized today to be alarmed when a man refuses to take "no" for an answer in the course of a seduction, but Narayan is writing in a tradition that assumes no woman worth caring about would openly invite a man into her room. We are supposed to understand at the end of Chapter 5 that Rosie has been seduced, not raped.

Chapter 6 continues the story of Raju's life in the village as its adopted holy man. Traditional festivals mark the passage of time, as if his life was one endless celebration. The Tamil New Year occurs in mid-April, and *Dasara* (also called *Dussehra* or *Durga Puja*)—devoted to the powerful goddess Durga—occurs in the autumn; *Deepavali* (or *Diwali*)—the festival of lights—comes in early November. Raju's self-centered nature is underlined by the fact that in this life of perpetual feasting, he has not noticed the region is suffering a severe drought. He is no peasant, but a city man, ignorant of the most basic things on which village life depends, and not inclined to educate himself about them. His suggestion that the weather has perhaps been affected by nuclear tests is not meant to illustrate extraordinary superstition, however; at the time many Westerners speculated about the effects of atomic bombs on climate. He could have run across such ideas in popular magazines and newspapers.

The rice riot illustrates the enormous gulf between Raju's comfortable existence and the daily struggle of the peasants to survive. Narayan rarely wrote about village life. Like Raju, he was a city man. However, here he reminds us powerfully how close to the brink of death traditional peasants are in rural India. But Raju views their disaster merely as an inconvenience to him personally, and he wishes they would "blow one another's brains out" (84) and spare him the trouble of dealing with their problems.

His attempt to settle their dispute by fasting is explicitly modeled on the tactic used by Mahatma Gandhi to quell fighting among his followers in the struggle for Indian independence. When Hindus and Muslims clashed in 1924, Gandhi fasted for three weeks, threatening to end his life if they did not agree to work peacefully together. He fasted again in the mid-1940s in protest of what South Asians call "communal" violence (violence between religious communities), and he effectively used fasting in other causes as well. The problem is that the peasants are not entirely clear about its significance. They tend to associate fasting with the austerities of traditional ascetic holy men who seek to create miracles by depriving themselves of food. Gandhi had taken a religious tradition and made it political, but the villagers drag Raju with them back in the direction of religion. Velan's brother is not alone in this misunderstanding, and Raju himself is partly at fault, for "not long ago he had spoken to them of such a penance, its value and technique" (95). The more he thinks and talks about food, the less the villagers are inclined to give him any.

In the second half of the novel, the increasing dilemma of Raju's forced fast is paralleled by the increasing complications of his earlier affair with Rosie. It is at the end of Chapter 6 that he begins to tell Velan the story of this affair, a recounting of which we have already read numerous bits earlier in the book. Chapter 7 finds him back with Marco and his wife as Raju learns that the best way to draw Rosie to him is to encourage her to resume her dancing career. The problem is that while for Rosie Bharata Natyam is a form of devotion ("Lover means always God," [110]), for Raju it is an erotic experience and—later—a source of cash.

The conflict in the last half of Chapter 7 between the lovers and Raju's mother is typical of Narayan's fiction in that there are no real villains in the story. His mother, who has almost never ventured out of the house, is typical of a well-off Brahmin wife of her generation, whereas Rosie is as far removed from such a role as possible. All of the characters actually like and care for each other, but their ideas about proper behavior are irreconcilable. If Raju is not actually villainous, however, he lets his passion carry him to extremes of heartless behavior toward his mother. Westerners are prone to think that parents need to learn to respect and accept their children's choices in partners. But in an Indian context where a marriage is more a merging of families than of individuals, the willingness to see a mother driven out of her own home by her son's beloved is shocking, without adding that Rosie is someone else's wife.

The sort of single-room household described in the novel is not only typical of many Indian homes even today, but of humanity generally around the world throughout history. Private bedrooms are largely a modern invention, formerly reserved for the wealthy. That a traditional Indian intergenerational extended family could find itself forced into such extreme intimacy naturally leads to conflict, even in so small a household as this.

Marco's reaction to learning about his wife's affair in the middle of this chapter is strikingly subdued, although it is good to remember we are getting the story from Raju, who was not present at the tumultuous confrontations between Rosie and her husband. His dismissal of her with the words "You can go where you please or do what you please" (133) is meant to indicate his basic lack of real affection for her rather than any sort of generosity. When he contrasts his behavior with that of Othello, who strangled his wife out of jealousy, we are not impressed because we know that whatever jealousy he feels is not grounded in true affection for Rosie.

The anecdotes that Raju's mother recounts include the story of Savitri, who saved her husband's life, first by fasting, then by trying to follow him into death. Seetha (more commonly spelled "Sita") remained faithful to her husband Lord Rama throughout her long captivity by the demon Ravana, and she demonstrated her virtue by leaping voluntarily into a fire. Such extreme examples are not likely to sway Raju from his affection for the very human Rosie.

Narayan does begin to remind us of Tolstoy in this section, as he traces the phases of the characters' feelings amid all this turmoil. By turns yearning and hostile toward her husband, it is only when Marco is rejecting Rosie that she becomes really drawn to him—but it is too late.

Raju's legal problems begin in Chapter 8, with his assault on the Sait; and at first we may suppose it was this that landed him in jail. But worse is to come. The irresponsible way in which Raju keeps welcoming the delays in his legal case sets the fatal pattern for the rest of the story. "Live for today" is not a wise motto when your affairs are as tangled as Raju's. With Rosie filling his field of vision, he has no room to consider anything else, but his passionate attachment to her is actually a form of self-absorption because he focuses almost entirely on his own needs and feelings. It takes a long time for him to realize she is not drawn to him as powerfully as he is to her.

His suggestion that she choose "Meena Kumari" as a stage name is meant to be comically inappropriate, because this was the name of an enormously popular Bombay film star at the time. It would be like a starlet naming herself "Marilyn Monroe" at the same period. Nalini Jaywant was also a popular film star in the 1940s and 1950s, but the first name is a fairly common one. Its primary meaning is "lotus blossom," which is a traditional religious symbol of purity. Thus, the name has "significance, poetry, and universality" (155).

Raju's vanity and selfishness are shown to be almost entirely responsible for the conflicts that cause them to fight. It is now that he begins to treat her like a wife rather than like an adored lover, with consequences fatal to their relationship. Raju is very clear about what he did wrong, and his striking frankness about his faults is the main reason we are able to still give him some measure of our sympathy, even when he finally declares himself to be lacking in "ordinary character" or basic human decency (195). Not only does he spoil their personal relationship, he spoils Rosie's pleasure in her own art by overcommercializing it. Rosie's only real salvation has been her passionate devotion to dance, and to deprive her of this is a real crime.

But the crime that lands Raju in jail—forgery—is committed on the flimsiest of impulses, out of mere greed (with perhaps a touch of jealousy). It is striking that even after Raju has clearly proved himself unworthy of Rosie and lost her love, she devotes herself to trying to keep him out of prison. Her generosity contrasts strongly with his selfishness.

The contrast takes on a darkly comic cast when she suggests they form a suicide pact and he shows he is all too likely to back out and let her die alone, as she suspects, by saying he wouldn't want to be burdened with disposing of her body—not an impressive form of defense against the accusation of self-centeredness.

The dance of the cobra that she performs just before his arrest takes up again imagery from earlier in the story. Raju had learned she was a dancer by watching her imitate the cobra he had found for her. The cobra that encircles Shiva and adorns Parvathi is a symbol of cosmic force, protective and creative rather than evil, as snakes are wont to be in the Judeo-Christian tradition. Her greatest artistic triumph precedes his deepest debasement. Not only is she shown to be morally superior to him; the balance of power in their relationship shifts in her direction, and he learns that he is superfluous—indeed, an obstacle—to both her prosperity and her happiness.

It may seem at first absurd that Raju turns out to be a model prisoner and is indeed quite happy in jail, but throughout the novel we have learned he is basically a creature of external influences. If there is going to be any structure in his life, it will have to be imposed from without. Not having to make his own choices—and his own mistakes—is undoubtedly a relief for him. This episode actually foreshadows his end, where he is again reduced to being a virtual prisoner of the expectations of the villagers during the drought. In both settings he is seen as a guide, but is in fact being constantly molded by circumstances. His sole form of creativity is rationalization.

The ending of the novel is read differently by different readers. Those with a strong interest in finding out the solution to fictional mysteries are baffled or irritated by the ending's ambiguity; which is a clearly inappropriate reaction. This is not the sort of novel one reads to find out "what happened." It is an exploration of a certain character and his relationships to those around him. His passive, vacillating character cannot logically lead to a definitive conclusion. To have him shift in one direction or another cannot at this point justify his existence or reveal the "truth" about him. Ambiguity is part of the essence of Raju.

Some critics have seen in Raju's final martyrdom a form of salvation, either social or spiritual. Some argue that although he may not in fact have succeeded in bringing about a miraculous rainfall, he has at least transcended his selfishness to embrace the good of his fellow human beings with an open heart. Those who argue for a religious interpretation, sometimes with elaborate references to various aspects of Hinduism, take Raju's conversion to the role of savior seriously.

However, a good deal of evidence supports the view of those who think he is deluded and a failure to the end. Vendors, newspaper reporters, and filmmakers gather noisily around him as his fast goes on, creating an incongruous atmosphere strikingly similar to the scene in Federico Fellini's *La Dolce Vita*—filmed just a few years later (1960)—of a young girl wildly chasing after her vision of the Virgin Mary in the glaring light of the clamorous press. It is often pointed out that an underlying poignancy lurks beneath much of Naryan's writing; but here the blend becomes strongly manifest as absurd dark comedy and tragedy jostle each other at the noisy, crowded, chaotic climax with almost unbearable intensity. When shortly before the end Raju tells the American film producer that he has always been "more or less" a Yogi, those of us who know him better are more likely to snort in derision rather than search for traces of spiritual tendencies we had not noticed earlier.

Do the rains come? Many readers conclude they have, but this seems like wishful thinking on the part of those who prefer "happy endings." After all, the rain is said to be happening off in the hills, not here where it can be witnessed and confirmed. It is more likely that it is the wetness of the river he is standing in creeping along his legs as he sinks down that deludes Raju into thinking the rain has come.

Does Raju die? As he traveled, people repeatedly asked Narayan whether Raju survived, but he refused to say. He did let interviewers know that Graham Greene had strongly recommended that he have his character die at the end of the novel, and he never indicated the ending was meant to leave open the possibility of survival. The whole novel has led up to this moment, narrowing down Raju's possibilities until he is forced to behave as a saint, even though he does not freely choose the role. His final decision to go along with the obsession of the villagers is probably partly prompted by a starvation-induced delirium rather than being a fully rational act of self-sacrifice. It is difficult to imagine a "happily ever after" ending to Raju's life at this point, and many readers feel the novel would be ruined if he were to recover. The downward spiral that has gripped him throughout the last part of his life has a powerful internal logic. The final sentence is not a hopeful one: "He sagged down."

Does this mean we are supposed to derive some sort of philosophical lesson from his experience? It seems unlikely. Narayan was insistent that his creations were not meant to be typical of India or illustrative of any particular philosophy, but merely portraits of interesting individuals. Narayan's outlook on life blended good humor with pessimism, religion with skepticism, irony with warmth. These qualities mingle in his fiction in different proportions. In *The Guide* we have followed an interesting thread—but only one—of the rich tapestry that is the world of Malgudi.

SELECTED BIBLIOGRAPHY

Holmstrom, Lakshmi. *The Novels of R. K. Narayan.* 2nd ed. Delhi: Writers Workshop, 1992.
    Contexts and analyses.

Kain, Geoffrey, ed. *R. K. Narayan: Contemporary Critical Essays.* East Lansing: Michigan State University Press, 1993.
    Recent essays plus a useful selected bibliography.

Narayan, R. K. *The Guide.* New York: Viking Press, 1958.
    The version used in this study is the 1988 Penguin reprint.

———. "Misguided 'Guide.'" *A Writer's Nightmare.* 206–17.

Amusing account of the mishaps surrounding the making of the film version of his novel.

———. *My Dateless Diary: A Journal of a Trip to the United States in October 1956.* New York: Pocket Book, 1960.

Entertaining sketches of his encounters with wide range of Americans.

———. *My Days: A Memoir.* New York: Viking Press, 1974.

Focuses on Narayan's early life.

———. "Reluctant Guru." *A Writer's Nightmare.* 99–105.

———. "When India Was a Colony." Originally published in the *New York Times Magazine* 16 Sept. 1984: 94; reprinted in *A Writer's Nightmare,* 222–32.

———. *A Writer's Nightmare: Selected Essays 1958–1988.* New Delhi: Penguin Books (India), 1988.

Pontes, Hilda. *R. K. Narayan (Bibliography of Indian Writing in English—1).* 1981. Atlantic Highlands, NJ: Humanities Press, 1983.

Detailed annotated primary and secondary annotated bibliography, including excerpts from reviews and other valuable information.

R. K. Narayan: India's Chekhov. Dir. Andrew Snell. Films for the Humanities, 1983.

Low-key interview with the author on location at his home. Location shots help Western viewers envision the settings of his novels.

Ram, Atma, ed. *Perspectives on R. K. Narayan.* Atlantic Highlands, NJ: Humanities Press, 1982.

Collection of original essays on various works by Narayan.

Sankaran, Chitra. "Patterns of Story-Telling in R. K. Narayan's *The Guide.*" *Journal of Commonwealth Literature* 26.1 (1991): 127–50.

The most useful of the religious interpretations of *The Guide,* with much helpful information about Indian traditions.

Swinden, Patrick. "Hindu Mythology in R. K. Narayan's *The Guide.*" *Journal of Commonwealth Literature* 34.1 (1999): 65–83.

Good also on the ambiguities in the novel.

Updike, John. "Alive and Free from Employment." *The New Yorker* 12 Sept. 1974: 80–82.

Review of *My Days,* containing an overview of the author's life and career.

Walsh, William. *R. K. Narayan: A Critical Appreciation.* London: Heinemann, 1982.

A survey by one of Narayan's finest critics.

Chapter 5

Attia Hosain: Sunlight on a Broken Column (1961)

A ttia Hosain was born in 1913 in Lucknow, into a wealthy, aristocratic family of Taluqdars, a class that owned much of the land in the region outright and ruled—like the *zamindars* elsewhere—almost as feudal lords under the British, paying taxes to the empire but administering their domains themselves. Her father had attended Cambridge and studied law at the Middle Temple in London. He was active in the movement for independence from the British and a close friend of Jawaharlal Nehru's father Motilal. Their home was frequently visited by distinguished political and cultural leaders. Her mother came from an old family steeped in the Persian and Urdu tradition of literature.

Attia and her four siblings lost their father when she was just eleven years old, and their mother took over not only the running of the family, but the running of the estate. She was brought up rather strictly, but her mother valued education and had her learn not only Urdu, Arabic, and English at home, but sent her to study at the famous La Martinière School in Lucknow and Isabella Thoburn College in Lucknow. She was the first woman from a Taluqdar family to graduate from college, where she distinguished herself well enough to win scholarships. Although Hosain was given regular study in the Qur'an and restricted in some ways (she was not allowed to attend Cambridge as her brother was), she was permitted to read freely in English literature. Against her mother's wishes, she married a cousin who had gone to Cambridge. Her husband's father was also a social activist and vice chancellor of the University of Lucknow.

As a young woman in the 1930s, Hosain was active in leftist politics, like many intellectuals, and attended the first Progressive Writers' Conference and the All India Women's Conference in Calcutta in 1933. Her early short stories attracted the interest of the activist writer Mulk Raj Anand, who says he prompted her to keep a journal that helped lead to the writing of her novel. She visited England when her husband was posted to the Indian High Commission there. When her country was split into Pakistan and India in 1947, her husband elected to become a Pakistani, but she maintained her identity as an Indian and remained in England with her children, where she supported herself through her own women's program on the Eastern Service of the British Broadcasting Corporation. She died in London in 1998.

Hosain produced only one novel and a volume of short stories, but she has always been considered an important contributor to South Asian fiction. Her collection of short stories, *Phoenix Fled,* first appeared in 1953, but gained a new readership when it was reprinted by Virago Press in 1988. These twelve stories already display some of the themes that were to characterize her major work. All but the last three focus on female characters and their problems. In fact, they deal with the disappointments and disasters of women's lives in traditional North India, particularly those caused by arranged marriages.

They also display an interest in all levels of society, from the humblest servant to the highest noble or government official, and in all ages: from small children to old people. Two of the stories, "Phoenix Fled" and "After the Storm," deal with violence that is probably meant to remind the reader of the 1947 Partition massacres. Some are simple character sketches or mood pieces; others have surprise twist endings. All are artfully written, displaying the creative talents that were to find their fullest expression in her single novel.

Sunlight on a Broken Column is frequently mentioned in surveys of notable Indian fiction. It has been translated into several languages, including Urdu, but it is seldom discussed in any detail. It is most often referred to as an early example of a "Partition" novel, but that label is quite misleading because the bulk of it is set before the division of British India into Pakistan and modern India in 1947, and the horrific violence that is the focus of most Partition novels is barely mentioned. Instead the novel depicts more gradual changes as a new generation arises in the 1930s to challenge the life patterns and beliefs of their elders. There is a certain amount of nostalgia in it for the departed glittering world of the old aristocracy; but that is balanced by profound criticisms of their way of life, particularly in its effects on the lives of women. For those who enjoy detailed evocations of upper-class settings in the past, it thus combines the pleasures of nostalgia with sharp social criticism.

It is written in a rather condensed style, with many brief scenes crowded together. It takes a certain amount of alertness to follow the action, but the novel is not otherwise difficult. A helpful list of the names of the major characters explaining their relationships appears at the front of the Penguin edition, followed by a few bits of vocabulary. Unfortunately this very incomplete glossary of non-English terms is not in alphabetical order, and more often than not it lacks the word the reader is looking for. Normally words defined in an author's glossary have been omitted from this volume's comprehensive glossary; but in this case I have made an exception to spare the reader the trials of using this awkward word list.

The distinguished novelist Anita Desai, in her very helpful introduction to the same edition, calls Hosain's writing "rich and ornate," which may make it sound more difficult than it is. She evokes some scenes in great detail, but for anyone comfortable reading traditional English literature it should pose no serious problems, although toward the end one has to remain alert to the shifts in chronology taking place from chapter to chapter.

The title—drawn from the T. S. Eliot passage that serves as the book's epigraph—suggests decaying aristocratic ruins, which is just what we see literally at the end of the novel. But it is obviously also meant to suggest the crumbling of a social class, the Taluqdars of Oudh (now Awadh), who have benefited mightily for the previous century by the presence of the British in their land, but who are now being swept up by the tides of change. Many in the younger generation yearn for freedoms that will undermine the authority of the elders in the old "joint-family" structure that has traditionally dominated Indian life. Hosain is particularly interested in exploring how these changes affect women, and her most interesting and fully realized characters are female.

When we first meet the narrator, Laila, she is a teenaged orphan being brought up by her old-fashioned grandfather, who disapproves of education for girls. By the standards of the culture at that time she is fast approaching marriageable age, and the planned marriage of her seventeen-year-old cousin Zahra to a "boy" of thirty is quite unexceptional. Even as the adults planning this union are looking forward to Zahra producing children for the family, we are reminded of how hazardous childbirth could be by the mention of the fact that the intended groom's mother died in childbirth. The adults make clear how unimportant the girl's opinions are in planning her own union. This is a merger of families in which the adults are presumed to know best.

Into this scene erupts the more unconventional story of the servant girl Nandi. Whereas Zahra is largely submissive and conformist, Nandi is rebellious and wild. Both of them are under constant pressure to remain "pure," but because the consequences for an lower-class girl are less, Nandi is able ultimately to get away with more than Zahra. Although both of them have disastrous relationships, Nandi at least follows her heart and can blame only herself for her bad choices, whereas Zahra is manipulated into throwing away her only chance at a happy marriage. In some ways, the servant girl is more free than the young lady.

But Nandi's lot is not sentimentalized. She will be beaten, seduced, abandoned, and mistreated in all manner of ways that make clear the wretched existence to which poor servants were routinely condemned. At this point she is being accused of a shamelessness that she is too young even to understand. Women who observed *purdah* were expected to avoid the company of unrelated men, and she has violated this rule by taking the driver his shirt in the garage. The adults see her as a potential "loose woman" in miniature, but she accuses Uncle Mohsin of having tried to seduce her, exposing the hypocrisy of their paternalism. The book suggests that instead of keeping her submissive, their restrictiveness will eventually drive her to rebellion. She reappears in the novel periodically to fill us in on yet more details of the humiliations inflicted on poor women.

At any rate, both Zahra and Nandi are being prodded toward conventionally proper female behavior by their elders, but Laila is busy discovering the secrets of her own heart in a way her family disapproves of: by reading. She tells herself that she is not heartless because she is moved by what she reads. The difference is, of course, that the relationships she explores in books are ones she can choose to enjoy freely rather than ones imposed on her by others.

The wretchedness of the poor in India is continually illustrated by the ongoing saga of Nandi, but it is treated in other ways as well. In Chapter 8, for instance, a scene of buying lavish jewelry for Zahra's marriage is paired with the ruthless eviction of a poor old woman from the family's land in an especially harsh contrast. This novel should not be mistaken for a simple sentimental reminiscence: it is a sustained social critique of a whole range of injustices.

In Chapter 4 we get a remembrance of the rich multicultural life of pre-independence Lucknow, in which the members of the community happily celebrated each other's religious holidays with little thought of the sort of sectarianism that was to cause so much trouble later. The holidays listed are all festive ones that would appeal to children, like Shubrat (*Shab-e-Baraat*), which is a day-of-the-dead festival somewhat analogous to American Halloween. For Laila, this is the positive side of having been a child in old Lucknow with her liberal, tolerant parents.

Later, when her grandfather dies during the ritual lamenting for Shi'ite martyrs on the tenth of Muharram, the younger people argue over the holiday, with Laila setting herself against the sort of sectarian hatred inflamed by the memory of old sufferings that has so often led to violent conflict. Many of the aspects of Islam illustrated in *Sunlight on a Broken Column* belong to the Shi'ite tradition dominant among much of the North Indian

Muslim population, which places great emphasis on the commemoration of ancient grievances. Later, when a Muslim procession damages a tree considered sacred by Hindus, the result is a bloody riot.

Earlier, also in Chapter 4, a relative is mentioned who participated in the Khilafat movement, which was organized in the wake of the collapse of the Ottoman Empire at the end of World War I under the leadership of Maulana Muhammad Ali and Maulana Shaukat Ali and flourished between 1919 and 1924. Working closely with the Hindu-dominated Congress Party against the British, it marked a high point in Muslim-Hindu cooperation. That it is only briefly alluded to here marks how times have changed, with the 1930s movement toward independence increasingly dividing Indians against each other along religious lines.

Hosain underlines resentment of and resistance to the British presence in India throughout her novel while also depicting characters who are happy to cooperate with and emulate their colonial rulers. When Laila's tutor, Mrs. Martin (who anglicizes her name as "Lily"), expresses the nostalgia for the old days before electric lights when the Muharram festivities were more colorful, the girl reminds her that in those days the Indians needed special passes issued by the British to attend the celebration if they were not wearing European clothes. This outspoken reaction leads Mrs. Martin to wonder if she has become a "Congress-wallah"—a participant in the independence movement—and indeed Laila is keenly aware of and interested in that movement. One of the principal themes of the novel is the spread of anticolonial sentiments among the young throughout the first half of the twentieth century.

With the death of her grandfather, Laila finds herself under the supervision of her Uncle Mohsin, who is in some ways more liberal—he believes in education for women—but who insists just as strongly as the older generation on the responsibility of parents to decide on their children's matrimonial futures, based largely on financial considerations. Asad, for instance, is forbidden to court Zahra, not because he is a distant relative—marriages between cousins are actually encouraged in this family—but because he is poor. As he puts it, a "wall of silver rupees" separates him from Laila and Zahra.

The combination of sophistication and traditionalism Uncle Mohsin exhibits is strongly reminiscent of the sort of upbringing given the author by her own widowed mother. Under a reproduction of the popular Victorian painting of Dante Alighieri falling in love with Beatrice (Henry Holiday's *The Meeting of Dante with Beatrice*), he dictates the terms according to which the female cousins under his care will marry. Romantic love such as the painting commemorates is out of the question. Zahra cannot follow her own desires; she is "the symbol of others' desires."

Zahra's total ignorance of sex on the eve of her marriage illustrates an ideal that was striven for in traditional families. The sequestration of women and powerful taboos against the public discussion of sexuality helped preserve girls in what is to modern readers an unnatural naiveté, but it has not been so long since European and American middle-class families strove to keep young girls in the same state of ignorance until their wedding nights.

It is ironic that in the colonial environment, upper-class social conservatism naturally led to contact with Western ideas that undermined their own traditions. The educations given to these privileged young people were not intended to turn them into radicals, but in many cases that is just what it did. Even Uncle Mohsin is aware of this trend as he forbids Asad to go study in Delhi where he may get involved in the political movements of the day. Asad's generation turned against not only the values of traditional India, but against their domination by the British, and this novel is largely concerned with these developments as India moved toward independence.

The brief passage toward the end of Chapter 17 contrasts two of the emerging streams of the independence movement: Marxism, which Hosain herself became involved in, and the nonviolent resistance (*satyagraha*) effort led by Gandhi and carried out by people like the *Satyagrahis* depicted in Chapter 5. Some of the young are filled with hope, others with despair, but no one of the rising generation can be fully shielded from what is happening.

In Part Two, Laila's life is no longer as circumscribed as it has been. The description of her circle of friends at college illustrates various aspects of the shifts occurring among young people. Nina expects her social activism to lead her to prison, like most of the Congress leadership. Nadira is fervently religious in a way that was emphasized as religious groups defined themselves more sharply in opposition to each other. Joan represents the Anglo-Indians, product of unions between English men and Indian women, who naturally found themselves sympathetic with the British, but whose ambiguous status made them distrusted by both sides in the independence struggle. Romana is the romantic who, cushioned by wealth and beauty, lives in a fantasy world that has already passed out of existence. The glimpses Hosain provides us of the world of young women at this time are interesting precisely because they emphasize variety, whereas the women in many South Asian novels depicting the period treat women principally as passive victims. These young women have minds of their own.

Laila has always been outspoken, but now she is sophisticated enough to confront the issues squarely, defending a Muslim girl who had run off with her Hindu lover because their families would never have tolerated an interfaith marriage. When challenged, she cites the romantic stories of love overcoming obstacles that made up the heart of the romantic literature dominating English-language education in India. Whereas for Romana, the idea of romantic love is an escapist dream, for Laila it is a vehicle for social criticism.

The preservation of women's "purity" above all does not only frustrate their longings for love in this novel; as the very next chapter illustrates, it can be deadly. Nandi's own mother dies because the family's ideas of shame prevent them from allowing her to be taken to a hospital during a difficult delivery.

One of the highlights of Part Two is the glittering reception held for the imperial viceroy, representative of the British government. But as usual Hosain is not content to wallow in the nostalgic glamor of the occasion. She points out that the elaborate *Baradari* (reception hall) used by the imperial government for the party was once part of the royal palace of the local ruler, Wajid Ali Shah, Nawab of Oudh, whose kingdom was seized by the British in the mid–nineteenth century when he was sent by them into exile. Soon thereafter, the English colonial government created a new local leadership loyal to themselves by elevating the status of the Taluqdars, the group to which Laila's family belongs and thereafter had a long history of close collaboration with the British. Thus everything about this party represents the corrupt, tangled alliance that Laila's generation is rebelling against, and a few of the young students shout the denunciation "toadies" (collaborators) during the ceremonies. Collaborators they may be, but they are not treated as equals. The palace is firmly in British hands. When Zahra proudly points out that the Taluqdars have a traditional right to audiences with the king of England, Laila recalls her own humiliation at school by a lowly English girl who called her "nigger."

It is ironic, of course, that this celebration of an old alliance provides the setting for Laila to literally fall into the arms of Ameer, the poor but idealistic young man she will marry in defiance of her family.

This celebration of Indian-British unity is followed closely by the massive student anti-British demonstrations in which Asad is wounded and Nita dies. The conflict is no longer a matter of mere theory to these young people; they have begun to suffer the consequences of the struggle directly.

The first chapter of Part Three is a farcical counterpoint to the romantic meeting in Part Two, as the family's two young men are welcomed home from the college and each pressured in turn to wed Laila in order to keep her inheritance in the family. Men have more choice in these matters than women, however. Fortunately for Laila they regard her more like a sister than a potential bride, leaving her free to dream of Ameer, but now she is all the more aware of how difficult it will be to marry him.

It is at the reception for her two cousins that Laila is able to become better acquainted with Ameer, for he is a close friend of Asad's. In a society where social dating simply does not exist, it is natural that a romance would blossom at a family party between a young woman and the friend of a male relative—one of the few unmarried men she would have the opportunity to speak with privately. Unfortunately, he belongs to an "inferior" branch of the family, lacking "breeding." Even as their forbidden love is beginning to blossom, we hear of another forbidden love, frustrated by religious differences, between Sita and Kemal. In this novel, love is constantly becoming entangled with the political situation surrounding the lovers.

Nandi is always ready to provide an earthy counterpoint to the negotiations over love and marriage taking place among her mistresses. She again shows her resourcefulness when she takes her vengeance on her old tormentor, Ghulam Ali, accusing him of attempted rape at the end of Chapter 11 of Part Three. She may be lying in this particular instance, but we know from her earlier complaints to Laila that he had in fact assaulted both her and the wretched Saliman in the past. She avenges Saliman's death by luring Ghulam Ali to her and then betraying him to the other servants. Given his misdeeds, it is hard to see Ghulam Ali as an innocent victim, and he takes his own terrible vengeance on her at the end of Chapter 16 of Part Three.

In the next chapter, as the political arguments become more heated, family members sharpen the differences among themselves. With the advantage of hindsight, Hosain can see that Islamic separatism had deeply conservative elements in it and that Hindus freed from British constraints may take the opportunity to avenge themselves for old grudges against Muslims. Uncle Hamid uses the traditional argument of an older privileged generation that is fighting to preserve its status: the young are not entitled to object to their feudal privileges while still benefiting from them. The argument has a certain force, but the fact is that the leaders of social revolutions have often been members of the prosperous middle classes. They have the education to learn what is possible and the freedom to make the possible real.

Chapter 14 of Part Three begins in 1937, when everything seems full of hope. But we cannot but remember that World War II will begin just two years in the future and ultimately lead to the collapse of the British Empire, independence, and the disasters accompanying the Partition of India into Hindu-dominated India and Muslim-dominated Pakistan. It is the unfolding of that story which provides the background for the rest of the book. At this point, of course, we don't yet know what consequences the war will have for Laila personally.

Uncle Hamid's triumph in the elections is portrayed as an illustration of the way the old Taluqdar class has managed to hang on to power, even in this modern age. Limited self-government is being granted by the British, but the votes are still counted in the colonial palace, where the great reception party had been held, by British colonial officers. This election does not mark the sort of independence Laila and her generation have yearned for, but is a continuation of the old British–Taluqdar collaboration by manipulating the democratic process. His triumph in the election will enable Uncle Hamid to maintain his feudal property rights.

But the election has one hopeful outcome, for once more, in the Baradari where Laila had first met Ameer, she encounters him again, and now he is at last in a position to claim her as his own. The older generation may be consolidating its power, but it will not have everything its way. Laila and Ameer are determined to be together; and they are old enough, courageous enough, and free enough to take their destiny into their own hands.

Unfortunately they are not free to transcend history, as we learn in Part Four. Up to this point *Sunlight on a Broken Column* has been told in a traditional, straightforward, even old-fashioned manner, with events unfolding in chronological order. But Part Four consists of a number of scenes told out of sequence, in an order determined by what aspects of the story Hosain wants to reveal to the reader at given points. The framework for these various flashbacks is a tour of the old house taken by Laila in 1952, after some of the principal characters of the story have died.

This narrative technique is somewhat reminiscent of Virginia Woolf's in one section of *To the Lighthouse,* where a house evokes powerful memories of the family that lived within it. Mulk Raj Anand claims to have introduced Hosain to Woolf when she was a young writer, so there may indeed have been some influence.

It is impossible to know exactly why Hosain decided to end her novel in such an unconventional fashion, but the huge, looming specter of Partition may have had something to do with it. Any book about the movement for Indian independence risks collapsing in despair in an account of the mutual slaughter that took place between Hindus and Muslims in 1947. The first draft of the novel in fact included an extensive account of Partition, but she was asked to remove it by Cecil Day Lewis, her editor at Chatto and Windus, perhaps because he thought it interfered with the deeply personal focus of the novel. Whatever his reasons, both Lewis and Hosain were later quoted as having regretted the decision.

But in the novel as it was published, she leaps right over the intervening fourteen years of the founding of modern India to portray Laila taking one last look at the old family home, confiscated when Saleem left for Pakistan. Partition divided properties as much as it did people (the old Rushdie family home in Bombay was similarly confiscated by the Indian government when Salman Rushdie's parents moved to Pakistan, even years after Partition, and he has only recently been able to reclaim it).

In an interesting passage near the beginning of Chapter 2 of Part Four, the author describes how the rising social class in independent India, which once looked to Europe for cultural models, is busily rediscovering its own roots. The somewhat acid tone in which she describes this development may be influenced by the fact that in India the revival of ancient traditions is often accompanied by a reinforcement of tensions. Insofar as India is defined as ancient Hindu India, it excludes or even opposes the Muslim minority within it. But she is careful to outline grievances on both sides. Clearly the stage is set for further conflict.

Chapter 3 takes us into Uncle Hamid's office, and back to 1937, where Laila explains to her guardian that she is determined to marry Ameer. It is not so much that he is convinced of the rightness of her decision as that now she has the maturity and the legal rights over her property to be able to exercise her own will. All that is arranged about her marriage is its timing, to obscure it by the splendor of another, more traditional, union.

The study remains the setting in which she reminisces about the rest of Uncle Hamid's life. She does not think vengefully about him, and Hosain is careful to portray a certain mellowing as characterizing his final years. The people in this novel are rarely purely villainous or purely heroic. Their complex humanity makes them more involving than if they were simple caricatures. But it is interesting to note that her final thoughts about him concern the freedom she enjoyed after he could no longer exercise control over her destiny.

Chapter 4 moves us to the dining room and to 1947, considering what the family members will do in the wake of Partition. This scene must have meant a good deal to Hosain, because she had enacted a version of it in her own family, opting like Laila to reject the newly created Muslim homeland of Pakistan and carve out her own destiny as an Indian of Muslim heritage.

Chapter 5 takes us into the pantry, once the domain of servants, where she recalls the story of Nandi, who has managed despite everything a kind of triumph, thanks partly to Laila's help. More than patronizing charity for an old family servant is involved, for Laila has seen Nandi as involved in the same struggles as herself to carve out a space in which a woman could make her own choices. It would be easy to dismiss this solution as leaving Nandi in a subservient position, but that is too facile. Her final treatment by Laila is both realistic and humane. This chapter also touches on the phenomenon of the neocolonial forces represented by the new dominant world power: America.

Chapter 6 is framed by a visit to the garden where Laila recollects the calamity of Zita's marriage, exactly the opposite of the devoted love match between Laila and Ameer. Chapter 7 continues in the same setting to present recollections of other old friends, including the formerly militant Muslim Nadira, who has now become an admirably compassionate worker for the poor in Pakistan. Note that Hosain is being careful not to portray her Indians and Pakistanis in simplistic ways, but to show the rich variety of reactions there were to Partition.

Chapter 8 begins by sketching the surprising successes of two more women, the poor singer, Zainab, and the glitzy international society life of the school beauty, Romana. Other characters' fates are tabulated as well. It is interesting to note that she discusses the women first.

In the final chapter, Laila returns from the sunlit garden into the death-like chill of her own room. By now we are naturally wondering what has happened to Ameer, and this is where we learn the story of their brief happy marriage. It is clear the story she has been telling is a lens through which she considers her continuing love for him. But having told that story in loving detail, she turns away, ready to move on.

SELECTED BIBLIOGRAPHY

Anand, Mulk. "Profile of Attia Hosain." *Commonwealth Quarterly* 3.9 (1978): 1–12.

    An interesting personal reminiscence of Hosain by a famous fellow author.

Hasan, Mushirul. "The Heart-in-Pieces Generation." *The Indian Express* 21 Feb. 1998. <http://www.financialexpress.com/ie/daily/19980221/05250374.html>.

    A brief article on Attia Hosain and Ahmed Ali, providing useful biographical details.

Hosain, Attia. *Phoenix Fled*. 1988. New York: Penguin, 1989.

———. *Sunlight on a Broken Column*. New York: Penguin, 1988.

Kaul, R. K., and Jasbir Jain. *Attia Hosain: A Diptych Volume*. Jaipur and New Delhi: Rawat Publications, 2001.

    Thus far the only book dedicated to Hosain, it is worth seeking out for much information unique to it and excellent bibliographies.

Chapter 6
Anita Desai: Games at Twilight *(1978)*

Even before the recent rise in the popularity of South Asian fiction, Anita Desai was one of India's best-known modern writers. Born in 1937 to a German mother and an Indian father, she learned German and Hindi as a child, but her education was in English, so it was only natural she should write in that language. Despite this fact, she has never been regarded as an "outsider" in India; unlike many other writers discussed in this book, she became famous in her homeland before she was known or published abroad. Although she remained in India much longer than many other authors, beginning in the late 1980s she has lived and worked mainly abroad, first in England, and now in the United States teaching at various colleges. Her film script based on her novel *In Custody* was directed by Ismail Merchant in 1993. Her youngest daughter, Kiran, published her comic first novel, *Hullabaloo in the Guava Orchard*, in 1998.

Desai is known principally for her novels, but the most striking features of her writing are those usually associated with short fiction. She strives to convey moods and settings more than she does to tell stories: several of her novels contain very little external action, although many of them end abruptly in a catastrophe. Her sensitive way of depicting settings and feelings is much admired by critics, who often compare her to novelists of the interior life like Virginia Woolf, but Desai herself says she has been most influenced by poets, and her writing often alludes to or quotes poetry.

Her first novel, *Cry, the Peacock* (1963), is characteristic of several of her works in depicting the anguish of an unhappily married woman. Because of her focus on the limitations Indian culture has placed on women, she has often been called a feminist, although she dislikes the term herself because she takes it to be exclusionary, and she points out that she has chosen to portray male protagonists in several of her novels and many of her stories. Yet Desai's portraits of women and girls have a great deal in common with avowedly feminist authors.

In *Cry, the Peacock,* Maya is a very young woman married to a cold, unfeeling judge twice her age. Several critics have echoed the fictional husband's criticism that she is suffering from a father complex, but this seems unfair. Although she has led a very sheltered life, it is clear that Maya loves her husband passionately, and her anguish stems largely from his inability— or unwillingness—to return that love. Her extreme sensitiveness puts off many readers—including Desai herself, who has since repudiated the anguished style of this work. But if the reader can set aside the concept that Maya is merely "crazy," there is much in the book to admire. Maya's madness expresses in an extreme form the yearnings and disappointments that many women have experienced.

Fire on the Mountain (1977) is similarly filled with anguish, this time that of an aging, bitter woman who has outlived her faithless husband and of her great-granddaughter, traumatized by a brutal father. At first it seems as if this might be a novel in the tradition of *Heidi:* bitter old age being redeemed by contact with lively youth. However, Desai is interested in depicting not therapeutic breakthroughs but mutual incomprehension. Like *Cry, the Peacock,* the novel ends in extreme, startling violence; but for much of its length the main interest of the narrative lies in the beauty and intensity of her portrait of the landscape in Kasauli, a far-northern region with which Desai has intense personal associations.

Many critics consider *Clear Light of Day* (1980) her most successful work. It combines a sensitive portrait of the interior life of its characters with vivid descriptions of their family home in Delhi. Unlike the earlier novels, the characters seem more balanced, capable of getting outside of themselves and changing in response to others. Bimala ("Bim") still lives in the family household, caring for her mentally handicapped brother, devoting herself to her teaching. Her younger sister Tara and her husband visit, and the two sisters explore the past, sorting out their feelings for each other. Anyone who has been caught in a family struggle between "the smart one" and "the pretty one" can relate to their feelings. Scene by scene, the narrative is interesting, the writing often beautiful, but the novel ends so ambiguously that critics do not agree on what precisely Bim finally realizes in the "clear light of day." For readers who do not insist on a decisive, revelatory ending, the work can provide a great deal of pleasure.

Baumgartner's Bombay (1988), written while Desai was teaching at Girton College, Cambridge, is in some ways an even more successful work. It is the story of a German Jew who was sent by his mother to India during the Nazi era to keep him out of the concentration camps. Ironically, he finds himself imprisoned by the Indian colonial government as an enemy alien in a camp largely run by its Nazi inmates. This tale is told retrospectively, from the point of view of the protagonist's old age as he wanders the streets of Delhi, begging for scraps to feed his beloved cats. Dozens of novels have been written about émigré Indians feeling alienated from the cultures to which they have moved, but Desai here does something new in reversing the pattern: this time it is the European who is alienated, misunderstood, and suffering.

With each of these works, Desai's craft has developed in breadth, flexibility, and complexity. Although Desai often says her novels grow spontaneously, without planning, the later ones are in fact carefully structured. *Baumgartner's Bombay* marks a high point in the way its rich, moving story is laid out. Like the early works, however, it ends catastrophically and may disturb readers who yearn for happy endings.

Much has been written about these novels, but relatively little about Desai's two volumes of short stories, *Games at Twilight and Other Stories* (1978) and *Diamond Dust and Other Stories* (2000), yet they are an excellent way to get to know the author. These are stories in the European tradition of sketches providing insight into characters rather than in the older tradition of the plot-driven "tale."

Many of the stories in the second volume lack Indian settings, and the following discussion concentrates instead on four stories from *Games at Twilight*. The title story from this volume begins with a rich evocation of tropical heat and childish energy:

It was still too hot to play outdoors. They had had their tea, they had been washed and had their hair brushed, and after the long day of confinement in the house that was not cool, but at least a protection from the sun, the children strained to get out. Their faces were red and bloated with the effort, but their mother would not open the door, everything was still curtained and shuttered in a way that stifled the children, made them feel that their lungs were stuffed with cotton wool and their noses with dust and if they didn't burst out into the light and see the sun and feel the air, they would choke.

'Please, ma, please,' they begged. 'We'll play in the veranda and porch—we won't go a step out of the porch.'

'You will, I know you will, and then—'

'No—we won't, we won't,' they wailed so horrendously that she actually let down the bolt of the front door so that they burst out like seeds from a crackling, over-ripe pod into the veranda, with such wild maniacal yells that she retreated to her bath and the shower of talcum powder and the fresh sari that were to help her face the summer evening. (1)

Little Ravi is so successful in the ensuing game of hide-and-seek that the other children forget all about him and leave him stifling in the dark, musty, spooky garage, turning his victory into humiliation. This is a story that could have been set anywhere, but Desai's poetic descriptions give it a vividness and intensity that make it into something special.

The second story in this volume, "Studies in the Park," is much more specifically Indian. Keep in mind that India still has a vast population of terribly impoverished citizens who struggle merely to survive from day to day. The small middle class that rises above the prevailing poverty can readily see the abyss yawning below it. Anxiety about success is pervasive, and the main path to success is through education. Parents place great stress on doing well in school and in passing the periodic uniform examinations that act as gateways to better jobs and family security. As a result, Indian students are pressured to work much harder at their studies than typical American students.

Suno, the boy who narrates the story, is the target of intense pressure from his family to do well in his upcoming "Inter" exams (slang for "intermediate" exams given in the second year of college that determine whether a student will be able to pursue a particular major or career). His learned father, who listens daily to the news in four languages, demands that he achieve a "first." In the traditional system inherited from the British, students are ranked within their classes when they pass exams. Getting a "first" means more than just getting an "A"—it means a student wrote the best exam in the class. The boy offering to sell him fritters (*dosai*—sliced vegetables dipped in batter and deep fried—a popular snack) in the tea shop illustrates the sort of job that boys who flunk their exams may be expected to hold. Even lower down on the scale is the completely uneducated street vendor who offers *gram* (roasted chickpeas), but a hint at the outcome of the story is given as he cheerfully whistles the tune "We are the *bul-buls* of our land, our land is Paradise" (23). The bulbul is a bird celebrated in ancient Persian poetry for its romantic song (often rendered in European translations as "nightingale" and serving much the same function in poetry), and the Persian-speaking Mughals brought the imagery associated with it to India where the bird is also native, and where it continues to flourish in poetry to this day. It is suggested that perhaps scholarship is not the only path to happiness.

At the beginning of the story, Desai vividly evokes the noisy household and Suno's impatience with both the pressure to study and the distractions that prevent him from doing so. The family lives in Old Delhi, the old walled city built by India's Mughal Muslim rulers long before the British developed the modern city of New Delhi surrounding it. Life there is crowded, lively, and full of diversions and distractions.

The twisting, narrow, crowded lanes are lined with homes and shops, even immediately surrounding the Jama (sometimes spelled "Jame") Masjid, the great mosque that serves as a center for the Muslim population of Old Delhi. It was built in the seventeenth century by Shah Jahan, the same ruler who also built the Taj Mahal. Nearby is Chandni Chowk, a market jammed with all manner of goods for sale, especially silver and rich textiles. Darya

Ganj Road abuts the park, and Mori Gate is a fourteenth-century ruin near the Red Fort, which is a popular tourist destination.

About 12 percent of Indians are Muslim, but in Old Delhi the concentration is much higher. It is natural that Suno would see mixed among the women wearing saris in the park, many wearing the traditional conservative Muslim female outer garment, the *borkha* (Arabic *burqa*), which completely envelops the wearer, hiding the body. Saris are often brilliantly colored and much more form fitting than borkhas, especially those worn on formal occasions. But here even the sari wearers cling to dowdy colors for their shapeless garments that cause Suno to call them "bag-like."

The "pyjamas" he sees men wearing in the park are not nightclothes, but traditional light summer day wear. The word comes to English directly from Hindi.

Although many students like himself are in the park, Suno also encounters other traditional disciplines: Hindu theology, yoga, and even wrestling. The world seems to be full of people earnestly following various pursuits while Sunil in contrast finds it impossible to concentrate on his own studies. (For more information on Vedanta, the Upanishads, and the Puranas, see the glossary.)

On first reading, it may seem that not much happens in this story. But its climax is not an exterior event. Irish novelist James Joyce used the religious term "epiphany" to label the sort of vivid experience that can transform a person's life. In Christian tradition, Epiphany, January 6, celebrates the day the world at large first encountered Christ in the form of the visit of the three Wise Men; but for modern writers it has taken on a much wider range of associations. Here, Suno's life is changed by an intense vision of human connectedness. He does not know whether the ill young Muslim woman he sees lying in the park is the daughter, wife, or lover of the older man who gently caresses her face—and it really doesn't matter. What strikes him about them is their wordless love for each other, so different from the relationships in his noisy, demanding family.

This scene is one that Desai says she encountered herself and moved her deeply. She used the identical scene again in her 1975 novel, *Where Shall We Go This Summer?* (145–46). In the novel an alienated wife tells her husband that witnessing this scene was the only happy moment of her life. But it also makes her feel shut out from their happiness, alienated from this almost unique tenderness. In the short story the identical scene connects Suno with the rest of humanity and seems to promise a happier life ahead—a fine example of how an author can shape her material in radically different ways depending on the needs of the work at hand. Fiction is rarely a mere transcript of reality.

Suno had come to the park to find the peace necessary for his studies, but he has learned something very different, which makes him become a "professional" inhabitant of the park: real life is about connection with other people. He begins to talk with all sorts of people in the park, and no longer takes seriously the preparation for his exams. Unlike Narayan's Raju, he is not a poor student for lack of academic talent; instead, he is a sensitive young man who is just learning how to live.

Will he in fact not take his exam? It is hard to believe he would abandon his academic career like Raju and turn into a hustling street merchant. He seems more likely to turn to literature, like Desai herself. Suno is from a Hindu family, as his name and various allusions indicate, but the vision that inspires him involves Muslims. This suggests that truth about life is to be sought not in the narrow doctrines of any one sect, but in the simple humanity surrounding him.

"The Accompanist" is another story that hinges on self-realization. Bhaiyya is a tanpura player, accompanying a master (*ustad*) of the most famous North Indian classical stringed instrument, the sitar. In standard performances, the sitar player is the star, choosing what rag to perform.

Indian classical music is largely improvised, but it is not totally free. The rag determines what scale will be used, its musical structure, both as it ascends and descends, and which notes are to be especially emphasized. The division of rags into six male *ragas* and thirty-six female *raginis* and into pieces suitable for performance at morning, evening, or other times of the day is more theoretical than something the average listener can actually hear, but musicians are always aware of them. Within the constraints imposed by the rag, the soloist, accompanied by the droning of the tanpura, typically begins his performance with the *alap* (literally, conversation) section of the piece, playing slowly, without any definite beat, thoughtfully exploring the relationship between notes. The alap is the part of the performance that Bhaiyya especially enjoys, because it allows the sitar player to show off his skill in subtle, sophisticated ways.

Less sophisticated listeners are likely to be restless until the set of two round-bottomed drums called the *tabla* enters, marking the beginning of the *gat,* a section whose rhythmic pattern is determined by the *tal* (*tala* in the South), meaning literally "rhythm." The rhythms of Indian classical music are the most complex in the world, often difficult patterns of odd-numbered beats (Indian popular and folk music rhythms are much simpler). The tabla player is second only to the soloist in prominence. He does not merely accompany the sitar, flute, or voice; he exchanges phrases with it. The sitar plays a rapid string of improvised notes and the tabla player quickly imitates it on the drums. The ever-accelerating gat becomes a kind of musical game of catch, with the soloist flinging out unexpected pitches that the tabla player must respond to. The flying fingers of the instrumentalists dazzle the audience, building to a wild, exciting climax. Watching a good raga performance is very much like watching a good jazz performance, with master soloists tossing ideas back and forth. This is the section that Bhaiyya considers as somewhat cheap and flashy compared to the alap.

So what is a tanpura (South Asian *tambura*)? It is a simple instrument with four to six strings steadily stroked by the fingers of the performer, creating a harmonic drone underneath the other instruments. Like most world music, Indian traditional music is basically monophonic (one note at a time) rather than homophonic (changing chords played beneath a melody). In Indian music, harmony is created both by the overlapping sounds of succeeding notes and by the drone of the tanpura. Playing it well takes more consistency and stamina than artistry, because performances of a single rag can go on for hours, and the same strings are plucked over and over in the same pattern by the tanpura player. Some idea of the simplicity of the instrument's role can be gathered by noting that many modern musicians dispense with a tanpura altogether, substituting a small electronic box that can be tuned to emit the desired tones to support any particular raga. There are no famous virtuosos among tanpura players.

Part of the reason Bhaiyya loves the alap more than the gat is that he and the Ustad share the spotlight in it, whereas the flashy tabla player is likely to capture the audience's attention during the concluding section. In addition, he adores his Ustad as a great musician whose genius should be appreciated on its own.

But Bhaiyya's friends are indignant that he has abandoned the possibility of a brilliant career as a soloist to devote himself to serving a master who is not even considerate of him, neglecting to inform him in advance what rag they will be playing, for instance. He is momentarily shaken by the thought that he might have become an ustad himself, on the sitar, or on other solo stringed instruments like the *sarod* or *vina*. But when he calms down he realizes his connection with the musical genius of the Ustad has given great meaning to his life, actually given him his identity. To symbolize this fact, Desai has him give us his name only when he tells of his "birth" as a tanpura player. His loud demand to be taken to join the Ustad is his reply to his friends' arguments. He may not be the star, but he is content to be a part of great musical performances.

Music is everything to him; his relationship to the Ustad is closer than marriage. He did not feel particularly close to his mother, although he enjoyed the candy she made. At first infatuated with Indian film stars like Meena Kumari (the same 1950s star whose name Raju had suggested Rosie adopt in *The Guide*), he turned from women when he took up his musical career, even dismissing his arranged marriage by saying of his wife "she does not bother me" (62). His abandonment of women for music is not as difficult to understand as it would be in the West because traditional Indian women do not date before marriage, and the choice of a bride is usually made by the groom's parents.

The more you know of Indian classical music, the more paradoxical this story may seem. Desai has deliberately chosen a very difficult task: to convince us that an intelligent, skilled man like Bhaiyya truly believes he has not wasted his life. She may not expect us to agree with him. But she wants us to understand the thinking of such a man whose devotion to the art of music is pure, undiluted by ego.

Although the story makes no allusion to the fact, it is some consolation to speculate that Bhaiyya might yet come into his own as an instrumentalist. He is only thirty, and plays with an ustad who was already elderly when he was just fifteen. He cannot accompany the old man forever. This would be a much sadder story if the narrator were in his sixties.

So far all these stories have featured male protagonists. Although Desai is famed for her sympathetic treatment of the inner lives of women and of the failures of their husbands to understand them, she prides herself on being able to adopt the points of view of male characters, and she does so much more often in her short fiction than in her novels.

The concluding story in *Games at Twilight,* "Scholar and Gypsy," is interesting in that it is told from the point of view of the husband with his wife initially being the object of his irritation. As they develop opposing reactions to India, however, she evolves into the more sympathetic figure of the two. (This same theme was developed further by Desai in her 1995 novel *Journey to Ithaca.*) David is an American graduate student trying to finish his doctoral dissertation on some unspecified subject involving India in Bombay, accompanied by his wife Pat, who at first hates everything about the country, including the food (her speculation that the dish offered her is made of goat is not paranoid: the "mutton" listed on Indian menus is usually goat meat). The vivid passages that convey her disgust with the sights, sounds, and smells of the country have offended some Indian readers, but this is not Desai's own view of India. She is skillfully imagining what it is like for foreigners unsympathetic to the culture to find themselves plunged into it, as she was to do even more strikingly in *Baumgartner's Bombay.*

Pat responds no better to the less humid but still oppressively hot climate of Delhi, and David finally suggests they seek the cooler region of the Kulu Valley in the far northern state of Himachal Pradesh, where the rich have traditionally gone to escape the heat of the lowlands in summer. They are re-enacting the annual migration of English wives of colonial officials who were sent to the "hill stations" in the foothills of the Himalayas while their husbands remained behind to work and swelter in Calcutta and Delhi. Women were considered too frail to stay behind. David, as a graduate student, is free to accompany his own wife. The result is a striking reversal of attitudes: she loves the little hill town of Manali and he hates it.

At first it would seem that the less educated Pat is simply clinging to what she finds familiar: Manali reminds her—with its majestic *deodar* cedar forests, apple orchards, and cuckoos—of her native Vermont. Their contrasting reactions to her discovery of the flower called jack-in-the-pulpit make clear their opposing feelings: she is delighted at finding a plant she knows, but he thinks of its hood as menacing, like that of an Indian cobra.

At first it seems as if this story is a satire on Pat, whose eager embrace of the land and culture of the Kulu Valley echoes the enthusiasm of the Western hippies who streamed into the region in the early 1970s, seeking Buddhism, *bhang* (tea made of marijuana), and bliss, with very little understanding of the people around them. They often confused the spiritual release of Nirvana with drug-induced intoxication. In Manali visitors are offered imported British treats like ginger biscuits (cookies) and Horlicks (a popular sweet malted milk drink among those who can afford imports). Restaurants provide the brown rice preferred by hippies influenced by the Japanese macrobiotic diet.

Although Buddhism originated in India and spread from there to pervade much of the Far East, it almost died out in most of India about eight centuries ago, with many of its leading characteristics absorbed and modified by Hinduism, the dominant religion. To the south, Sri Lanka remained heavily Buddhist; but in India only in the far northern Himalayan hills adjacent to Buddhist Tibet did the religion continue to thrive. One of Manali's nicknames is in fact "Gateway to the Himalayas," and travelers from the town reach the Tibetan city of Lahaul by going through the nearby Rothang Pass.

There is a substantial revival of Buddhism within India today, but Buddhist visitors to the country are often surprised to find how scanty are the traces of their faith in the land of Gautama Buddha's birth. Even at Sarnath, where the Buddha began his mission and where once a vast Buddhist monastery thrived, the only contemporary temples have been built using funds provided by foreign devotees.

So it is natural that many Indians view the touristic interest in Indian Buddhism as superficial. But the fact is that Buddhism is one of the great gifts of India to the world, one of the most successful religions the world has ever seen partly because of its flexibility, which allows it to attract a wide variety of people from all sorts of cultures. The major elements of Buddhism are closely related to similar ideas in Hinduism, and the Buddha is even conventionally regarded by Hindus—although not usually worshiped—as an incarnation of the god Shiva.

When Pat finds herself drawn to the Buddhism pursued by the visiting Westerners, she is going beyond her nostalgia for Vermont to embrace a tradition that is at least Indian in its roots, and she is quite correct when she rebukes her husband: "you don't even know it's possible to find Buddha in a Hindu temple" (137). Although early in the story she had seemed to be the more naïve of the two, it is David who now proves himself limited in his ability to relate to his surroundings: his negative reactions to Manali are as vividly described as were Pat's earlier reactions to Bombay and Delhi. It is difficult to maintain our respect for his superior knowledge of the culture partly because we are given few examples of it (we never do learn the subject of his thesis), and he loses credibility entirely as his interest even in pursuing his research wanes. She has studied enough to pick up Hindu concepts like *prana*—the spiritual force that energizes the body, literally "life." They have exchanged roles: she is now the eager student while he is the depressed one, alienated from his surroundings.

It is too simple to say that Pat is "right" and David "wrong" in their reactions to India. The culture is too complex, too varied for a single reaction to be appropriate to all of it—that is part of the point of the story. Both of these characters have blind spots and deficiencies. The story is not about discovering what is genuinely Indian, whatever that may mean, but about the way in which two people drift apart because of their opposing sensitivities and interests. It is strikingly reminiscent in this way of Raja Rao's complex philosophical 1960 novel *The Serpent and the Rope,* in which the Hindu protagonist studying medieval European religion is progressively drawn back to his Hindu roots while his European wife embraces Buddhism, which is to him an alien faith.

A subtle racial theme runs through the story as well. Pat, who was repelled by the exposed brown flesh of the women in Bombay, turns brown herself in the sun and happily makes friends with a fellow pilgrim from Harlem while David's failure to fit in is symbolized by the purple disinfectant splashed on his wounds. We are told that when the bus radiator exploded he considered it only from his own point of view, as *his* accident: "He quite forgot to ask about the driver or his brainless help or the hapless bystanders who had been standing too close to the boiling radiator" (135). He leaves Manali marked like a baboon, totally alienated from his wife, more concerned with his own bizarre appearance than with the fact that she has left him.

In this he is like most of the husbands in Desai's fiction, who fail—or never even try—to see the world from their suffering wives' point of view. Passionate identification with women's plights and sensitive descriptions of their surroundings are the most striking characteristics of Desai's fiction; but as is clear from the other stories discussed earlier, she is quite capable of sympathizing with men as well, and her works are enjoyed by a wide variety of readers.

SELECTED BIBLIOGRAPHY

Desai, Anita. *Baumgartner's Bombay.* London: Heinemann, 1987.
———. *Clear Light of Day.* London: Heinemann, 1980.
———. *Cry, the Peacock.* London: Peter Owen, 1963.
———. *Diamond Dust and Other Stories.* London: Chatto and Windus, 2000.
———. *Fire on the Mountain.* London: Heinemann, 1977.
———. *Games at Twilight and Other Stories.* London: Heinemann, 1978.
Jaggi, Maya. "A Passage from India." *The Guardian* 19 June 1999. <http://www.guardian.co.uk/booker/Story/0,2763,201690,00.html>.
    A detailed portrait of the author and her career, based on an interview with her.

Lewis, Robin Jared. "Anita Desai: *Fire on the Mountain* and *Games at Twilight.*" *Masterworks of Asian Literature in Comparative Perspective: A Guide for Teaching.* Ed. Barbara Stoler Miller. Armonk, NY: M. E. Sharpe, 1994.
This entire volume is an invaluable resource for anyone interested in Asian literature. The article on Desai has a good selective bibliography.

Rajendra Prasad, V. V. N. *The Self, the Family, and Society in Five Indian Novelists: Rajan, Raja Rao, Narayan, Arun Joshi, Anita Desai.* New Delhi: Prestige, 1990.
Contains a good section on Desai.

Ray, Sangeeta. "Gender and the Discourse of Nationalism in Anita Desai's *Clear Light of Day.*" *Eroticism and Containment: Notes from the Flood Plain.* Ed. Carol Siegel and Ann Kibbey. New York: New York UP, 1994. 96–119.
Useful if you can handle the jargon.

Chapter 7
Bapsi Sidhwa:
Cracking India *(1988)*

apsi Sidhwa is the most eminent author who began her career in
Pakistan now writing fiction in English about South Asia. She was
born August 11, 1938, in Karachi, into in a Gujurati-speaking Parsi
family, and raised in Lahore. The Parsis (also spelled "Parsees") are descen-
dants of Zoroastrians who fled Persia when it was conquered by Islam in the
seventh century. Of the few who survive today, the largest concentration
lives in Bombay; but Sidhwa's family belongs to a tiny fragment of the community: some two hundred Parsis living in Lahore out of a population of five
million, most of whom are Muslims.

Upon India's independence from England in 1947, Pakistan was created
as a homeland for Muslims, who constituted a minority in India as a whole
and many of whom feared discrimination. Although Gandhi and the
Congress Party argued for a united, secular Indian state in which people of
all faiths could live side by side, many Muslims distrusted the largely
Hindu-led independence movement. Although Muslims and Hindus had
coexisted peaceably for many years in South Asia, Muslim rulers had dominated much of Hindu India during the earlier Mughal period. Long-sim-
mering antagonism between the two groups has tended to surface in times
of tension, and during the lengthy struggle for independence several out-
breaks of what South Asians call "communal violence" broke out: fighting
between Muslims and Hindus.

When the British withdrew and certain northern provinces of India were
formed into Pakistan under the leadership of Mohammad Ali Jinnah, disaster struck. As millions of Muslims fled to Pakistan and millions of Hindus

fled to India, mutual massacres broke out. To complicate matters, the Sikhs, whose dominant territory was divided between the two nations, also attacked their Muslim neighbors (for further background, see Chapter 3 on Khushwant Singh's *Train to Pakistan*). "Partition," as it is called, was a bloodbath of unprecedented proportions, blighting the independence celebrations and reinforcing hatreds that continue to erupt from time to time in the region. So shameful is the memory of the Partition violence that it has been seldom written about.

Sidhwa witnessed some of that violence close up. As a nine-year-old child, she saw the flames burning parts of Lahore and encountered shouting mobs (and learned to shout slogans that would agree with each mob's politics). When a servant was escorting her to her tutor's, he pushed over a gunny sack left sitting in the road, and out tumbled the dead body of a young man whose waist had been carved away. Sikh friends who had lived next door entrusted their property to the family and fled south, never to be heard from again.

She was educated by tutors when she was young because she had contracted polio at age three and was not allowed to attend school until she was fifteen years old. Her well-to-do family could afford an *ayah* (nanny), other servants, and a private education, but even the high walls of the family compound could not entirely shut out the turmoil in the world around her.

The family spoke Gujarati at home, and Urdu (the official language of Pakistan) was her second tongue, but much of her education took place in English. A tutor gave her a copy of *Little Women* on her tenth birthday, which set her off over the next several years on a course of intensive reading that influenced her profoundly and provided her with the background she would need to become an English-language author herself. Having largely overcome the disability that had weakened her legs, she studied at and graduated from the Kinnaird College for Women in Lahore.

Traditional Parsis try to maintain their community by insisting on marriage inside the faith and not accepting converts. Given the small numbers of Parsis in Lahore, it is understandable that she was married at the age of nineteen to a Parsi in Bombay, where the community was much bigger. She found the experience of living in a large community of her own people stimulating, but was even more exhilarated to be thrust into a sophisticated social setting where men and women mingled together after being largely segregated as an unmarried girl from the world outside the family.

Divorced after five years, she married a Parsi businessman, Noshir Sidhwa, in Pakistan. At the age of twenty-six, now the mother of two children, she heard the story of a young Punjabi girl who had been forced to marry a jealous and violent husband in the remote Karakoram Mountains on the border with China. The girl ran away from her abusive spouse, but was tracked down and beheaded by him. Sidhwa felt she had to tell the girl's story. She secretly began work on her first novel, *The Bride,* which would take four years to write and even longer to publish.

Numerous publishers rejected this grim story, and Sidhwa set about writing *The Crow Eaters,* a considerably more lighthearted novel. Yet it too met rejection everywhere, leading Sidhwa to print and market it herself in Pakistan. The British firm of Jonathan Cape finally published *The Crow Eaters* in 1980 to very positive reviews abroad, and Sidhwa was launched on her career as an internationally celebrated author. *The Bride* was published in 1983, followed by her most famous novel, *Cracking India* (originally *Ice-Candy-Man*), in 1988, and her most recent work, *An American Brat,* in 1993.

Sidhwa was active in various political causes in Pakistan as a young woman, and she represented her nation at the 1975 international Asian Women's Congress in Kazakhstan. She also worked on an advisory committee to Prime Minister Benazir Bhutto on women's development. In 1983 she moved with her husband and children to the United States where she began a distinguished career teaching creative writing at colleges such as Mt. Holyoke, the University of Houston, and Brandeis and Columbia. Although she became a U.S. citizen in 1992, she retained dual Pakistani citizenship, and returns for months at a time annually to her homeland, often identifying herself as a Pakistani writer, but now preferring to be regarded as an American. Although female authors are rare in Pakistan and she has been very critical of some aspects of Pakistani culture, Sidhwa was awarded the nation's highest arts honor, the Sitara-I-Imtiaz, in 1991. She has noted that she is able to write about subjects in English that would bring down the wrath of the censor were she to write about them in Urdu, which is read by far more people in Pakistan. In addition to several other honors, in 1994 she received the major Lila Wallace-*Reader's Digest* Award. Her works have been translated into German, French, Italian, Greek, and Russian.

The Bride begins as the story of Qasim, a ten-year-old boy belonging to the hill-country Kohistan tribe in the mountains bordering Afghanistan married off to a horrified teenaged bride to settle his father's debt. After this disastrous beginning, he eventually matures enough to appreciate and love his wife, having five children by her, three of whom survive when the rest—and his wife— are struck down by typhoid fever. This disaster is followed by the murderous chaos of Partition, in which Qasim is swept up, murdering a Hindu who had insulted him by calling him a "filthy son of a Muslim mountain hog."

Yet Qasim has his compassionate side. He rescues a little girl whose parents have been killed in the rioting and raises her as his own, naming her after his own beloved daughter, Zaitoon. As the novel develops, it is Zaitoon who gradually develops into the book's protagonist, becoming at last the bride of the title. Yet much of the first half of the novel is a portrait of Qasim, who consistently combines qualities of kindness and generosity with ferocity and murderous violence. He makes his fortune as a contract killer but acts tenderly toward Zaitoon, and he seems to cherish her as if she were truly his own.

In Chapter 10, the novel's focus shifts to the girl, now fifteen. Her developing sexual feelings are described, although she understands nothing of what she is experiencing. Disaster strikes the next year when Qasim decides to marry Zaitoon to a fellow Kohistani tribesman. It is not entirely clear in the context of the novel why he makes this drastic decision, abruptly taking the young girl whom he seems so attached to off to a distant region she knows nothing of to wed a man she has never met. Sidhwa has explained in a private communication that Pakistani readers would have known that members of the mountain Pathan tribes seldom marry women outside their own tribe. Thus the marriage Qasim plans would have been regarded as more or less automatic.

Within the context of the novel, Qasim explains his decision to himself as a need to reaffirm his roots, to reconnect with his people; but it is also suggested that the substantial bride price the groom is willing to pay has something to do with his decision in the matter. In most of South Asia, a young girl is a financial burden because her husband's family expects a large dowry; marrying Zaitoon to a Kohistani transforms her from a liability into an asset.

Clearly Qasim thinks he is acting as a loving and responsible father, just as her new husband Sakhi believes himself to be a loving and responsible husband. Their tradition-bound minds prevent them from understanding the horrific suffering they are inflicting on Zaitoon. Although the girl discovers intense pleasure in lovemaking during her honeymoon, her groom's brutish behavior quickly destroys the love she is developing for him.

On the way to meet her future husband, the young girl had encountered a very different "mixed marriage" between Carol, a blond Californian, and Farukh, a young Pakistani foreign student. The differences in their background become apparent when they return to begin married life together in Pakistan, and Carol rejects the possessiveness of her husband, insisting on the right to her personal freedom, eventually taking a lover and rejecting her husband altogether. She can get away with this because she is older and Western. Zaitoon, severely beaten by her jealous husband, has stronger grounds for leaving her marriage, but less opportunity for doing so. Whereas Carol seems capricious and self-centered, Zaitoon emerges as a true heroine. The harrowing story of her grueling escape brings to life the story of the girl Sidhwa had heard about on her second honeymoon, but with a surprise twist at the end.

The novel is written simply and straightforwardly, with great power and economy of expression. Urdu words and expressions are sprinkled throughout, but usually in a context that makes them self-explanatory. Like all her later novels, *The Bride* is punctuated by expository passages that explain aspects of the culture and language to the foreign reader, a pattern that annoys some South Asian readers but for which others may be grateful. It is also marked by Sidhwa's interest in female sexuality, a theme that will pervade her later novels.

The Bride is both a lament for women's powerlessness and a tribute to women's courage. It may not have been seen in Pakistan as a sweeping indictment of men because Qasim and Sakhi are despised "tribals." Yet Sidhwa was to make clear in her other writings that the oppression of women in Pakistan is not confined to such groups. The scenes among the Kohistani have been objected to by Pakistani critics, who found them stereotypical, and the reader should be aware that such murderous traditions are not universal among them. However, it is also true that numerous instances of such "honor killings" have been reported, even quite recently, in the more rural regions of Pakistan.

The title of *The Crow Eaters* comes from a popular expression, which says of especially talkative persons that they must have "eaten a crow." The chattiness of Parsis is noted but made little of in the novel. It was an odd and perhaps unfortunate choice of titles that earned Sidhwa's book widespread criticism among her fellow Parsis when it appeared. Many of them mistakenly assumed she was referring to the traditional Parsi method of disposing of the dead by leaving their corpses in open towers to be consumed by carrion birds. Other Parsis accused her of exposing a traditionally private, vulnerable community to ridicule. These accusations plagued Sidhwa earlier in her career, but she now seems to have been embraced by many in her community as a representative to be proud of.

The comic tone of this work contrasts strikingly with the grim story in *The Bride*. The central figure of the first part of the novel is Faredoon Junglewalla, who moves his pregnant wife, his baby girl, and mother-in-law Jerbanoo from their home in central India to Lahore to seek his fortune. Jerbanoo is a wildly selfish, domineering woman who does battle with Faredoon throughout the novel. At one point he tries to solve his two most urgent problems by setting fire to his business, hoping to cash in on his insurance and kill off Jerbanoo at the same time.

If the novel were told in the same tone as *The Bride*, it would be a powerful indictment of male selfishness, for Faredoon not only attempts murder, but betrays his wife and heartlessly tells his young son Yazdi to forget the girl he has set his heart on because she is a prostitute—Faredoon can prove it because he has slept with the girl himself. Although the novel was welcomed by most reviewers as the rollicking, bawdy tale of a lovable rascal, Faredoon continually tests the limits of our tolerance by his outrageous behavior. The young girl, for instance, has been forced into prostitution by her family, and she clearly suffers intensely.

His favorite son dies early. Yazdi, revolted by his father's heartless behavior, rebels by abandoning the family for the life of a self-sacrificing ascetic. It is the remaining son, Behram (called "Billy"), who becomes the center of the last part of the novel. Building on his father's fortune, he becomes tight-fisted and selfish, constantly struggling over the family budget with his free-spending bride, Tanya. He had outrageously made a bid for her after being formally introduced as a potential bridegroom to her pockmarked, flat-chested older sister. He lacks his father's charm because his misdeeds reflect a meanness foreign to the impulsive Faredoon.

The novel is saturated with an intensely earthy physicality, especially reflecting Sidhwa's interest in sex. Sidhwa has commented that the fiercely puritanical official culture of Pakistan results in a strong repressed sexuality that bubbles up in all sorts of ways. Her account of Billy and Tanya's honeymoon is quite explicit, detailing both the joys and failings of the pair who have been shielded from all knowledge of the acts they are expected to engage in as a married couple. Sidhwa's criticisms of Pakistani sexual repressiveness strongly resemble those made by Khuswant Singh in other contexts, and this novel might have been written by a such a man, for there is nothing obviously feminine (or feminist) about it. In fact, Sidhwa was pleased to note that several early reviewers of the book assumed the author was male.

One particularly interesting episode in *The Crow Eaters* depicts Faredoon taking his family to England, where his mother-in-law deliberately outrages their hosts' sensitivities. Faredoon loses much of his respect for the British, finding they can be as poor, dirty, and ignorant as any Indian. It is a recurrent theme in Sidhwa's fiction that British pretensions to superiority in India were fueled mainly by money, power, and arrogance, with little basis in reality.

After satirizing various aspects of Lahore Parsi culture in *The Crow Eaters*, Sidhwa depicts them far more positively in *Cracking India*. She originally titled the book *Ice-Candy-Man* after the vicious popsicle vendor who features in it. Her American publishers found the title off-putting, some even imagining it might be misunderstood as a drug reference, and the work was given its more widely known title.

Cracking India is based on Sidhwa's own experience of Partition, the violence accompanying the "cracking" of Pakistan off from India in 1947. She chose to tell the story through the eyes of a young girl with polio partly because it came naturally to her to draw on her own life, but also because she reasoned that such a girl might spend more time with adults than most children and plausibly have the opportunity to witness and understand what was going on around her. In fact, Sidhwa herself as a young girl understood little of the events surrounding Partition at the time, and her parents were not prone to confide in her. Many readers have felt that Lenny, the little girl in the book, is too knowing, displaying at times a distinctly adult understanding of her surroundings. Others argue that we are supposed to understand there is a second narrative voice in the novel, the adult Lenny, commenting on matters she had not understood as a child. In any case, Lenny emerges as a convincing and moving character, striving to make sense of a world in which both love and hate threaten disruption and loss.

Public catastrophes are often narrated through the eyes of children because our natural sympathy for their status as innocent victims brings home and reinforces the horror of the deeds committed by adults. Although Lenny escapes the worst of the violence surrounding her, we naturally fear for her, so we are drawn powerfully into the perils she faces.

Whereas Khushwant Singh's *Train to Pakistan* portrays Partition from an Indian perspective, with unimaginable slaughter taking place off across the border in Pakistan, Sidhwa gives us a Pakistani perspective. Not that she holds her countrymen blameless, but she provides vivid details of the horrors inflicted by Indian on Muslims in a way that has made her book more readily accepted in Pakistan.

Much of the story centers on Lenny's teenaged nursemaid, named Shanta but normally referred to by her title as "Ayah." This is not meant to depersonalize the girl but to indicate intimacy, because family members are normally referred to by their roles rather than their names, much as a very small American child might refer to "Mommy" and "Daddy" without being sure of their actual given names.

Ayah's natural beauty and sensuality naturally attract men, and the young Lenny perceives this as an intriguing source of magnetic power. Meanwhile Lenny's little cousin (called simply "Cousin") is similarly besotted with Lenny and introduces her to sex play in ways that she finds both alarming and fascinating. Cousin is himself fairly naïve, not much older than Lenny, and he is treated in the novel less as a villain than as a comic foil. Right to the end of the novel Lenny remains ignorant of how the sexual act is performed, but she is acutely attuned to the erotic currents flowing around her.

It is tempting to read this work as a study in the loss of innocence: the adults engage in bloodshed and rape while Lenny is violated. But Sidhwa presents these themes more complexly than we might expect. Cousin is presented as more inept than threatening. His infatuation with her gives her a sense of power, and Lenny credits him with arousing her lifelong fascination with men. (It's worth noting that Sidhwa says Cousin is a wholly invented character, not based on anyone from her own childhood.) Less ambiguous is the figure of the cook, Imam Din, a dirty old man who plays "naughty games" with the family children on his lap. Their complaints about him have no effect. But even he is not painted as a complete monster. When Lenny's parents allow him to travel alone with her to visit family members in a nearby village, nothing untoward happens, surprising the reader who expects a traumatic follow-up to earlier comments about him.

Lenny's main traumatic experiences center on Ayah. The first is her own involuntary betrayal of the girl when a hostile Muslim mob comes looking to kill Hindus in their home. This incident is based on a real occurrence in which such a mob came to her parents' home, but in that case their Muslim cook saved the day by assuring the crowd that his employers were Parsis, not Hindus. Sidhwa combines this incident with another real story, about an

Indian Sikh who kidnapped and forcibly married a Muslim woman during Partition. She managed to get away from him and go to Pakistan where she remarried. He followed her and committed suicide. When, in Chapter 29, Lenny realizes the full extent of Ice-Candy-Man's villainy, her shock is described in powerful terms for which "loss of innocence" is an inadequate label. Whereas in *Train to Pakistan* interfaith romance was a redemptive force in the face of violence, here it is an integral part of the violence. The name she has been given, "Mumtaz"—recalling the beloved wife of Shah Jahan in whose memory the Taj Mahal was built—is bitterly ironic.

Clearly Sidhwa considerably has reshaped events from her own life to convey the experience of the period. Ayah comes to stand for the innocent victims of all violence, and her earlier role in the home reflects the long period of peaceful coexistence among Muslims, Hindus, and Parsis so tragically interrupted by Partition. Sidhwa vividly depicts how, as the moment of independence drew near, people began to turn to their own communities, emphasizing their differences, becoming more "pious" in ways that cut themselves off from their neighbors. Earlier her Parsi family had been happy to celebrate Christian holidays like Christmas and Easter, Muslim holidays like Eid, and Hindu holidays like Diwali—a widespread phenomenon commented on as well by Salman Rushdie in reference to his own childhood. Now religions draw tight lines around themselves to keep others out. Sidhwa states in Chapter 10, "People shrink, dwindling into symbols." Enraged Muslims who had probably participated in the popular pastime of squirting colored water on passersby during the joyous Hindu holiday of Holi now threaten their old neighbors by saying they will "play Holi with their blood."

Lenny begins to notice little differences, like the way young Sikh boys wear a traditional tuft of hair on their otherwise shaven heads. She is treated to the standard repertoire of jokes depicting Sikhs as comically foolish and unsophisticated, as well as jibes at Muslims and Parsis. She is shocked to realize that a Brahmin feels he must throw away food uneaten that has been rendered unclean by her shadow. Although it is not clear how much influence these prejudices have on Lenny's own thinking, one can see how mutual distrust and hatred is being nurtured in the culture.

Sidhwa is eager to rebut Indian views of Jinnah, the founding father of Pakistan, by portraying him as more rational and responsible than has been common in earlier Indian accounts of Partition, and humanizing him by telling of his marriage to a Parsi. Gandhi, in contrast, is criticized for having incorporated too much of Hinduism into his movement, despite his efforts to reach out to Muslims. Among the list of prominent names also mentioned in Chapter 10 is that of Muhammad Iqbal, poet and prominent advocate of a separate homeland for Muslims. Of the others, Tara Singh (born Nanak Chand Malhotra) was an important Sikh leader during Partition, and Lord Louis Mountbatten was the British diplomat dispatched to negotiate

India's independence. Also discussed in the novel is the notorious affair his wife Edwina was alleged to have carried on with Jahawarlal Nehru, chief disciple of Gandhi, leader of the Hindu Congress Party, and later, India's first premier.

We don't learn much of Ayah's interior life, and that is natural given that we see her through Lenny's eyes. We get a considerably more detailed portrait of Lenny herself, including the way in which she childishly manipulates her handicap to arouse sympathy and secure privileges. The passages concerning Lenny's polio are among the most effective in the book. Despite her apparent helplessness, Lenny is never depicted as pure victim. Caressed and fawned over by both mother and Ayah, she has a strong ego that sees her through the scarifying events to come.

Just as Cousin is not pure villain at the childish level, neither is Ice-Candy-Man at the adult level. He both rescues and destroys Ayah, loves and exploits her. Lenny is haunted not only by Ayah's dehumanization at his hands, but by his own dehumanization through the power of his desire for her. Erotic attraction has enormous power in this novel, both creative and destructive. It is not easy to sort one out neatly from the other. Sex is love, but it is also an instrument of hate. Images of burgeoning life and brutal death mingle. Lenny wonderingly caresses her newly grown breasts while other women are being raped and having theirs cut off.

Such power as Ayah exercises through her attractiveness is involuntary. She doesn't mean to draw men to her, and in the end her attractiveness is her undoing. Her erotic magnetism binds her as much as it does her admirers. In some ways she is less free than Popoo, the young servant girl who retains her defiant spirit despite frequent severe beatings by her deranged mother, although Popoo ultimately finds herself drugged and married off to a deformed old man, dashing her hopes for a better life through marriage. Even Lenny's own mother, who at first would seem to have security in an ideal loving marriage, has to suffer both the infidelities and blows of her husband, or so the narrative suggests. Sidhwa conveys an almost classical Greek attitude toward Eros as a powerful force that inspires respect and fear as much as desire.

Women's subjection is presented in a multiplicity of ways in the novel. At the bottom of the family hierarchy is "Slavesister," given a nickname invented by Sidhwa to express a dim, unmarriageable old maid's subjection to her domineering sister, turned into a virtual slave working for the other more favored members of the extended family. So far is she outside the circle of Lenny's affections that she is treated almost comically. But she is part of the pattern of oppression that haunts all women in this novel, from highest to lowest, including the little girls of the family whose complaints about the dirty old man who rubs them on his lap are ignored. Queen Victoria's statue is banished from the landscape at independence, but so are most Pakistani women, and the ones who remain are kept close to home. Lenny's education in womanhood is a series of lessons in the limits of the possible for females in her culture. Only the fact that Lenny is narrating this story years later suggests that she may have transcended those limits.

Not only does Sidhwa reshape and enhance the materials that she draws on from her personal life. She also remolds history significantly by deliberately setting Mahatma Gandhi's famous salt march campaign fifteen years later than it actually took place in a bit of tinkering not unlike Salman Rushdie's chronological changes to the same historical period in *Midnight's Children*.

Those who are dissatisfied with the rather distanced picture of the chaos of Partition depicted in *Train to Pakistan* will find plenty of gruesome details in *Cracking India,* particularly in a section narrated by a young Muslim boy who was scalped and left for dead before escaping to Pakistan. The details are scrupulously accurate, including the description of the boy— his story is based on a real-life original.

For a while, Lenny suspects her family of involvement in the arson destroying Lahore, but when she learns the truth it reinforces the general pattern of Parsi innocence that emerges from the story of Partition. Parsis were neither targets nor activists in the conflict, but Sidhwa does not let her own ethnic group off entirely. The Parsis were well known for accommodating their allegiances to whomever happened to be in power. During the Raj, they had been among the strongest supporters of the British, and risked losing a good deal through independence. Sidhwa paints a vivid scene in which the leaders of the Parsi community resolve to side with whoever emerges triumphant. Preservation of their community is more important than creating principled alliances. Yet she also creates in Lenny's own family a group of idealists, willing to go to considerable lengths to rescue threatened Hindus in a nation suddenly dominated by Muslims.

In 1999 *Cracking India* was adapted into a successful film entitled *Earth* (in South Asia released as *Earth, 1947*) by the distinguished Indian-Canadian woman director Deepa Mehta. Ice-Candy-Man is in this version a rather more sympathetic character, and the ending is reshaped to create a more abrupt ending. Romance is in the air more than the raw sex so pervasive in the novel. The sexual awakening theme connected with Lenny is almost entirely eliminated, with some mildly erotic lovemaking on the part of Ayah being added. Sidhwa was consulted during the making of the film and approved the final version, whose plot differs somewhat from her work. Readers will recognize most of the scenes and characters easily (Sidhwa herself plays the brief role of the adult Lenny). A showing of the film would be an excellent introduction to a discussion of Partition as it has been treated by Indian writers. Unrated in the United States, it probably would have garnered a PG-13 because of some strong language used in anger during an early confrontation between an Englishman and a Sikh at a dinner party.

Sidhwa's next novel, *An American Brat,* tells the story of Feroza Ginwalla, a teenaged Parsi girl from Lahore descended from the Junglewalla family depicted in *The Crow Eaters,* whose growing conservatism is worrying her mother in the increasingly repressive climate of modern Pakistan. Feroza has even begun to criticize her mother's traditional mode of dress as "immodest." Hoping to open her horizons, she sends the girl off to visit an uncle just a few years older, studying at MIT. After a humiliating encounter with immigration officials in New York, she is introduced to the perils and delights of America. She sees the worst of the grubby, violent side of 1970s New York, including the squalor of the notorious Port Authority bus station. Her mother's plan backfires because she is not only drawn into American life but decides to stay and enter college herself, undergoing various adventures over the next four years that would have been a nightmare for her parents had they known about them.

The culminating disaster is her love affair with and engagement to a wonderful young Jewish student. Marriage outside the Parsi faith means not only exile from the family but eternal damnation according to her parents' theology, and her mother is determined to prevent the impending marriage.

Although *An American Brat* was well received by most Western reviewers, some Indian readers objected to what they took to be its patronizing and stereotypical view of an Indian student. Note that Feroza is far younger (sixteen) than most South Asian students at U.S. colleges. The majority are graduate students, many of them much more knowledgeable about life in America than the heroine. Families who can afford to send their children abroad are usually part of a network of acquaintances and relatives, many of whom will have lived and worked abroad. Feroza is not precisely a self-portrait. The author was in her second marriage, with three children, when she moved to the United States. However, she has said that the novel is loosely based on the experiences of herself and her daughters.

Yet in its portrait of the difficulties faced in America by someone from a traditional culture that seeks above all to keep girls "pure" before marriage, it can show American readers to some degree how their culture looks from outside. Sidhwa presents plenty of criticisms of her adopted country and its culture; this is no one-side love story; but neither is it an indictment. Ultimately we can see both what makes the country so attractive to Feroza and so frightening to her mother. As always in Sidhwa's fiction the depictions of sexuality are vivid and realistically detailed. Clearly one aspect of life in the United States that the author treasures is the ability to write frankly about sex.

An American Brat has a detailed glossary of terms near the end of the book that will be welcome and useful to readers less familiar with the culture. Sidhwa adapted the novel to an English setting for a dramatic version to be performed in London in 2003, retitled *Sock 'em with Honey.*

It is striking that the best known Pakistani author writing fiction set in the country should be a member of a non-Muslim minority and a woman also, but neither of those facts seem to have interfered with her reputation. With the release of the film based on *Cracking India,* her work continues to reach large audiences, both east and west.

SELECTED BIBLIOGRAPHY

Dhawan, R. K., and Novy Kapadia, eds. *The Novels of Bapsi Sidhwa.* New Delhi: Prestige, 1996.
  Outstanding collection of essays on Sidhwa's works, many of them unavailable elsewhere.
Earth. Dir. Deepa Mehta. New Yorker Video, 1999.
  Film version of *Cracking India.*
Graeber, Laurel. "The Seeds of Partition." Rev. of *Cracking India. New York Times Book Review* 6 Oct. 1991: 11.
Milkweed Publications. "Curriculum Guide for *Cracking India.*" Available in .pdf format at <http://www.milkweed.org/4_catalog/4_1_1_3565.html>.
  Discussion guides, study questions, and vocabulary from the original publishers of Sidhwa's most famous novel.
Rajan, Julie. "Cracking Sidhwa." Monsoon 3 (2000). <http://www.monsoonmag.com/interviews/i3inter_sidhwa.html>.
  Interesting interview with the author.
Sidhwa, Bapsi "Amazon.com Talks to Bapsi Sidhwa." <http://www.amazon.com/exec/obidos/show-interview/s-b-idhwaapsi/>.
  Another interview with the author.
———. *An American Brat.* Minneapolis: Milkweed Editions, 1993.
———. *The Bride.* New York: St. Martin's Press, 1983.
———. *Cracking India.* Minneapolis: Milkweed Editions, 1991. Rpt. of *Ice-Candy-Man.* 1988.
———. *The Crow Eaters.* 1980. Minneapolis: Milkweed Editions, 1992.
———. "New Neighbors." *Time* (special South Asian edition commemorating the fiftieth anniversary of Indian independence) 11 Aug. 1997: 47+. <http://www.time.com/time/magazine/1997/int/970811/spl.neighbors.html>.
  Interview about Sidhwa's personal experience of Partition. This piece did not appear in the United States, so the Web alternative will be the most accessible for U.S. readers.
———. "Short Biography." <http://members.aol.com/_ht_a/bsidhwa/>.
  Sidhwa's own personal Website, containing a biographical sketch and other useful materials.
Tharoor, Shashi. "Life with Electric-Aunt and Slavesister." *New York Times Book Review* 6 Oct. 1991: 4.
  Review of *Cracking India.*

Chapter 8

Bharati Mukherjee:
Jasmine (1989)

It is unfortunate that the term "identity politics" has been claimed by
conservatives opposed to it, because it is a good label for much of the
controversy that swirls around authors like Bharati Mukherjee. On the
one hand, members of various minorities seek to shed the stereotypes that
lump them together with others sharing the same origins and work to be
recognized instead as individuals. On the other hand, they strive to recover
their roots and create new group identities that can give them a sense of heritage and worth. Although these are not really contradictory impulses, and
they do not cancel each other out, there is always a tension between them,
and this tension is strongly apparent whenever a writer is singled out by the
majority as a recognized representative of a minority struggling for self-
expression.

A writer like Mukherjee longs to speak in her own voice, give her personal
version of what it means to be an emigrant from India, an Indian Canadian, and
a new American. But her fellow South Asians look on anxiously, concerned that
in giving her own version of their shared reality she may be distorting what they
perceive to be the truth, or even reinforcing dominant negative stereotypes.
This is a common dilemma, not confined to recent times. James Joyce and
William Faulkner were assailed for decades by their compatriots for presenting
slanderous pictures of—respectively—Ireland and Mississippi.

But some authors seem to cause this sort of irritation more than most:
Maxine Hong Kingston and Bharati Mukherjee are perhaps the two most
prominent examples among modern writers with Asian heritages. The conflicts swirling around them are exacerbated by the fact that the majority

readership that loves their writing remains serenely unaware of the angry critics rejecting and attacking them. The very fact of their high visibility means that other voices with different views are not heard, so that—far from feeling represented by such writers—many members of minority communities feel silenced by them.

Why should authors who are not warmly embraced by the communities they come from be so popular among dominant-culture readers? One commonly given answer is that writers like Mukherjee depict an image that is already well entrenched in the majority imagination: in her case a backward, squalid, crime-ridden, sexist India in desperate need of Westernization. Her fans are more apt to like her because she is a vivid, moving writer, her prose sings, and her characters are lively and interesting. Some readers feel that both are true. Mukherjee has a talent for hitting the very sore spots that are bothering South Asians while brilliantly conveying a personal vision that contains a great deal of truth.

Mukherjee burst on the international scene with her powerful first novel, based loosely on her own life and family: *Tiger's Daughter* (1972). Her protagonist Tara, like Mukherjee herself, has grown up as the pampered, sheltered daughter of a Calcutta manufacturer, but has departed from family expectations by marrying an American. She has returned to Bengal to visit her family and assess her relationship to her land of birth. The book is filled with vivid details, many of them exceedingly repellent, as she finds herself largely alienated from her former homeland. Although Western readers embraced the novel as a lively, entertaining, and unsparing critique of Indian culture, many Indians were understandably outraged by what they took to be an act of betrayal. In this novel Mukherjee introduced South Asian fiction to a vast Western audience in a way that began an intense debate over her work that continues to this day.

In the 1970s Calcutta had become an international symbol for decay and degradation, and Mukherjee's portrait of it reinforced the image held by the world at large, adding details about the idleness, frivolity, and corruption of the prosperous class to which her own family belonged. Although it is nonfiction, readers interested in Mukherjee's career should also read *Days and Nights in Calcutta* (1977), an account of a lengthy visit to her family in India by the author and her husband, writer Clark Blaise, in the year following the publication of her first novel. It provides a great deal of detail for understanding the setting and characters of *Tiger's Daughter.* Mukherjee insists that Tara in her novel is not to be confused with herself, but the portrait of Calcutta society in the two books is essentially the same.

Wife (1975) might also be called *Cry of the Peacock Goes to New York* because like Anita Desai's novel it features a young woman slowly going mad in a loveless marriage, with a similarly violent conclusion. Yet whereas Desai's novel remains claustrophobically contained within the imagination of its protagonist, Mukherjee's work portrays a wider range of characters and pays more attention to external settings. The wife in her novel is too sheltered and ignorant to understand the radical disorientation she feels, whereas the one in Desai's story has a fairly clear grasp of what is bothering her. Because Mukherjee's novel is told so tightly from the protagonist's point of view, we also do not completely grasp the significance of her experiences. Is the book primarily a statement about marriage, about emigration, about gender roles, or about self-destructive neurosis? It's difficult to say. The novel's brutal ending shocked and repelled many Indian readers, although it evoked a strong positive response in a U.S. audience influenced by the burgeoning women's liberation movement of the 1970s as yet another depiction of the ways in which women are channeled into restrictive roles. Novels in which women break violently out of rigid patriarchal confines were a common feature of the decade, and Mukherjee's work fit in well with other such novels for Westerners even while it appalled many South Asians.

For the next decade, Mukherjee concentrated on polishing her art in writing short stories, collected into two volumes: *Darkness* (1985) and *The Middleman and Other Stories* (1988). Her writing strengthened impressively in power and beauty during this period. It is often remarked that the gloomy stories in the first volume, dating mainly from her frustrating time in Canada, give way to tales with a more optimistic outlook in the second, after she and her husband had moved to the United States. Mukherjee found Canada's approach to multiculturalism at that time deeply racist, imprisoning her in an identity she refused to embrace. In contrast, the U.S. tendency to encourage immigrants to blend into the dominant culture as quickly as possible appealed to her as far more welcoming—in contrast to many other writers who feel such attitudes are bent on robbing them of their identities. (It is worth noting that she has recently acknowledged Canada has made great progress in recent decades toward accommodating its immigrant population.)

Mukherjee has frequently proclaimed that she now views herself not as a South Asian, nor as an Asian American, but simply as an American writer. She has repeatedly argued that immigrants should avoid living in isolated communities dedicated to preserving their old ways of life and instead seek to enter the mainstream of their new homeland. These arguments have been heatedly denounced by other Asian immigrants, but she defiantly rejects their criticisms, insisting on the validity of her own vision of reality.

As if she had not stirred up enough controversy with her take on national identity politics, she has often portrayed gender roles in ways that have rubbed feminists the wrong way. In the second half of her career, sexual relationships are often portrayed as a vehicle of liberation, and she has chosen some very controversial examples: illegal immigrant domestics having affairs with their married employers, a pregnant young woman deserting the loving but wheelchair-bound father of her child for an old lover passing through, and a woman captive in a harem enthralled by a despotic raja. Most contemporary women authors would have depicted these relationships with horror, but Mukherjee celebrates them. Her female characters are commonly extremely beautiful, and they gain a good deal of their power from their ability to entice others with their "exotic" glamour—a pattern that echoes traditional male-dominated fiction.

Especially striking is the story "Jasmine" from *Middleman*. In it a young, beautiful woman of African heritage from Trinidad leaves the land of her birth with no regrets and energetically builds a new life for herself in America. In these short stories the principal characters, although mostly South Asian, come from a variety of minority backgrounds. Mukherjee had begun by this time a systematic program of creating a new, richer palette for American fiction that embraced Asians as part of the normal fabric of American culture. She is not interested in detailing the sort of immigrant life depicted in *Wife*, confined largely to immigrants who hesitate to blend with the larger society. In her stories Asians encounter Caucasians in all sorts of settings, routinely work side by side, and fall in love with each other—as she had herself. They do not blend into the majority in a bland uniformity, however; rather each individual injects a new, individual note into the overall mix that shifts in a distinctly Asian direction.

When Jasmine becomes the live-in maid for a young professor and his performance artist wife, the stage would seem to be set for a tragic tale of exploitation and grief. Instead, after the wife blithely abandons her home to go on the road for her art, Jasmine is thrilled to be embraced by the lonely husband. The story ends on a note of exhilaration as they make love for the first time: "His hand moved up her throat and forced her lips apart and it felt so good, so right, that she forgot all the dreariness of her new life and gave herself up to it." It would be difficult to imagine a conclusion more out of step with the dominant feminist view of such relationships in which the power of the man is usually seen as making impossible any true consent by the dominated woman. Mukherjee is clearly rejecting this analysis, saying, "Sometimes this sort of thing works out just fine." The figure of Jasmine continued to haunt Mukherjee's imagination until she decided to rework her story in her next novel, also called *Jasmine* (1989) (discussed at more length later).

The Holder of the World (1993) is a fantastic historical novel set in a science fictional framework. A rebellious Puritan woman in colonial America abandons her home for an Indian (Native American) lover, and her daughter goes even further—to India, where she becomes the devoted lover of an East Indian rajah. The story is rich and complex, the main character appealing, but the novel breaks with the realistic framework that characterized Mukherjee's earlier works.

Leave It to Me (1997), although it returns us to a contemporary setting, is even more fantastic. A young woman adopted as a child by an American couple from an Indian orphanage goes looking for her birth parents and discovers them to have been a crazed American hippie and her serial-killer Indian guru: a cross between Rajneesh and Charles Manson. She seems to be totally amoral: seducing her parole officer, setting fire to a faithless lover's house, and murdering several people. A strain of violence is an often-noted constant in Mukherjee's fiction, but whereas her early protagonists had been timid and confused, this one is filled with ferocious energy and entirely destructive rage. Over the course of her career, Mukherjee's always negative portrait of India became more and more harsh until in *Leave It to Me* it developed into a nightmarish caricature, a living hell whose curse can reach out of the distant past to wreck the life of someone who has only the slightest of memories linking her to it.

Her latest novel, *Desirable Daughters* (2002), marks a sharp change in direction. After a beautifully written, wildly exotic introduction portraying the origins of a mythical Hindu saint, it develops into a compelling woman-in-peril thriller exploring the varied lives of three sisters from Calcutta, the central one of whom is a wealthy divorced wife and mother living in San Francisco. Like most of her principal female characters, all three of the sisters are ravishingly beautiful, and—also typical of her characters—their various sexual relationships, both negative and positive, play a major role in the story. In this novel Mukherjee finally presents a more nuanced vision of life in India, which actually becomes a plausible environment in which to live. The extreme violence that characterizes all of her novels is here, but so are many wonderful touches of satire and not a little romance.

But it is *Jasmine* that continues to be the popular favorite. It has given many Western readers their introduction to South Asian literature. The accusation that it provides a narrow and warped window on India is less relevant now that a wide variety of South Asian authors has attracted a popular audience. The novel is actually centered not in India, but in Iowa, where Mukherjee lived for several years after going there to study creative writing, and where she met and married her husband. The novel focuses not on some South Asian rural famine, but on the ongoing farm crisis that erupted into the American national consciousness in the mid-1980s. After a brief introduction, the work begins, constantly returns to, and ends in Iowa, with the rest of the story told in flashbacks.

The Iowa countryside of *Jasmine* is plagued by bankruptcies, broken homes, suicides, and murders. Antisemitic right-wing fanatics prey on the fears of impoverished farmers. These people may be far better off than the typical rural Indian family the protagonist comes from, but by American standards, they are in desperate straits, and she sympathizes with them, illustrating painstakingly many aspects of their struggle to survive.

This aspect of the novel tends to be forgotten because Jasmine herself (also called at various point "Jyoti," "Jazzy," "Jas," and "Jane") undergoes sufferings so intense and sensational that the farm crisis tends to pale in comparison. She begins life as a spirited young girl from a rural Indian family who defies her destiny from earliest childhood, constantly seeking to create new identities for herself and carve out her place in the world. Like her namesake in the earlier short story, she also discovers a sense of freedom and fulfillment in sex. She is compared in the book to a tornado, roaring through the landscape, leaving bodies and broken hearts strewn in her wake.

She is presented neither as typical nor as a role model, but as an intense, inventive survivor. In this she resembles most fictional Indian heroines less than she does a female adventurer like Daniel Defoe's *Moll Flanders* (1722). The literary term associated with this sort of character is *picaro* (although picaros are traditionally male). Like Moll, Jasmine can be tender and loving, but ruthless when her self-preservation is at stake. Also like Moll, she is attractive to men and knows how to use her attractiveness to her own advantage, although Jasmine is rather less manipulative in this regard than Moll. Picaros like Moll and Jasmine are constantly on the move, taking on identity after identity, earning their way however they can, committing crimes when they must, but always meaning well. Looked at objectively, they may be seen as dangerous, even frightening, women, but as we hear their adventures from their own lips, we are inevitably drawn into their own view of themselves. We may not approve of everything they do, but it is difficult not to admire their spirit. No wonder readers who would never dream of imitating her have found *Jasmine* exciting and even inspiring.

The novel opens in the small Punjab village of Hasnapur, chosen by Mukherjee because it was the ancestral home of the family of the prominent Trinidad-born novelist V. S. Naipaul. Early in her career Mukherjee admired Naipaul greatly, but she came to be irritated by his overbearing pessimism about the possibilities inherent in impoverished countries like Trinidad and India. She was determined in the novel to create a character who could break free of her background and triumph against seemingly overwhelming odds.

Despite her decision to let Jasmine shape her own life, she begins by following the literary tradition according to which an astrologer successfully forecasts her character's fate. But it is in fact this curse hanging over her that will fire Jasmine's determination to rebel and forms the character that will allow her to survive when the foretold disaster arrives. When the astrologer warns her that she cannot escape her fate by reminding her of the myth of Behula, whose husband Lakhindar was killed by a snakebite on their wedding night, Mukherjee probably expects at least some of her readers to remember that Behula did not submit meekly, but defiantly dragged her bridegroom's body before the gods and persuaded them to restore him to life. In this brief opening chapter, Jasmine/Jyoti is depicted not as simply haunted by death, but as defiant. Its last sentence is "I know what I don't want to become."

One of the aspects of the novel that has disturbed many readers is Jasmine's desertion of the loving, supportive Bud Ripplemeyer as she carries the child he yearns for, sitting shattered, alone, in his wheelchair. Mukherjee knows she is setting up a situation in which her protagonist might lose the reader's sympathy entirely, so she takes several steps to brace us for this action, including telling us up front—on the second page of the second chapter—that she has already left him. Her departure is not meant to be a shock; instead we are compelled to keep reading to find out what would lead Jasmine to such a seemingly heartless act of abandonment.

American farmers don't live in isolation from modern life. Bud measures the size of his farm by comparing it with the distance between the older and newer Chicago baseball fields: Wrigley Field and Comiskey Park; their home is equipped with the latest electronic equipment; and their neighbor Darrel dreams of opening a Radio Shack franchise. Yet urbanization is also a threat to the farming way of life: housing developments and golf courses are invading the landscape. These changes are hard to resist in the face of falling commodity prices added to the traditional threats posed by nature such as the winter storms swooping down from Canada called "Alberta clippers" by the natives, one of which has driven Darrel's girlfriend away from him to sunny Texas.

It is typical of Mukherjee that rather than presenting her tale from the perspective of a struggling farmer, she chooses a banker and strives to render him as sympathetically as possible. Being well off does not automatically condemn characters in her novels to heartlessness, although she has also created her share of empty-headed, coldhearted rich people. Bud tries hard but is ultimately unable to rescue the farmers whose plight he sympathizes with, just as he cannot "save" Jasmine or Du, the Vietnamese orphan they have adopted. Bud is a big strong man with an influential institution in back of him, but in the end he is far less powerful than the slender, wily survivor Jasmine, who feels "potent, like a goddess." It seems clear it is Bud's love that is largely responsible for this feeling. Jasmine loves him less for himself than for how he feels about her. Anyone who could so transfix a man must be a goddess. When, near the end of the chapter, she watches a televised monster truck competition with Bud and Du, she identifies with the names that reflect her own sense of power: *"Nitro Express, Brawling Babe, Insane Expectations."*

The description of how Jasmine and Bud came to be lovers reflects this power imbalance: he begins as "a tall, fit, fifty-year-old banker" and is transformed quickly by his encounter with Jasmine: divorced, having lost his home, confined to a wheelchair. The fragility of the men in the novel is contrasted with the hardiness of the women, like Bud's mother, who at seventy-six still is active and stylish. Even Bud's abandoned wife is a survivor, working for a suicide crisis line and clearly able to step back into Bud's life when Jasmine leaves. Mukherjee is frank in her admiration for a country that is so much more favorable to women than her native India, contrasting Mother Ripplemeyer with a girl from Hasnapur who had committed suicide at twenty-two when her husband died of typhoid fever. It is this sort of stark contrast that arouses the ire of Mukherjee's Indian readers, but there is undeniably a degree of truth in the comparison.

Bud is not the perfect lover, however. He always sees Jasmine as the lovely, exotic foreigner whose real name he cannot pronounce. He can never know her as well she knows him. She is convinced he could never bear to hear her real story. Part of his self-protection against her alienness is the name he gives her: "Jane." He jokes, "me Bud, you Jane," alluding to the familiar scene in the old *Tarzan* stories in which the ape man first encounters his enticing mate from abroad. She enjoys their lovemaking, but in the end her energy leaps beyond his, so that at the end of Chapter 5 she feels like a sprouting crop ripping its way through the parched soil of Iowa. She moves about while he sleeps on, unaware.

At the heart of the secret she shields from Bud is her violent illegal entry into the United States. When she views Americans interviewed on television portraying themselves as the victims of illegal immigration she is enraged at their self-absorption, their inability to truly understand the experiences of desperately poor people struggling to establish a toehold in the country at enormous cost to themselves. She does not dismiss the suffering of middle-class Americans as insignificant, but she does try to put it in perspective.

The limits of American understanding are further underlined in the story of the teacher who tries out "a little Vietnamese" on Du in school, not realizing that by doing so he is revealing himself as one of the soldiers who helped make Du into a refugee in the first place. If America is the land of new beginnings, it is also the land of easy forgettings, of historical amnesia. For people like Jasmine and Du, such blank unawareness of foreign pasts rises like a wall of incomprehension, shutting them out.

In this novel Mukherjee pursues her project of depicting the Asian threads in the contemporary American tapestry. Besides Jasmine herself, this rural town includes both a Chinese-born doctor who doesn't understand the allusion to the old "Dick and Jane" books, which children of Bud's generation were taught to read from, and enough Laotian Hmong refugees to form an entire church of their own. Without being overly insistent, Mukherjee simply continues to point out that Asian immigrants pervade U.S. life even in its traditional heartland.

Only with Chapter 6 does the tale move back to its chronological beginning, to the birth of Jyoti in Hasnapur. This is her first birth, compared to a lush crop, implicitly linked with the imagery of agricultural rebirth contained in the final lines of Chapter 5. From this point on, the story proceeds mainly chronologically, with frequent returns to "now" in Iowa, but also skipping ahead from time to time with glimpses of scenes to come. In most summaries of the novel, this tangled structure is ironed out flat and made considerably less interesting than it is. Jasmine's story is a layered one, reflected in the novel's epigraph by James Gleick: "twisted, tangled, and intertwined." The violence, the fear, and the passion of moments in her past lurk beneath her daily existence in New York and in Iowa. Despite her rejection of the way her father clung to the past (described at the end of Chapter 6), she cannot "move on" neatly from one epoch in her life to the next, and the way she tells her story reflects this fact.

Much is made in the work—and in the criticism of it—of the imagery of reincarnation. Mukherjee has often said that the only aspect of Hinduism she really clings to is the idea of reincarnation—not in its literal sense, but as an image of the possibility of personal reinvention. But the persistence of memory is just as powerful in *Jasmine* as change. Indeed, change here is frequently driven by memories, by forces from the past.

It is only at this point that we learn little Jyoti was almost murdered at birth by her own mother, but that—unlike the maniacal infanticide attempt in *Leave It to Me*—Jasmine regards this as an act of love. This shocking detail is followed by an allusion to the notorious "dowry deaths" of India in which young brides who bring insufficient resources into a marriage may be murdered by their in-laws in ways designed to look like accidents. Such sensational passages, although reflecting real patterns in Indian life, lead Mukherjee's critics to accuse her of warping Western views of their culture by stressing its violent and repressive aspects. It would be highly unfair to derive from such passages an image of the typical life of a female in India, but Jasmine and her creator are not alone in loathing these very real misogynistic patterns in their homeland. If female infanticide is somewhat less common in India today than it used to be, that is largely due to modern technology, which allows many families to abort female fetuses while they await the conception of a longed-for boy.

This passage also alludes to a tragedy that affected both sexes and all ages: the Partition riots of 1947, discussed in Chapter 3 on Khushwant Singh's *Train to Pakistan*. Jyoti's father blames the riots partly on Mahatma Gandhi's reluctant agreement to the splitting of her native Punjab between India and Pakistan—a prejudice that many would see as wildly unfair given that Gandhi fought Partition as long as he could and his heart was broken by the riots he could not stop (he was assassinated by a Hindu fanatic who considered him too conciliatory toward the Muslims). Piece by piece, an image is being assembled of modern India as a historical nightmare that continues to haunt Jasmine in her new homeland.

Chapter 7 depicts her childhood, including her first introduction to American culture, the 1954 Stanley Donen musical *Seven Brides for Seven Brothers,* misremembered by her under the much more Indian-sounding title *Seven Village Girls Find Seven Boys to Marry.* This exactly inverts the plot of the original, in which the seven Pontipee brothers, desperate to get married, kidnap and woo seven attractive but recalcitrant young women. India is traditionally a land in which it is women—not men—who are desperate for spouses.

The fact that her first experience of television includes viewing a video on family planning reminds us that the date is 1965, in the early phases of Indira Gandhi's birth control campaign, which was to turn notoriously coercive a few years later. The medium seems to have influenced her more than the intended message, because as a teenaged bride she will yearn for pregnancy in the traditional way of her culture, and she is spared the dangers inherent in childbirth at a tender age only by the reluctance of her more Westernized husband.

At first her rebelliousness is channeled in acceptable ways—pasteurizing the milk, admiring a widow who eats forbidden onions—but when she expresses the wish to be a doctor she is leaping out of the realm of her family's expectations into a very different world—although not necessarily a Western one. Although Mukherjee makes nothing of it in the novel, it is well to remember that India was governed at this point by a very powerful woman. Her relatives think she is insane, but she actually sees further into contemporary reality than they. She will never be a doctor, but she has developed a sense of possibility that will drive her for the rest of her life.

We are also introduced to the threat of Sikh separatists, responsible for a number of terrorist acts in northern India. They had felt betrayed by all parties at Partition, with their homeland split between India and Pakistan, rendering them a tiny minority in both countries. Groups like the "Khalsa Lions" campaigned for "Khalistan," a separate nation for Sikhs. It is well to be aware that Mukherjee's roots are in the old Hindu establishment of northern India, and in her fiction she consistently depicts the rise of rival forces like the Marxist Naxalites and the Sikh separatists as destructive. Many Indians would agree with her, but hers is but one possible view of modern Indian politics.

The reference at the end of Chapter 7 to "Kali Yuga" is sometimes taken to indicate that Mukherjee has a shallow knowledge of Hinduism. She implies that Kali Yuga (the age of deterioration and destruction embodied in the fearsome demon-slaying goddess Kali) is an awaited future event, akin to the Christian Armageddon, when in fact most Hindus consider that humanity has been experiencing the Kali Yuga already for many thousands of years and we are approaching its end. This is not a serious error, but it is a reminder that we should not trust entirely to novelists to instruct us on the finer points of an alien religion.

The image of Kali with blood dripping from her tongue is what will inspire Jyoti/Jasmine later in her act of murderous revenge against Half-Face. Her childhood is punctuated by incidents illustrating her fierce courage, like the killing of the mad dog, which will prepare us to accept her as an avenging spirit. Her grandmother's spiteful rejection of her triumph is based on the traditional view that salvation lies beyond the grave, not in achievements within life—a view Mukherjee and Jasmine alike reject.

In the opening of Chapter 9 the death of her father is tangled up with her later love for Taylor and for Prakash. Having come to marriageable age, her future relationships come flooding into the story as her parents' relationship is breaking up. It is important to understand that her mother's attempt to commit *sati*—ritual suicide—is not typical of the behavior of a modern Indian widow. *Sati,* illegal in India for a century and a half, is extremely rare, a point that Mukherjee's critics insist on strongly. (Americans prone to look down on Indian culture should remember that suicide in the wake of the death of a spouse is not exactly unknown in the United States.) But everyone in the culture is familiar with the tradition, and her mother's gesture undoubtedly helps inspire Jasmine in her own suicidal plans later. At the beginning of the next chapter she performs an individual ritual by burning her beloved English books, symbolizing her attachment to the father who rejected her foreign learning. This is only the first of the "self-murders" she will commit as she repeatedly reinvents herself.

But the next stage in Jasmine's life is initiated by her brothers as they set about the task of finding her a suitable husband. Unfortunately, this romantic quest is interwined with her first encounter with the man who will wreck her marriage, the fanatical Sukhwinder. He has visited the Sikh revolutionary Sant Bhindranwale, who was to gather an armed force in the Sikh Golden Temple in Amritsar in May 1984. On June 5 of that year, Indira Gandhi sent troops in Operation Bluestar to drive the insurgents out of the temple, creating a shock that was to lead eventually to her own assassination by her Sikh bodyguards. Because this assault has not happened yet in the novel, we must be some time earlier, probably when Bhindranwale was simply a Sikh leader preaching at the temple rather than an insurgent occupying it.

It is the deep, tolerant voice of her future husband, Prakash, that rejects the fanatic's rantings, simultaneously earning Jasmine's love and Sukhwinder's hate. Prakash has a bent for technology associated in the modern American mind with Indians, but her adopted son Du will have the same leaning. To be drawn to machinery is to be drawn to the West, and he has ambitions to study abroad that will eventually lead Jasmine to Florida. It is ironic that the sentence she chooses to practice her English on at the beginning of Chapter 11 celebrates the rejection of foreign expertise and technology. Again, the content has no impact on her; English is her vehicle for leaving India.

Jasmine is lucky in that she has developed a crush on the very man chosen to be her husband. In her family, arranged marriages are still expected, and a young girl of her inexperience would not normally choose her own spouse. The trip to the cinema is a comic misadventure, but its outcome is determined by Prakash's kindness in rescuing her from her confusion. The family approves, she loves him—what could be more perfect?

"Jasmine," the name we have been using for the girl originally called "Jyoti," is actually given her by her husband, and it is a symbol of her abiding love for his memory that this is the name by which she is called in the novel's title. He becomes her Professor Higgins, although less overbearing than the mentor in George Bernard Shaw's *Pygmalion* (which inspired the musical *My Fair Lady*). He helps her reinvent herself as a sophisticated young urban woman. He pushes her toward regarding herself as his equal: "Vijh & Vijh." It is her modernization at his hands that outrages Sukhwinder and ironically leads to her husband's death when the young fanatic tries to assassinate her, partly because she is abandoning the traditionally more modest *salwar kameez* for a stylish, more revealing sari.

Against all odds, it seemed Jasmine was headed for a happy life. Still a fragile and volatile teenager, she rages first for revenge, then for annihilation. Her bizarre plan to immolate herself in Florida on his suit is not an example of traditional *sati*, nor a reasonable way to escape the pain of her present situation. Why put herself to enormous expense and acute suffering far from home only to kill herself? Such a decision can only be explained as the product of a wildly fevered adolescent romanticism.

Mukherjee keeps us from asking too many questions about this bizarre plan by keeping it hidden from us until just before it is abandoned. We know Jasmine is determined to go to the campus where Prakash had been admitted to study, but we don't know why. When we learn why, it is in the midst of such horror that her original motivation is the least of our concerns. The author has succeeded in transporting her protagonist to the United States, and ultimately that is all that is important.

Presumably Jasmine could have traveled as an ordinary tourist had she not been underage. It is this one fact that forces her to take the route followed by underground immigrants, through Germany, smuggled by a literally rapacious pirate into Florida. However irrational her decisions may be, she certainly undergoes many of the trials experienced by others who leave comfortable middle-class existences to suffer extreme hardship in order to start a new life in America. The motivation for her odyssey may be implausible, but her sufferings are all too familiar.

Half-Face, her tormentor, is a vicious former Vietnam vet who once fought to keep his country safe from Asian communism and who now makes his living smuggling Asians into it. His cruel rape of her is so vividly described that it is often overlooked that he had previously battered her head so hard against a television screen that he cracked it. This man is obviously a menace to her life as well as her virtue, explaining in part her determination to kill him. Of course logically, because she was originally bent on killing herself, it could be argued that her ferocious self-defense is self-defeating. But clearly she has changed. Her suicide was to be a romantic gesture that would unite her with Prakash for eternity, but Half-Face has ruined that plan, dressing in the suit that for her has come to embody her late husband's memory and menacing her with a meaningless, degrading death. The result is to shock her back into life.

The extravagant gesture of slicing her tongue to resemble the demon-slaying Kali is wildly cinematic, but it fits with her present frame of mind. She waits until after this climactic encounter to tell us that she had been repeatedly raped on her voyage to America, giving the scene its maximum dramatic effect. The killing of Half-Face is the peak of her frenzy, and it seems to purge her madness, so for the rest of the novel she comes across as basically sensible and practical, although thirsty for new experiences.

Chapter 18 begins the story of her several American incarnations ironically, in her encounter with the Iowa professor mad about exploring her past lives. America looks east for wisdom while Asia flees west for survival, and the two meet over lunch at the University Club so Mary Webb can tell Jasmine about her experiences channeling an Australian aborigine. Her explorations seem frivolous and vaguely insulting compared with Jasmine's fear-driven transformations.

Lillian Gordon, who runs an underground railroad station for illegal immigrants, is probably meant to resemble the many activists who joined the Sanctuary Movement organized around liberal churches in the 1980s that sheltered Central American war refugees as a form of protest against U.S. policies in that region. Jasmine finds herself among another sort of "Indians"—the Mayan Kanjobals from Guatemala. Already in the voyage over she had begun to think of herself less as a Punjabi, or even Indian, than as part of the mass of illegal immigrants scrambling to survive in the United States.

Jasmine's life with "Professor" Vadhera's family in Flushing represents the sort of ingrown community, clinging desperately to its old culture, that Mukherjee had rejected in *Wife*. Immigrants have always been torn between preserving the old and assimilating to the new. America would not be the rich cultural tapestry it is if everyone was as bent on assimilation as Jasmine, but her attitudes are certainly typical of large categories of people who cannot shed fast enough their accents, their tastes—their old identities. What seems to stay longest with Jasmine is her taste for Indian food and her memories—and her fondest memories are tied up with a man who pushed her to the West.

Again, comedy erupts in the novel as Jasmine discovers that Vadhera is a fake engaged in selling immigrant women's hair, an occupation that not only degrades him, but reminds us of the grinding poverty that makes Indian women's hair a marketable commodity. A former scientist, his story is only too typical of that of many immigrant professionals who find themselves trapped at the bottom of America's economy, like the former doctor from Afghanistan who has become a taxi driver in New York and delivers her to the Vadheras' door. She begins her account of her five months with them by describing her flight from them on the subway.

As Jasmine tells us of her attempts to patch together a life, she punctuates the narrative at the beginning of Chapter 21 with an account of Du's experiments in patching together technology, not all of which make practical sense but that clearly symbolize cultural fusion—or, as the fashionable label for this sort of thing calls it, "hybridity." But the chapter is dominated by news of drought, bankruptcy, and menacing hate groups. Jasmine's story is not, as it is often taken to be, a simple progress from benighted India to the glorious United States. Step by step, the story of her discovery of the delights of her new homeland is punctuated by accounts of its darker side, where failure seems more likely than success. It would be a mistake to think of this as a simple Horatio Alger tale celebrating the American dream. Never is Jasmine truly prosperous, and her very survival is often in question. It's in the middle of talking with Du about his "recombinant electronics" that she learns he too, like her, has killed to survive.

In the hands of most authors, the story of Jasmine's career as an au pair nanny would be presented as a tale of degrading, underpaid exploitation by irresponsible employers leading to her ultimate betrayal at the hands of a lustful husband. Mukherjee does not conceal that Taylor and Wylie Hayes are saving money by taking advantage of her illegal immigrant status to get cheap, trustworthy labor, but she makes them basically kind people. She shows us Jasmine as determining her own fate, gleefully embracing her life with them and her first attempt at motherhood in caring for their daughter, Duff. Much of the Americanization of Jasmine while living with the Hayes family is in Mukherjee's comic mode, and it provides a striking contrast with the grimness of her life until now. Despite occasional satirical touches, most of this episode has the same optimistic quality as the original short story "Jasmine" that preceded it. It is not an exposé, but a celebration.

Even Taylor's declaration of love for her is portrayed not as sexual exploitation, but as a promising idyll encouraged by his wife, interrupted by the discovery in Central Park of the man who had originally aimed to kill her back home. This encounter may seem like a wild coincidence, but anyone who has lived for a time in the magnetic center that is New York City has tales of improbable encounters on the streets of Manhattan with people from home.

This is the second time that Sukhwinder has blasted a moment of great happiness for Jasmine, and it is not surprising that she flees all the way to Iowa, where Duff was born. Even though she has to leave the girl herself, she is making a pilgrimage to her birthplace. But we already know that Iowa is no sanctuary, and the very next chapter begins with the story of the shooting that cripples Bud there. She will be haunted for the rest of her life by her failure to pick up the signal from Bud that she should call the sheriff. Despite her devotion to him after this disaster, his crumpled body is a constant reminder of her failure, and she may be staying with him more out of guilt and pity than out of love.

Only after giving us the worst does Mukherjee show us Bud and Jasmine's romance at its peak. It is notable that although Jasmine could easily be depicted as a disgustingly greedy home wrecker (and Bud's wife Karin clearly views her that way), her feelings during the early stages of the relationship are deliberately left unstated. It is Bud's desire for her glamour, her exotic beauty, that determines their destiny. She is not an "undesirable alien" but a highly desirable one. He chooses her; she merely acquiesces, at least so far as we know.

She does distrust the strength of his desire for her, using traditional Hindu wording to suggest that too much attachment is a hazard that will lead to disillusionment. She has learned this bitter lesson not in a Hindu ashram, but by letting herself become attached first to Prakash, and then to Taylor and Duff. Jasmine conceals so many essential truths about herself from Bud that their relationship is largely a creation of his own mind that fails to encompass large parts of who she is. He is pathetically grateful for her presence in his life, but pathos is not romance, and Jasmine has already known romance and yearns for it again.

Her temptation to leave Bud and rejoin Taylor and Duff becomes intertwined with Du's own plans to escape from Iowa when he discovers her postcard from her former employer at the end of Chapter 24. His joke about "Mr. T" alludes to a character in the 1980s television series *The A-Team,* not unlike Du in his ability with machinery and in being always on the run. The family that Bud strove so hard to invent is falling apart. Darrel's subsequent attempt at seduction is unwelcome, but reminds her of the limitations of her life with Bud, and must make life with Taylor seem all the more attractive.

We may not sympathize entirely with Jasmine and Du in deserting Bud, but we need to understand them. Jasmine tries hard to settle down, but her heart is elsewhere, and Bud can never love her for who she really is. Du always felt out of place in the Ripplemeyer household. They may be a pair of home wreckers, but they are also a pair of home *builders:* Du wants to rejoin his sister, and Jasmine wants to rejoin him, with her new family. Mukherjee portrays Karin as still in love with Bud, to prevent him from seeming too bereft, and she even has the ex-wife absolve Jasmine of guilt in the last pages of the novel.

It is often pointed out that the final flight toward California echoes the cliché of American fiction dating back to *Huckleberry Finn* in which freedom lies to the west. The fact that this is a national myth should tell us that it has more than a little truth in it. New York and the West Coast have always been more hospitable to self-reinvention than the Midwest. Darrel has been longing to move west as well in search of a better life. His shocking death (ironically just as his loan has been approved) is an omen to Jasmine, a warning to get out before she too is crushed by the cascade of disasters that have come down around her. In the choice between duty and hope, she has chosen hope.

Nothing implies that Jasmine's career is meant to provide a role model for immigrants or for young women generally, but it is emblematic of the sort of restless search for freedom that has always characterized Americans, often abandoning old responsibilities for new possibilities, not perhaps exactly inspiring, but certainly exhilarating.

SELECTED BIBLIOGRAPHY

Alam, Fakrul. *Bharati Mukherjee*. New York: Twayne, 1996.
    The essential book on Mukherjee. Clearly written; fine analyses of the works through *Holder of the World* and a useful bibliography.

Chen, Tina, and S. X. Goudie. "Holders of the Word: An Interview with Bharati Mukherjee." *Jouvert: A Journal of Postcolonial Studies* 1.1 (1997): 104. <http://social.chass.ncsu.edu/jouvert/v1il/bharat.htm>.
    A spirited defense of her work against criticisms made by "postcolonial" and Marxist critics. Contains many interesting and provocative comments on *Jasmine*.

Jain, Anapuma. "Re-Reading beyond Third World Difference: The Case of Bharati Mukherjee's *Jasmine*." *Weber Studies: An Interdisciplinary Humanities Journal* 15.1 (Winter 1998): 117–26. <http://weberstudies.weber.edu/archive/Vol.%2015.1/15.1Jain.htm>.
    Answers many of her critics with an interesting analysis if the reader can penetrate the academic jargon in which it is written.

Mukherjee, Bharati. *The Holder of the World*. New York: Knopf, 1993.
———. "Immigrants and Novels." *Newsweek* 27 Sept. 1997: 58.
    Good brief interview presenting her views.

———."Immigrant Writing: Give Us Your Maximalists!" *New York Times Book Review* 28 Aug. 1988: 1, 28–29.
    A much-discussed rejection of the theme of "exile" in favor of a literature of immigration.

———. *Jasmine*. New York: Grove Weidenfeld, 1989.
———. *The Middleman and Other Stories*. New York: Grove Press, 1988.
———. *The Tiger's Daughter*. Boston: Houghton Mifflin, 1972.
———. "Two Ways to Belong in America." *New York Times* 22 Sept. 1996, sec. E: 13.
    An op-ed piece in which Mukherjee contrasts her own attitude toward immigration with that of her sister Mira.

———. *Wife*. Boston: Houghton Mifflin, 1975.
Mukherjee, Bharati, and Clark Blaise. *Days and Nights in Calcutta*. 1977. Harmondsworth: Penguin, 1986.
Nelson, Emmanuel S., ed. *Bharati Mukherjee: Critical Perspectives*. New York: Garland, 1993.
    A collection of representative scholarship, focusing especially on *Jasmine*.

Shankar, Lavina Dhingra. "Activism, 'Feminisms' and Americanization in Bharati Mukherjee's *Wife* and *Jasmine*." *Hitting Critical Mass: A Journal of Asian*

American Cultural Criticism 3.1 (Winter 1995): 61–84. <http:// socrates.berkeley.edu/~critmass/v3n1/shankar1.html>.

A representative critique of *Wife* and *Jasmine* from a feminist perspective, rejecting the view that their protagonists'murderous acts should be seen as liberating.

Warwick, Ronald. "Bengali Brahmin Meets Berkeley: Bharati Mukherjee: Perspective." *New York Times* 20 Oct. 1995, *Times Higher Education Supplement:* 18.

Another classic statement of Mukherjee's stance on immigrant literature, rejecting "postcolonialism."

Chapter 9
Salman Rushdie:
*E*ast, West *(1994)*

S alman Rushdie is the most influential writer to come out of South Asia
since Tagore (see Chapter 1), and in many ways his influence has been
even more profound. Although his first novel, a bizarre, rather ponderous fantasy titled *Grimus* (1975), failed to attract much notice, his second,
Midnight's Children, appeared in 1981 to widespread acclaim, winning the
British Booker Prize for fiction and in the process revolutionizing South
Asian fiction. The explosively lively language, daring depictions of sexual relationships, and complexly patterned structure of the novel were unprecedented. Not only were his stylistic and subject-matter innovations to be
widely imitated, but he inspired others to explore many other styles and
themes. Perhaps most important, his success created a vast market for fiction
from the region, which continues to encourage new writers to enter the field.

Rushdie is also known to a vast audience that has never read a word he
has written because of the virulent attacks on him and his novel *The Satanic
Verses* (1988) by Muslim extremists. His eloquent defense of that novel in a
lecture entitled "In Good Faith" sums up some of the most important characteristics of not only *The Satanic Verses,* but of all his fiction:

Standing at the centre of the novel is a group of characters most of whom are British
Muslims, or not particularly religious persons of Muslim background, struggling
with just the sort of great problems that have arisen to surround the book, problems
of hybridization and ghettoization, of reconciling the old and the new. Those who
oppose the novel most vociferously today are of the opinion that intermingling with
a different culture will inevitably weaken and ruin their own. I am of the opposite

opinion. *The Satanic Verses* celebrates hybridity, impurity, intermingling, the transformation that comes of new and unexpected combinations of human beings, cultures, ideas, politics, movies, songs. It rejoices in mongrelization and fears the absolutism of the Pure. *Mélange,* hotchpotch, a bit of this and a bit of that is *how newness enters the world.* It is the great possibility that mass migration gives the world, and I have tried to embrace it. *The Satanic Verses* is for change-by-fusion, change-by-conjoining. It is a love-song to our mongrel selves.

These themes of fusion, hybridity, "mongrelization," are present in all of Rushdie's works, including *Midnight's Children*. For Rushdie, India is above all a rich and varied collection of cultures, peoples, and languages. It is truest to itself, he thinks, when it celebrates that fact, and it betrays its own history when it tries to create a uniform culture that celebrates some tendencies while ignoring others. In 1993 the Booker Prize committee observed the twenty-fifth anniversary of its founding by choosing this novel as the best published in Britain during that time.

It is a long book, and not an easy one to read. Rushdie's style does not appeal to everyone. He infuriates or bores some readers while he thrills and amuses many others. To judge for yourself, try the following paragraph, from early in the novel:

One Kashmiri morning in the early spring of 1915, my grandfather Aadam Aziz hit his nose against a frost-hardened tussock of earth while attempting to pray. Three drops of blood plopped out of his left nostril, hardened instantly in the brittle air and lay before his eyes on the prayer-mat, transformed into rubies. Lurching back until he knelt with his head once more upright, he found that the tears which had sprung to his eyes had solidified too; and at that moment, as he brushed diamonds contemptuously from his lashes, he resolved never again to kiss earth for any god or man. This decision, however, made a hole in him, a vacancy in a vital inner chamber, leaving him vulnerable to women and history. (8)

If this passage seems silly or deplorably blasphemous, Rushdie may not be for you. But if you find it amusing or intriguing, try reading on. You don't need to know exactly where Kashmir is (straddling the border between modern Pakistan and India) or grasp that the name of the first man in this story is supposed to remind the reader of Adam—the first of all men—to enjoy Rushdie's prose. *Midnight's Children* can be read in many different ways, and the more one knows of Indian culture and history, the richer the experience will be; but it is filled with enough colorful characters and events to intrigue even those who lack such knowledge.

The most obvious characteristic of the preceding passage is its whimsically fantastic subject, but the whimsy conveys a more serious meaning. One needn't believe that Aadam Aziz's blood and tears actually became jewels to understand that this character has undergone a profound loss of faith that will influence him for the rest of his life. It is simultaneously sad and ludicrous. This sort of combination of amusing fantastic symbolism with deeply serious feelings is characteristic of certain writers of what is called "magical realism," particularly in the works of Günter Grass *(The Tin Drum,* 1979) and Gabriel García Márquez *(One Hundred Years of Solitude,* 1967), both of whom Rushdie has discussed repeatedly as important influences on *Midnight's Children.* Fantastic events are presented as routine parts of everyday life, and ordinary events, like a nosebleed, are transformed into wonders. The result is a poetic intensification of the significance and impact of actions in striking ways that traditional realism cannot convey.

Midnight's Children also shares with *One Hundred Years of Solitude* a tendency to anticipate later events in the narrative by glancing suddenly forward, then back again, although Rushdie takes this tendency to far greater extremes than had the Colombian author. At times he seems to be scrambling to hold his wildly thrashing novel together by continuously resummarizing it, as if without his efforts it would threaten to disintegrate, like India itself.

Rushdie's decision to write the chronicle of an ordinary man who is not even the hero of his own life—and who is surrounded by a host of other characters more lively and interesting than himself—was stimulated by Laurence Sterne's comic classic, *Tristram Shandy* (1767), a vast, digressive ragbag of a novel stuffed with all manner of surprising entertainments.

The style of the work, thick with literary and historical allusions and puns expressed in popular street language, owes a great debt to James Joyce, especially to his *Ulysses* (1922). But whereas Joyce had drawn mainly on Western European sources for his allusions, Rushdie loves to mix Indian and Western allusions in his works in a cross-pollination of images that reflects his identity as a writer belonging to both worlds, although his allusions are generally less obscure than Joyce's.

The spoken language of much of the novel is Indian urban street talk, drawn partly from the pages of the popular film magazines that chronicle the vast and colorful Bombay movie industry known affectionately as "Bollywood." Dialogue in earlier Indian fiction had often been rather stiff and formal, reflecting the nineteenth-century patterns of the English novels that were studied in South Asian schools. D. V. Desani had experimented with Indian colloquial language in *About H. Haterr* (1948), and Rushdie credits Desani's example with inspiring him in his own writing. Plenty of English and South Asian writers had quoted fractured "babu" English in their works, but usually to ridicule the speakers for their ignorance of "proper" usage. Instead, Rushdie makes this street dialect into a lively and energetic means of expression, filled with wit and creativity.

South Asian critics point out that it makes little sense to render speeches that would have been uttered originally in Hindi or Urdu in such "Hinglish," and Rushdie does occasionally fall into that pattern. But most of the time the characters speaking are precisely the sort to whom such language would come naturally.

Given that Rushdie has freely acknowledged his many debts to earlier writers, it is not surprising that some readers reproach him with a lack of true originality, but he has provided his own best defense in the passage quoted at the beginning of this chapter: newness enters the world not through the creation of novelty out of nothingness, but through novel recombinations of preexisting elements. His language reflects his theme: the richest sort of experience comes not from clinging to narrow tradition but from gleefully combining diverse ingredients, what Rushdie calls "chutnification," after the complex condiments of Indian cuisine called chutneys.

Part of this technique consists of sprinkling Hindi and Urdu names and allusions to Muslim and Hindu legends and myths in his works alongside references to European classics and popular Hollywood movies. So dense does this allusiveness become at times that a detailed commentary explicating all the references in *Midnight's Children* would be almost as long as the novel itself. Yet it is not necessary to catch all of his allusions to enjoy the book; he explains many of them himself or puts them in such a context that they are easy to understand. Indeed, some Indian critics reproach him with bending over backward in this regard, boring them with what to them are explanations of ordinary bits of language and daily life. But Western readers are more likely to feel that he leaves far more unexplained than most South Asian writers. Indeed, he quite consciously chooses to throw Western readers off balance, expecting them to experience some of the same bewilderment that an Indian reader may feel on encountering modern colloquialisms in contemporary Western fiction. It is not necessary to understand every word to enjoy his work, but delving into Indian culture and history can considerably enrich one's experience of Rushdie's writing.

It is worth noting that Rushdie himself often analyzes his own work within the framework of the novel itself. Look for passages in which he explains how one event leads to another, what names signify, and how patterns emerge throughout the novel.

History, of course, is the main subject of *Midnight's Children*. Simply summarized, this is the story of modern India, from the eve of independence in 1947 through the highly controversial "Emergency" declared by Prime Minister Indira Gandhi in 1975 in which she assumed dictatorial powers. The historical events are told through the experiences of a single family, most of which is destroyed in one catastrophe after another. Even the narrator himself is literally disintegrating at the end of the book.

It is tempting to sum up the novel's message as a simple cry of anguish at the failures of modern India to live up to its initial promise. After the inspiring events of the resistance movement (most famously led by Mohandas K. Gandhi, a figure rarely appearing in Rushdie's works), great things seemed possible, symbolized in the novel by the supernatural gifts of the thousand and one children born simultaneously with the nation. This ancient land, rich in traditions and culture, could undergo a new golden age. Yet Partition—the

1947 creation of Pakistan out of parts of the territory of traditional India—was accompanied by ghastly bloodshed among Hindus, Muslims, and Sikhs, as has been discussed in Chapter 3 on Singh's *Train to Pakistan*. Fanaticism, the determination to exclude those who are different and cling to one's own tradition, is always a destructive force in Rushdie's work, and here it is exemplified by the "midnight's children" squandering their gifts in pointless conflict with each other.

Family members in *Midnight's Children* also betray each other, turn on each other, and tyrannize over each other just as Indians at large had done. In the end the rich promise of the independence movement is wasted in a series of cataclysmic riots and oppressive acts that threaten the very survival of the nation, with the only hope given at the end of the novel being provided by the potential of Aadam Sinai (a hope that Rushdie cynically crushes in his later novel, *The Moor's Last Sigh*).

Such a summary does not do justice to Indian history, of course. The recent past of the world's largest democracy cannot be reduced only to its disasters. During the decades Rushdie depicts, industries were built, art and fiction were created, and a rich and vital culture evolved that was to produce people like Rushdie himself. Political satire is not the same as history. For a more balanced view of modern India, read a traditional history book. *Midnight's Children* articulates a very special view of the nation, filled with anguish over the many wounds it has suffered, many of them self-inflicted. (Although he mocks the tendency of some Indians to cling to English ways, this is not a particularly anticolonial novel; he holds the Indians responsible for their own destiny.)

Yet Rushdie is no historian, nor a writer of bald political satire; he is above all a storyteller. He loves to spin yarns, taking as his model Scheherazade, narrator of *The Thousand and One Nights*—a text to which he frequently alludes. To reduce his works down to their political message is to ignore their essence. They are brimming with fantastic adventures, marvels, portraits of colorful characters, wild romances and comic pratfalls. Readers who entirely ignore his political themes are missing much of the point of his works; but readers who approach Rushdie only for sober political messages are bound to be disappointed. He is first and foremost a storyteller.

Summaries of the novel's plot are freely available in various study guides, but a bare recital of the events in the novel conveys very little of the experience of reading it. Some books are like a warm bath that you relax into and luxuriate in. Others are like a wild roller-coaster ride in which you flip the pages as rapidly as possible to find out what happens next. But some, like *Midnight's Children*, more closely resemble an elaborate role-playing fantasy game in which puzzles must be solved, connections made, and symbolism grasped. All of Rushdie's writing demands that the reader be actively engaged with the text: remembering, anticipating, and questioning. It is aimed at people who enjoy stretching their brains, for whom mental exercise is fun. Because of the demands he places on readers, Rushdie is more famous than popular; but for those who enjoy this sort of thing, he has few peers.

Although the characters in *Midnight's Children* are largely imaginary (with the notable exception of his fierce satire on Indira Gandhi as "the Widow"), the story does reflect elements of Rushdie's own family history. His ancestors were Muslims from Kashmir, but he grew up in cosmopolitan Bombay, far to the south. However, while he was away at school in England, his parents moved the family to Pakistan, a move that Rushdie bitterly resented as a betrayal of his roots and is clearly alluded to in the middle portion of the novel. The passages about Pakistan foreshadow the portrait of that nation he would create in his next novel.

Shame (1983) is a scarifying satire of the history of Pakistan. It is a much shorter novel than *Midnight's Children,* and it is tempting to recommend beginners to start with it; yet it lacks much of the charm and humor of his earlier novel. If Rushdie has a love/hate relationship with India, his feelings toward Pakistan are much more unambiguous.

Rushdie's personal animosity to the country's government is expressed by making the members of two linked families into substitutes for several important figures in Pakistani history: Zulfikar Ali Bhutto (Iskander Harappa), Benazir Bhutto (Arjumand "Virgin Ironpants" Harappa), and Zia Ul-Haq (Raza Hyder). Because it assumes a good deal of knowledge of Pakistan's actual history, it is somewhat harder to read for the beginner. Do not assume that everything said about the characters in the novel is true of their real-life counterparts. This is the extreme form of satire known as *lampoon.* Also note that the novel was completed before Benazir Bhutto began her own controversial reign as Pakistan's prime minister.

Whereas the main flaw of India in *Midnight's Children* is "communalism" (sectarian hatred and violence), in *Shame* governmental corruption and repression are the main destructive forces at work. Rushdie's hostility to Islamic "fundamentalism" is striking and found fuller expression in *The Satanic Verses.*

The novel's title reflects another important theme: the connection between shame and violence, particularly as it affects women. Rushdie has often been criticized for his depiction of women. Most of them are either wildly sexual or severely antisexual, destructive or submissive. They lack the complexity and varied natures of his male characters. Early feminist critics argued that the only kind of freedom he seemed to advocate for women was sexual freedom—of direct benefit to men.

Yet this is too simple. Rushdie cares passionately about the humiliations and agonies inflicted on women in traditional South Asian cultures. Sufiya Zenobia, although a cartoon of a woman, forcefully represents the destructive effect of a system in which women's chastity is deemed more important than their happiness, or even than their survival. What may have seemed exaggerated when the book first appeared seems less so as we read of contemporary "honor killings" in countries like Pakistan where any slight suspicion of unchastity may obligate a man to murder his own wife or daughter in an attempt to redeem his sense of honor. It was just such a killing that served as one of the main inspirations for the book.

In this novel Rushdie continued his crusade to explore sexual topics frankly (although not in particularly graphic language), inspiring many followers, such as Khushwant Singh (*Delhi,* 1990) and Upamanyu Chatterjee (*English, August,* 1988). But sex in Rushdie is associated primarily not with pleasure, or even with love. Instead it is linked to the struggle for freedom, both personal and political. More often than not, it is the jealous or heartless attitudes of their husbands and lovers that create the sufferings of women in Rushdie's fiction. He defends women not by idealizing them, but by criticizing men.

As for the ferocious side of some of his female characters, it is worth noting that he creates male monsters too, and that he did not make up such real-life characters as Indira Gandhi, Benazir Bhutto, and Margaret Thatcher. Women whom he believes to have abused their power are held responsible for their misdeeds just like men.

The time sequence in the novel is severely distorted. The reader has to keep a sharp eye out for shifts into the future and back into the past. Even more than in *Midnight's Children,* events are often foreshadowed. It is also punctuated by autobiographical notes and what amount to nonfictional essays expressing Rushdie's own ideas.

Rushdie's fierce satire on Indira Gandhi led to a successful lawsuit by her supporters in India, and his satire on Pakistani politicians unsurprisingly caused *Shame* to be banned in that country. But none of this hostility deterred the author from proceeding to create the most inflammatory novel of the late twentieth century: *The Satanic Verses* (1988).

This novel is principally about the experiences of immigrants living in England and struggling with questions of prejudice, self-definition, and change. But threaded through this contemporary matter are various fantastic tales dealing with Muslim fanaticism, including a satirical portrait of Muhammad, the founder of Islam, as "Mahound." By Western standards, the satire is mild and respectful: he is seen as flawed and imperfect, but also as idealistic and well meaning. But there is no tradition in Islam of satire that dares to call into question the divine inspiration of prophets and the purity of their acts the way there has been in Christianity since at least the Middle Ages, and particularly since the eighteenth-century Enlightenment, which featured fierce opponents of the Church like Voltaire mocking the Bible, the saints, and even God himself in hugely popular writings—often censored and repressed, but nevertheless widely reprinted and read.

In conservative Muslim countries, in contrast, statements perceived as critical of the Prophet Muhammad or of the Qur'an can arouse violent passions and lead on occasion to deadly riots. In such countries, fiction has no special privileges, and blasphemy is taken very seriously indeed.

Fanaticism—or even piety—did not feature in Rushdie's own early religious background. In the essay "In God We Trust," he writes,

My relationship with formal religious belief has been somewhat chequered. I was brought up in an Indian Muslim household, but while both my parents were believers neither was insistent or doctrinaire. Two or three times a year, at the big Eid festivals, I would wake up to find new clothes at the foot of my bed, dress and go with my father to the great prayer-*maidan* outside the Friday Mosque in Bombay, and rise and fall with the multitude, mumbling my way through the uncomprehended Arabic much as Catholic children do—or used to do—with Latin. The rest of the year religion took a back seat. I had a Christian ayah (nanny), for whom at Christmas we would put up a tree and sing carols about baby Jesus without feeling in the least ill-at-ease. My friends were Hindus, Sikhs, Parsis, and none of this struck me as being particularly important. (376–77)

Many Indians of the same generation report not being aware when they were young of which of their friends were Muslim and which Hindu. For such people the inflammatory religious passions that have bitterly divided the two groups in contemporary India is a tragedy. As at least a nominal Muslim, Rushdie felt it his duty to challenge the forces inside Islam that were exacerbating these passions. He satirizes both the founders of Islam and—much more fiercely—the modern leaders like the Ayatollah Khomeni who have built repressive regimes on religious intolerance. It is ironic that the Iranian leader very probably condemned Rushdie to death for having written *The Satanic Verses* without realizing it contains a fierce satire on Khomeni himself, for few of the novel's Muslim critics have read more than a few selected excerpts held to be especially shocking to the faith. Yet, had they read them in context, they would not likely have been mollified, for the novel does indeed question the divine inspiration of the Qur'an and satirizes several of Muhammad's teachings.

Less commented on is a subplot in which an idealistic young woman believes she can cause the waves of the Arabian Sea to part as she leads a group foot pilgrimage to Mecca, a story based on an actual incident Rushdie had read about in the news. The story of the fatal idealism of Ayesha is one of the richest, mostly delicately nuanced, and most moving in the book. Its attack on extremism did not provoke the hostile reaction of the passages concerning Muhammad because it does not challenge religion itself, but its distortion by fanatics.

But *The Satanic Verses* is not primarily about religion at all. The main plot concerns the struggles of two Indian immigrants, a voice-over artist who prides himself on having shed his Indian identity (Saladin Chamcha) and an irresponsible, self-centered Bollywood star (Gibreel Farishta). They find themselves by pure chance together in an airplane that has been hijacked by

Sikh terrorists and is blown up in the first lines of the novel. Instead of plummeting to their deaths, they land miraculously unharmed. But in the ensuing pages they undergo a series of transformations: the destructive Gibreel acquiring a halo and the timid Saladin growing devil's horns. The latter change is a concretization of the currently popular phrase "demonization of the other." The English make immigrants into devils by their prejudices against them.

The immigrants' critique of British insularity in the wake of the collapse of their empire is voiced in a witticism uttered by a minor character (his name mirrors his stammer), S. S. Sisodia: "The trouble with the Engenglish is that their hiss hiss history happened overseas, so they dodo don't know what it means."

The novel was written shortly after riots in various cities revealed how tense racial relations actually were in modern Britain, and such a riot features at the climax of the book. Rushdie was deeply disappointed to be attacked by the very immigrant community he had written the novel to defend. But this is no narrowly political treatise: black nationalists, Trotskyite revolutionaries, and anarchists are all satirized at one point or another. In fact, this is by far the most humorously satirical of Rushdie's books, filled with jokes, puns, and scenes of pure farce. All forms of rigid fanaticism are attacked in this novel: political, racial, and religious.

For that reason, it would be a good work for the beginning Rushdie reader not offended by such satire to explore, for it does not require the detailed knowledge of South Asian history important for understanding the full significance of *Midnight's Children* and *Shame*. Only two scenes are set in India, and the second of the two is more personal than political. A network of cross-references, duplicated names, and echoed images knits the various strands of the novel together. Running through all the varied plots of the book is an argument for blended identity, flexibility, and openness to change versus stereotypes and rigidity. Again, a bare plot summary would convey very little of the book's impact. Although few people who picked it up out of curiosity over the controversy penetrated past the first few pages, more and more critics have begun to consider it one of his finest achievements. More than any of his works, it repays careful, engaged reading and rereading.

On February 14, 1989, the Ayatollah Khomeni transformed Rushdie's life by issuing a *fatwa* (judgment) calling on faithful Muslims to hunt him down and kill him. This is not the sort of fame that any novelist dreams of, and the ensuing years were grueling ones, involving constant police protection and frequent changes of address. The highly gregarious author found himself unable to attend movies, go to parties, and tour on behalf of his own book. His marriage had been disintegrating before the *fatwa*, but going underground meant that he also lost contact with his son Zafar. As a way of staying in touch with the boy, he wrote a short children's novel for him entitled *Haroun and the Sea of Stories* (1991). *Haroun* is also an affectionate tribute to Rushdie's own father, who loved to tell his children complex and endless bedtime stories.

Rushdie has always insisted that the story, involving a fiendish plot to deprive the world of fiction, was not inspired by the protests against his own novel, but few readers doubt that the censorious villain Khattam-Shud is at least partly a satire on Khomeni. The novel is much less densely allusive than his other works, providing few difficulties for the young reader and sufficient entertainment for older ones. Those who do not disdain young adult fantasy can find a lot to enjoy in these pages. Reading the appendix, "About the Names in this Book," helps the reader understand various in-jokes involving the names of characters and places.

His next novel, *The Moor's Last Sigh,* appeared to generally positive reviews in 1995. As rich as any of the earlier books in details and incident, it is not perhaps as heartfelt. He creates a family very different from his own, a Jewish–Muslim–Christian mixture representing the old interreligious interracial culture of medieval Moorish Spain, depicted as a multicultural paradise lost to fanaticism. But Moorish Spain really stands in for the fondly remembered tolerant Bombay of his youth. Toward the end of the novel he engages in a fierce satire on Shiv Sena leader Bal Thackaray in the shape of "Raman Fielding," a rabid Hindu nationalist.

Hinduism has often been regarded as a highly tolerant religion, open to all varieties of faith and lacking any central dogmas, but in contemporary India fiercely anti-Muslim political leaders like Thackaray have risen to power. Bombay itself was plunged into interreligious bloody riots and bombings in 1993 in the wake of the destruction of a mosque in the city of Ayodhya by Hindu fanatics who believed it to have been built on the site of the birthplace of Rama, the famous warrior god.

In his books set in India, Rushdie makes historical events more vivid and personal by embedding them in the personal lives of his central characters. Whereas in *Midnight's Children* the claim that the events of Indian history were all caused by the narrator's family are obviously delusional, in *The Moor's Last Sigh* the crediting of the 1993 violence to members of the narrator's family seems to play down their significance rather than magnify it, for this is much more a family saga than a national one.

The novel is also a veritable catalog of taboo passions. All of Rushdie's fiction deals with forbidden desires and relationships. Even *Haroun and the Sea of Stories* begins with the main character's mother abandoning her family for an affair with a neighbor. Rushdie determinedly set himself to write more explicit erotic passages in the novel than he had done previously, and much of it has the feeling of deliberately willed rather than spontaneous sexuality. In addition, the Jewish and Christian identity of the characters seems forced for symbolic reasons, not a natural product of his experience.

The Moor's Last Sigh, however, is a rich book and would probably have a higher reputation had he not already written *Midnight's Children* and *The*

Satanic Verses. Its greatest significance was in proving that the *fatwa* had not prevented him from creating another big ambitious novel.

Beginning with this work, minor characters from earlier novels began to reappear in new settings. It marks his deep disillusionment with Indian politics that the sole surviving family member who symbolized hope for the future at the end of *Midnight's Children* is destroyed in *The Moor's Last Sigh.*

Rushdie has said of *The Ground Beneath Her Feet* (1999) that it marks his farewell to the Bombay of his youth and his transition to writing novels set in the West, where he now lives. Despite this fact, more of it is set in India than *The Satanic Verses,* but with an emphasis on the penetration of Western culture, especially rock music, into his home city in the 1950s and 1960s. It concerns the tortured love triangle among musicians Vina Apsara, Ormus Cama, and the photographer who loves them both: Rai. After a detailed account of their early days in Bombay, the rest of the novel takes place largely in London and New York, in the world of international pop music.

Considerably less complex in style and structure than most of his earlier works, it goes to even greater extremes than his earlier novels in playing games with history. Few of the historical characters alluded to are given their real names, and fictional characters are treated as if they were real. Events like the Kennedy assassination are whimsically rearranged or revised. But whereas in his other novels these departures from the historical record usually had a clear purpose, here they often seem willfully arbitrary.

The Ground Beneath Her Feet is long, but it seems stretched rather than stuffed. There are not so many obscure allusions (and fewer of them are South Asian), and the puns and other word games lack the explosive energy of books like *Midnight's Children* and *The Satanic Verses.* Clearly Rushdie hoped some of the power of the music he loves would flow into his novel, but his attempts to convince us that this fictional couple from India were bigger than the Beatles fell flat because we can't really *hear* them, even in our imaginations. The rock group U2 did make a recording of the "title song" from the novel, but it was not a notable success either.

Fury (2001) is a peculiar novel unlikely to be ranked among Rushdie's best by most readers. The main character is a middle-aged Pakistani who has fled his wife and son to live (like Rushdie) in Manhattan. He dates gorgeous women including (like Rushdie) a South Asian model. But Malik Solanka is no self-portrait. He is far less genial and gregarious than his creator, filled with a wide-ranging rage at popular culture, American materialism, and himself. None of the characters is particularly well defined, and one tasteless decision makes a highly educated African American character speak in nineteenth-century black dialect—wildly implausible even as a joke.

Long passages of the novel consist of simple evocations of pop culture icons from Monica Lewinsky to Alan Greenspan, and they seem more like attempts by Rushdie to show how hip he is than constituting a real portrait of a time. The novel depicts New York at the peak of the turn-of-the-century stock market bubble and was published just ten days before September 11, 2001, when the World Trade Center Towers attacks instantly rendered his depiction of Manhattan both sadly dated and irrelevant. They also prevented him—already a prominent target of Muslim extremists— from touring in support of the novel.

Unlike the allusions in his other writings, those in this novel are trivia taken directly from the mass media, without the magical realism transformations he had performed in his earlier works. Although it contains some vivid and funny passages, on the whole most readers have found it his least satisfying work.

Those who don't feel ready to tackle *Midnight's Children* or *The Satanic Verses* can get a taste of Rushdie's style from reading the first few stories from the collection *East, West* (1994). These are mostly simple, straightforward tales, some of them written early in his career.

"Good Advice Is Rarer Than Rubies" is a very simple twist-ending story that was originally published in *The New Yorker* (June 22, 1987). The setting is presumably Karachi. Rushdie effectively evokes the colorful street life of the city. A young Pakistani woman finds a convenient way to avoid the arranged marriage into which she has been destined by her parents, using the notorious skepticism of British immigration officials, which she learns about free of charge from an "advice-wallah" (a man unofficially selling advice about emigration outside the British consulate). This would-be con man not only fails to charge his usual fee because he is so charmed by the beauty of the young woman, but she makes completely unexpected use of his expertise. Little of Rushdie's characteristic wit appears in this story except for this sarcastic comment: "England is a great nation full of the coldest fish in the world." However, it is difficult to know whether the advice-wallah is referring to the English themselves or to the produce of the North Sea, although Rushdie himself undoubtedly means to allude to the English. In *The Satanic Verses* Rushdie compared England to a kipper (smoked herring), peculiar tasting and "full of spikes and bones."

"The Free Radio" (first published in *The Atlantic Monthly,* June 1982) was inspired by the aggressive family planning campaign carried on under the leadership of Sanjay Gandhi (son of Indira) in the 1970s. Various techniques including money payments and the gifts of pocket radios were used to persuade both men and women to volunteer for sterilization, and not a few were tricked or even coerced into it. This was one of several factors that led to popular resentment of the Gandhi government and ultimately to its downfall. Traditionally upper-caste widows have been expected to devote themselves to a life of simplicity and abstinence (when they were not—in earlier times—burned alive on their husbands' funeral pyres in the ritual called *sati*). The narrator argues that a good widow would go to live out her days in devotion in the sacred city of Benares (the British name for the holiest city for Hindus; Indians call it "Varanasi"). This is still considered an ideal way for a devout Hindu to end his or her days, and a good number do even now.

Ramani may be a fool when it comes to getting what he wants in the world (a wife, a radio), but he has a terrific imagination. By the end of the story he has graduated from listening to an imaginary radio to leading an imaginary existence as a Bombay film star. Who can say that he has not achieved happiness, even if he has had to invent it in his mind?

"The Prophet's Hair" is the single story that makes the best possible brief introduction to Rushdie. It is filled with wit, magic, and beautiful language, which lends itself particularly well to being read aloud. The few terms unfamiliar to most Western readers are annotated at the end of this book (see the glossary), but the tale is not at all difficult to follow. It also makes compelling reading, for it is very much influenced by the tradition of the tale of adventure from the *Thousand and One Nights,* like "Ali Baba and the Forty Thieves."

However, it is more than a mere piece of entertainment. Rushdie is satirizing certain tendencies toward Islamic fanaticism he was later to experience in all too personal a fashion. "The Prophet's Hair" (*London Review of Books,* 1981) was based on an actual incident. At the Hazratbal shrine in Srinagar, on December 27, 1963, it was disclosed that the day before a hair reputedly from the beard of the Prophet Muhammad (known as the *Moe-i-Muqaddas*) had disappeared. It had been kept in a small glass tube secured inside two wooden cupboards from which it was normally removed for display only ten times a year. It was widely rumored that supporters of a prominent leftist leader, Bakshi Ghulam Mohammad, were involved; and enraged mobs set fire to movie theaters and other properties belonging to his family.

Hundreds of thousands of protesters poured into Srinigar and milled about, marching and rioting, paralyzing the city and resulting in the imposition of a curfew to maintain order. Mysteriously—and some thought, conveniently—it was announced on January 3, 1964, that the relic had reappeared. It took a special verification ceremony to convince skeptics that this was indeed the very hair of Muhammad and not a substitute hastily procured by frustrated officials. It has been said that this incident marked the beginning of the phase of violent protest and combat in Kashmir that continues to this day.

The Valley of Kashmir has historically been considered one of the greatest beauty spots on earth, often compared to Paradise. Rushdie has a personal connection with the area because his ancestors had emigrated from the area to Bombay. But at Partition, Kashmir was divided between Pakistan and India and became the subject of a passionate and often violent struggle (indeed, during June 2002, the world was to witness the two nations edging toward the brink of a nuclear exchange over Kashmir).

The whole episode struck the skeptical Rushdie as an entertaining example of religious fanaticism, and he touched on it briefly in *Midnight's*

Children. Later, he decided to rework the incident as the darkly comic tale that now features in *East, West*.

He begins in the middle of the action, gripping our attention at once by the intriguing situation of Atta's seemingly insane quest for a professional thief, only gradually revealing the strange story that has led up to this desperate move. The rest of the story involves a series of unfortunate miracles, which—although not directly calling into question the possibility of the miraculous—certainly subject it to a certain amount of ridicule.

This is a family that has no particularly strong religious background. Hashim's embarrassment at the piety of his sons reflects the experiences of many secularized or liberal Muslims, especially common in the immigrant community Rushdie knows so well, where young men frustrated with their lot in life have joined Islamic fundamentalist movements. For an entertaining example of this sort of intergenerational conflict, see the film *My Son the Fanatic*, from a script by Hanif Kureishi (1998). When Hashim argues that his high interest rates could be seen as a useful lesson in the value of money, he is flagrantly flaunting the law of Islam, which does in fact forbid not just usury (the taking of excessive interest) but the charging of any interest at all.

Muslims, unlike Buddhists and Catholics, have not traditionally venerated sacred relics; indeed Islam strictly forbids the worshipper to think of the Prophet as divine. But in Kashmir, the veneration of such relics is an ancient tradition.

The stolen hair inspires the formerly thoroughly secular Hashim to begin observing the standard five prayers per day and to become fanatical about those aspects of Islam that result in restrictions on his wife and daughter without inspiring him to obey the prohibition against lending money for interest; indeed, he becomes more rapaciously grasping than ever. He has also turned against the cinema because some—but by no means all—Muslims consider movies a violation of the Islamic prohibition against the creation of images of living beings. Hashim has become "religious" in the worst possible way, adopting restrictions that make him oppressive and mean rather than loving and generous.

The mutilation of children to make them into more pathetic beggars is a frequently reported if not exactly common practice in places in South Asia, often criticized in fiction (see Rohinton Mistry's *A Fine Balance*, for instance). It is commonly associated with professional criminals.

This story belongs to the long tradition of tales in which a magical gift has unexpectedly harmful consequences, in which apparent blessings turn into curses. It may even be that Rushdie is suggesting that the fervent devotion with which Muslims and Hindus alike adore Kashmir has backfired to make it a nightmarish battlefield. Its very sacred beauty has made it cursed.

One story from the "West" section of the collection, "At the Auction of the Ruby Slippers" (*Granta*, April 1992), is especially interesting because Rushdie was enthralled at an early age by viewing the classic movie of *The*

Wizard of Oz, and he has often connected Dorothy's journey with the trans-formations undergone by emigrants like himself. It is also interesting because it is at least in part a response to those who attacked him over *The Satanic Verses:*

We, the public, are easily, lethally offended. We have come to think of taking offence as a fundamental right. We value very little more highly than our rage, which gives us, in our opinion, the high moral ground. From this high ground we can shoot down at our enemies and inflict heavy fatalities. We take pride in our short fuses. Our anger elevates, transcends. (89–90)

This highly interesting experimental ("postmodern") story is not discussed further here because it has no direct relevance to South Asia, but it is one of his most artful and often-analyzed stories.

The section of the book titled "East, West" is devoted to stories involving South Asian immigrants living in England. "The Harmony of the Spheres" and "Chekov and Zulu" are both brilliant examples of Rushdie's mature style, full of clever twists, told in sparkling language, and packed with allu-sions. The second of the two also contains a good deal of dialect that may not be easy going for the beginning Rushdie reader. Both are worth explor-ing, but have less immediate relevance to South Asia than the final story, "The Courter," which appeared for the first time in this volume.

Here Rushdie is drawing on details from his own life, for after he went to Britain at the age of thirteen, in 1961, to attend the famous school at Rugby, his parents and three sisters emigrated the following year to join him. He became a British citizen thanks to more liberal passport laws than those that were to apply later; and the family did have a Christian ayah, although he has never said publicly whether the character in this story has anything else in common with the woman who helped rear him. As noted earlier, the fam-ily celebrated the Christmas holiday with her as well as observing Eid at the conclusion of the Muslim holiday of Ramadan.

Anyone who has tried to speak in an incompletely mastered language will have noticed how much less sophisticated and intelligent one appears than when speaking in one's own native tongue. The father of the family is laughed at by his children for using the wrong word in a pharmacy, although he is an educated man. This effect is even stronger in the mangled English with which Certainly-Mary expresses herself—she is constantly struggling to convey her thoughts in this alien medium, with mixed success. As with the stuttering S. S. Sisodia in *The Satanic Verses,* Rushdie enjoys playing games with Mary's speech defect. Satirical use has long been made of immigrant dialects, often in a mocking manner; but Rushdie's portrait of these diffi-culties is clearly affectionate. He goes out of his way to have his narrator acknowledge his own linguistic pratfalls. The porter's own crippled speech is a result of a stroke. But despite their handicaps, the two manage to fall in love, even in old age—a coming together of Eastern Europe and South Asia in the heart of London.

The story contains several references to songs popular during the early 1960s, most of them easy to identify and track down. The old slave cotton-picking song "Pick a Bale of Cotton" was popularized in a 1952 recording by Huddie "Lead Belly" Ledbetter and even more by Harry Belafonte in 1955. "Jumble-Aya" is a pun on the Cajun tune "Jumbalaya," a lively Cajun dance tune made famous in 1952 by Hank Williams, although he used the spelling "Jambalaya." "Unzip a Banana" was a suggestive Trinidadian calypso, later used as an advertising slogan to promote the sale of bananas. Presumably it is one of the posters from that ad campaign that Mixed-Up reads as he goes up the escalator.

The story is threaded through with the rising adolescent desires of the narrator, whose frank but frustrated yearning for sex contrasts strongly with the more subdued affection between the two old people. But these two threads have in common a lack of consummation. The adults feel too old to marry or have an affair, and the narrator is too young.

Rushdie likes to jump not only from generation to generation, but from culture to culture, moving on a single page from a reference to the famous Tottenham Spurs soccer team to classical Odissi dance (originating in the southern Indian state of Orissa). This rich celebratory east–west multiculturalism is a Rushdie trademark. Each is associated with a different girl desired by the narrator, one Polish, the other Indian. The latter is associated with rivers east and west: the sacred Ganges and "Moon River" (title of the theme song composed by Henry Mancini for *Breakfast at Tiffany's* and loaded with romantic associations).

The name "Charles Lutwidge-Dodgson" is an in-joke; this was the actual name of Lewis Carroll, author of *Alice in Wonderland,* whose main character was modeled on a little girl named "Alice Liddell," so Rushdie makes his housekeeper into a Mrs. Liddell. The real little Alice had trouble pronouncing Dodgson's name; she called him "Dodo"; and he therefore put a dodo into his story, based on himself. In Carroll's second Alice book, *Through the Looking Glass,* the entire plot is structured as a chess game. Carroll was a graduate of Rugby, like Rushdie.

The rather sordid story of the two emigrant maharajas and their involvement with the underworld clashes disastrously but also somewhat comically with the genteel romance of the two old people. But its main function is to demonstrate that the courtliness of the "courter" extends beyond mere courtesy to true chivalry as he risks his own life to protect Mary.

Although this story may on the surface seem to satirize South Asians, note that they have to deal with vicious racism directed against them in London, both on television and in real life, in the form of the English gangsters who can't be bothered to distinguish one Indian from another. The first gangsters are dressed as "Mods," an incongruously neat form of dress adopted by certain young hoodlums in the early 1960s in England. Their scruffier opponents were the "Rockers," and the two styles were reflected in the clothing of the early Beatles and Rolling Stones.

It is unclear whether Mary's flight from England is entirely caused by the assaults of the racist Mods and Rockers, but they certainly precipitate her decision. But the narrator, like Rushdie, insists that for himself he cannot choose between East and West. He embraces both, and millions of readers are grateful he has done so.

SELECTED BIBLIOGRAPHY

Blaise, Clark. "A Novel of India's Coming of Age." Rev. of *Midnight's Children*. *New York Times Book Review* 19 Apr. 1981: 1, 18–19. <http://www. nytimes.com/books/99/04/18/specials/rushdie-midnight.html>.

Brians, Paul. "Notes on Salman Rushdie: *The Satanic Verses* (1988)." <http:// www.wsu.edu/~brians/anglophone/satanic_verses/index.html>.

Detailed annotations and other materials to support the reading of this novel, with an extensive bibliography and an essay explaining the novel's structure. Revised 14 June 2002.

Chauhan, Pradyumna S. *Salman Rushdie Interviews: A Sourcebook of His Ideas*. Westport, CT: Greenwood Press, 2001.

Despite a few transcription errors, this helpfully annotated collection of radio, television, and print interviews is a great source. Covers the fiction through *The Ground Beneath Her Feet*. Surprisingly little overlap with Reder.

Cundy, Catherine. *Salman Rushdie*. Manchester: Manchester University Press, 1996.

Aimed at an audience familiar with contemporary critical and theoretical debates, this is still the most useful study of Rushdie's fiction for the general reader, through *The Moor's Last Sigh*. Contains an excellent review of earlier scholarship.

Fletcher, D. M., ed. *Reading Rushdie: Perspectives on the Fiction of Salman Rushdie*. Amsterdam: Rodopi, 1994.

Outstanding anthology of scholarly articles on the fiction from *Grimus* through *Haroun and the Sea of Stories*. Some knowledge of the terminology of contemporary literary theory is required for the reader to benefit fully. The annotated bibliography helpfully summarizes the main points of each book or article cited.

Goonetilleke, D. C. R. A. *Salman Rushdie*. New York: St. Martin's Press, 1998.

Very good overview of Rushdie's writing through *The Moor's Last Sigh*.

Grant, Damian. *Salman Rushdie*. Plymouth: Northcote House, 1999.

For more advanced readers. Chapter 1 is a very useful survey of Rushdie scholarship. This volume discusses issues in the fiction through *The Moor's Last Sigh*.

Harrison, James. *Salman Rushdie*. New York: Twayne, 1992.

The best introduction to Rushdie's novels from *Grimus* through *The Satanic Verses*.

Jussawala, Feroza. "Rushdie's *Dastan-e-Dilruba: The Satanic Verses* as Rushdie's Love Letter to Islam." *Diacritics* 26.1 (1996): 50–73. <http://muse. jhu.edu/demo/dia/26.1jussawalla.html>.

An important article on Rushdie's most controversial novel.

Reder, Michael R., ed. *Conversations with Salman Rushdie.* Jackson: University of Mississippi, 2000.

Outstanding collection of interviews with the author from throughout his career, many of them otherwise difficult to find.

Richards, Fiona. "The Desecrated Shrine: Movable Icons and Literary Irreverence in Salman Rushdie's "The Prophet's Hair." *SOAS Literary Review* 2 (July 2000). <http://www.soas.ac.uk/soaslit/issue2/contents.html>.

This somewhat ponderous analysis of the story contains useful details and references.

Rushdie, Salman. *East, West.* London: New York: Pantheon, 1984.

———. *Fury.* New York: Random House, 2001.

———. *Grimus.* London: Gollancz, 1975.

———. *The Ground Beneath Her Feet.* New York: Henry Holt, 1999.

———. *Haroun and the Sea of Stories.* New York: Viking Penguin, 1990.

———. *Imaginary Homeland: Essays and Criticism, 1981–1991.* New York: Granta, 1991.

The essays in this volume include some of Rushdie's most eloquent explanations of his own works, especially of *The Satanic Verses.* The first edition also contains the notorious essay "Why I Have Embraced Islam," which was composed by Islamic clerics who argued that if he would sign it, he might escape the *fatwa* hanging over his head. He subsequently regretted this act, and in later editions the essay is removed and replaced by "One Thousand Days in a Balloon," his own account of the "Rushdie Affair."

———. *Midnight's Children.* New York: Knopf, 1980.

———. *The Moor's Last Sigh.* New York: Pantheon, 1995.

———. *The Satanic Verses.* New York: Viking Penguin, 1989.

———. *Shame.* New York: Knopf, 1983.

Chapter 10
Shyam Selvadurai: Funny Boy *(1994)*

Sri Lanka has produced a number of notable authors writing in English, the most famous of whom is Michael Ondaatje (see Chapter 13 on his fine novel, *Anil's Ghost*). However, a good introduction to Sri Lankan literature in English for those not ready to tackle Ondaatje's sometimes difficult prose is the fiction of Shyam Selvadurai.

Because his first novel is saturated with Sri Lankan history, it is important to begin with some background on his homeland. Sri Lanka (formerly Ceylon) is a large island situated off the southern tip of the Indian subcontinent. For centuries it was known chiefly for the export of spices, especially cinnamon, and in more modern times for the growing of coffee and tea. To the Arab traders it was known as "Serendib," a place of legendary beauty (the word "serendipity" is derived from this name). In Hindu mythology the island has traditionally been identified with the land of Lanka in the *Ramayana* where Lord Rama, accompanied by Hanuman the monkey-warrior, went to rescue his wife Sita from the demon Ravana.

Although Sri Lanka shares a great deal culturally with India, it has always been independent from it politically. One obvious difference between the two countries is that whereas the majority of Indians are Hindus, the majority of Sri Lankans are Buddhists. When the faith founded by Gautama Siddhartha Buddha almost entirely died out in India in the twelfth century, it continued to prosper in Sri Lanka, following the ancient traditions of Theravada Buddhism. Early on, substantial kingdoms were built with great and distinctive achievements in art and architecture.

When Portuguese explorers arrived in the early sixteenth century, they brought with them missionaries who converted a substantial number of people to Catholicism. They built their first fortress in the city of Kolomba (which the Portuguese rendered as "Colombo"), and it became the capital of the island and still is the heart of its business life, although the governmental capital has now been moved to nearby Kotte. There are still many Portuguese place names and family names in Sri Lanka.

An invading Dutch fleet conquered the Portuguese territories in 1638, dominating the trade in spices until the British arrived and drove them out in 1796. The memory of their presence persists in personal names like "Ondaatje" and in the members of the social class called "burghers," who trace their ancestry back to the Dutch and who have held prominent social and economic positions on the island ever since.

Neither the Portuguese nor the Dutch were much interested in the interior of the island, being mainly concerned with controlling its lucrative spice trade. It was the English who made Sri Lanka an integral part of their empire, exploiting the land agriculturally and imposing heavy taxes on the inhabitants. Although they granted limited self-government to the Sri Lankans in 1900, full independence was only attained in 1948, just after India's. An English-speaking elite of about 7 percent subsequently controlled much of the power in the country.

But the new government was dominated by Sinhala speakers who made Buddhism the official state religion and Sinhala the sole official language. This greatly offended and distressed the substantial minorities of Hindus, Muslims, and Christians, many of whom had formerly dominated the economy. Since then, Sri Lanka has been the site of many bitter struggles stemming from a pattern common around the world: when a new democracy is used by a majority group to impose its will on a formerly dominant minority, the latter react bitterly. Particularly virulent has been the resistance of the speakers of Tamil (about 18 percent of the population). The Tamils in Sri Lanka have close linguistic and cultural ties with the Tamils of South India, and they are therefore sometimes portrayed by the Sinhala as outsiders, although many Tamil families have lived on the island for centuries.

Most of the Tamils are Hindus, although some are Christian, and about 7 percent of the population is Tamil Muslim. Tamils dominate only the two northeastern provinces of the island, with the rest dominated by the Sinhala majority. In the 1980s continued Tamil resentment and frustration against the central government led to the forming of various resistance groups, notably the Liberation Tigers of Tamil Eelam (LTTE; known popularly as the "Tamil Tigers"), who launched an insurrection in 1987 aiming at establishing a separate Tamil state. The Sinhala government fiercely resisted this rebellion and instituted draconic measures against Tamils, crushing their uprising but exacerbating tensions between the two groups. The Tigers began to engage in terrorist acts, and they became notorious for assassinations and suicide bombings (over two hundred so far) and later for kidnapping Tamil children and forcing them into their army. Throughout this struggle, the Sinhalese responded with their own massacres, tortures, and persecutions. The island has been essentially in a state of civil war ever since, with so many atrocities committed on both sides that mutual recriminations and hatred make it difficult to visualize any lasting peace in the near future, although in December 2001, the Tigers declared a cease-fire whose permanence remains to be seen.

Tensions were exacerbated in the late 1980s by the intervention of the government of India under Rajiv Gandhi, which sent troops to act as peace-keepers in Tamil regions but ended by battling with the Sri Lankan army. This catastrophic intervention convinced many Sinhala even more that the Tamil deserved to be treated as outsiders. Hundreds of thousands of Tamils—including Selvadurai's family—fled Sri Lanka for India and countries in the West, and tens of thousands have died in the continuing conflict. India has since repudiated the Tigers.

Modern Sri Lankan history is also notable for the election of the world's first female democratic head of state, Sirimavo Bandaranaike, widow of a former socialist prime minister who was assassinated by Buddhist extremists in 1959. She governed the country from 1960 to 1965 and again from 1970 to 1977. She was removed from office and stripped of her civil rights by Parliament in a corruption scandal that is briefly alluded to in *Funny Boy* near the beginning of the third chapter. She ultimately regained her rights and became prime minister for the third time in 1995, dying in office at age eighty-four, in 2000.

Selvadurai was born in Colombo, Sri Lanka, in 1965 to a prosperous family. His father was Tamil, his mother Sinhala. Theirs was a love match in which family resistance had to be overcome, so it is not surprising that he has been particularly interested in the many ways in which the sectarian violence pervading modern Sri Lankan history has torn people apart. One can sense the poignancy with which loving relationships in his works are distorted and destroyed by prejudice and violence on both sides.

In addition, as a youth slowly discovering he was gay in a country where such leanings were little understood and strongly deplored, Selvadurai has clearly felt torn by contending forces of several kinds and thoroughly isolated. The appearance of *Funny Boy* was hailed as the first gay novel from South Asia, and its opening and concluding sections do indeed focus on that theme, but they are only part of a larger picture in which religious and political difference looms more menacingly.

Note that the novel has a glossary explaining most of its non-English vocabulary. Words and phrases explained there are not included in the glossary at the end of this book.

After the family emigrated to Canada to escape the riots of 1983, Selvadurai was able to look back on his early years with some perspective. He wanted to understand better the events that had resulted in his family's exile, so he began to research various aspects of the conflict, weaving them eventually into his first novel.

Funny Boy is composed of five discrete chapters plus an epilogue, each with its own plot, so it can be read almost like a short story collection. But together they comprise the story of Arjie Chelvaratnam and his family, beginning when he is seven years old, in 1977. Arjie's preference for the company of girls and his delight in dressing up as a bride mark him as a "funny boy" in a way that alarms his family, but the most striking aspect of the youngster's story is his persistent determination to go his own way. He frustrates his father's attempts to straighten him out by deliberately failing at cricket, just as he will later frustrate the school principal's attempts to use him by deliberately failing in his recitation at the award ceremony. Arjie is at first confused, unsure of his identity, and oblivious to his family's fears about his sexual orientation (he knows "pansy" is an insult, but he doesn't know what it means), but he always pursues his own path.

The images of a romantic young boy parading in a worn-out sari are deliberately described in a humorous fashion. Events that another author might have treated as soul-killing trauma become instead an amusing celebration of individuality. Although he is exiled at the end of "Pigs Can't Fly" from both the boys' and the girls' worlds, we see him not crushed, but trudging stolidly off toward the future.

"Radha Aunty" takes place immediately after the events in the first chapter, in 1978, as Arjie finds a companion and ally in his Westernized, bell-bottom-wearing aunt. The story of her romance with a Sinhala boy is the first in the series of relationships destroyed by events stemming from Sri Lankan politics. That she meets him in a production of *The King and I* is particularly ironic because the latter stresses the importance of overcoming racial prejudices (although not, as the novel points out, to the extent of having Anna and the king actually marry). Radha is not only an ally, but a role model for Arjie as she determinedly pursues her romance with Anil in defiance of her family's opposition and interference. It is true that Arjie learns from her experience that love does not necessarily conquer all, but he does not acquiesce in her ultimate submission.

Set in 1979, "See No Evil, Hear No Evil" takes the theme of forbidden love to a more serious level in two ways: it involves Arjie's own mother, and it involves the death of the beloved. Whereas Radha's beloved was Sinhalese, Amma's is a burgher investigating the abuses of the Sinhala government against Tamils. Selvadurai artfully depicts the slowly dawning realization of Arjie that despite the fact that she disagrees with Daryl Uncle's politics, his mother is having an affair with him. Their story is told in a way that vividly conveys a childish loss of innocence.

Like Radha Aunty, Daryl Uncle is a sympathetic adult who has lived abroad and helps open up the world of possibility for Arjie, in this case by validating his love for Louisa May Alcott's novels. This time the outcome of the romance is determined by forces beyond the family. Each chapter is growing successively more entangled with Sri Lankan ethnic and religious tensions. Arjie realizes much more this time how thoroughly love has been overwhelmed by hatred and violence.

In "Small Choices," set in 1982, Selvadurai dives straight to the heart of the national conflict by introducing the character of Jegan, an admirable young man who—like Velutha in Roy's *The God of Small Things*—has radical connections. He formerly belonged to the Tigers, and this history condemns him forever in the eyes of the Sinhala police, although he has left them for the more benevolent charity organization specializing in assistance to Tamil children victimized by the violence, the Gandhiyam movement. Selvadurai is careful to apportion blame for unjust violence to both the Sinhala and the Tamil factions in society.

The failed relationship in this case is not a romance, but the friendship between Arjie's father and his late friend, Jegan's father. Amma's betrayal of her husband is not portrayed as harshly as is the father's betrayal of Jegan, for she acts out of love, and he acts out of cowardice. Indeed, Amma again proves to be a fearless investigator of injustice in this story just as she had been in the previous one. Quite unintentionally she is modeling for her son the virtue of defiant courage in the face of oppression.

Jegan also plays a role in the story of Arjie's maturation, for at age thirteen the boy is beginning to feel attracted to men. Whereas his affection for Daryl Uncle was straightforwardly childish, he feels more complicated emotions for Jegan. Whatever sympathy we might have felt for Father because of his wife's affair is blunted by the revelation in this chapter that he had himself had an affair with an English girl, and his feelings about her are much more crass and selfish than those Amma felt for Daryl.

"The Best School of All" is the bitterly ironic title of the chapter depicting the nightmare that is the Victoria Academy (set in early 1983). Arjie is sent there much as a boy considered weak in another society might be sent to a military academy, "to make a man of him." But this attempt by his father to steer his son away from homosexuality fares no better than did his earlier determination to force him to play cricket. Not only does he defy the sadistic principal and his follow students, Arjie finally finds a lover of his own at the academy: Shehan Soyza, who is actively gay and unapologetic about it.

The violence practiced on the boys at the school may strike contemporary readers as grotesque, but a few generations ago the beating of schoolboys with switches for minor infractions was routine in Europe and America. A standard cartoon stereotype humorously depicted the "bad boy" as having to eat his dinner off the mantelpiece because he had been switched so hard that he couldn't sit down. The principal seems genuinely vicious, but his actions would not have been considered bizarre in the context of a traditional private school. Selvadurai has said that Black Tie was an amalgam of various teachers he suffered under in three different Sri Lankan schools.

His initiation into sex by Shehan is again sensitively depicted. Arjie is simultaneously attracted and frightened. He has feelings he doesn't completely understand, and the surprising actions that result from those feelings are messy, uncomfortable, and disturbing. But they are also exciting. Any young person who has struggled with similar feelings of repulsion and desire—whether gay or heterosexual—can identify with Arjie's story. But again Arjie does not let himself be defeated. He moves past his initial revulsion to enter into a true love affair—the first of his life. Selvadurai does not sentimentalize this affair. The two will part on an unsatisfactory note that reflects adult ambivalence rather than childlike black-and-white thinking.

This chapter marks the coming together of the two main strands of the work: Arjie's maturation and Sri Lanka's civil turmoil. Tamil-Sinhala animosity pervades the academy, and Arjie almost becomes its victim. Yet, as in the other stories, love struggles with hatred. Love may be defeated in that the two young lovers will be parted by sectarian violence, but at the end of the chapter they are walking side by side, united, out of the shambles of the ceremony. Arjie realizes the experience has changed him forever, that he is no longer a part of his family, but inhabits another world alien to them.

In the closing epilogue (set in the summer of 1983), the narration focuses on the terrors inflicted on the Tamils by the Sinhala population. Arjie's father's earlier resistance to emigration is destroyed along with their home. The violence that has swirled around the family strikes directly at it. Selvadurai has said that although his own family also left Sri Lanka in the wake of the anti-Tamil riots of 1983, the circumstances were quite different. He did extensive research to create a vivid picture of what Tamils actually experienced during this period. As in earlier chapters, Arjie is depicted at the end as going off down the road, wounded, but not destroyed. We know he will grow up to be the man who will tell this story with understanding and compassion.

Selvadurai's second work, *Cinnamon Gardens,* appeared to generally favorable if not enthusiastic reviews in 1999. It is a historical novel depicting a wealthy family in Sri Lanka in the 1920s, and it partly concerns a married man struggling with his continued feelings for a man he had an affair with in his youth. The novel is a classic study of various would-be lovers struggling with parental interference, and it is generally well written, but it lacks the warmth and vividness of *Funny Boy.*

Funny Boy resembles Arundhati Roy's *The God of Small Things* in several ways. Both involve children swept up in social conflicts they don't understand, and both sensitively depict the world as seen through childish eyes. Both tell the stories of mothers having affairs with forbidden men. Love struggles with hatred in both. But whereas Estha and Rahel are grievously maimed by their experiences, Selvadurai implies that Arjie will learn from his experiences, survive, and grow.

SELECTED BIBLIOGRAPHY

Christensen, Peter G. "Shyam Selvadurai." *Asian-American Novelists: A Bio-Bibliographical Critical Sourcebook.* Westport, CT: Greenwood Press, 2000. 332–38.

Selvadurai, Shyam. *Cinnamon Gardens.* New York: Hyperion, 1999.

———. *Funny Boy.* New York: Morrow, 1996.

———. "Shyam Selvadurai's Personal Website." <http://www.interlog.com/~funnyboy/>. Web site published 1999.

This site, created by the author, presents some useful background for reading *Funny Boy.*

Wijesinha, Rajiva. "Aberrations and Excesses: Sri Lanka Substantiated by the Funny Boy." *Miscelanea: A Journal of English and American Studies* 18 (1997): 347–56. <http://fyl.unizar.es/MISCELANEA/ARTICULOS_18/ABSTRACTS_18.HTML#anchor195698>.

This article by another Sri Lankan novelist places the various themes of *Funny Boy* in context and discusses the reception of the work in Sri Lanka.

Chapter 11
Rohinton Mistry:
A Fine Balance *(1996)*

Rohinton Mistry was born into a Parsi family in Bombay in 1952. (For more about Parsis, see Chapter 7 on Bapsi Sidhwa.) As a teenager, he was an aspiring musician, performing Bob Dylan–influenced songs on his guitar around the city. Following the wishes of his family, he studied math and economics at Bombay University, although he was always interested in writing. In 1975, at the age of twenty-three, he emigrated to Toronto. After completing a BA at York University and the University of Toronto, he began working in a bank, but pursued his literary interests by taking courses in night school, leading finally in 1983 to another BA in English from Woodsworth College. Also in 1983 his wife, a schoolteacher, suggested he enter one of the stories he had written in the Hart House Literary Contest, and he won that year and the same prize for a different story the following year, beginning a long series of awards and honors that has continued to the present.

Mistry rarely visits India, but follows events there closely, and he chooses to place almost all of his fiction in Indian settings. Unlike several other non-resident Indians (commonly referred to by themselves as NRIs), he has chosen not to concentrate on life outside of South Asia and works hard to make his settings as convincing as possible. His tastes in literature are conservative, and he writes in a straightforward manner, with a good deal of humor and a strong emphasis on plot and character, which has led him to be compared repeatedly to Charles Dickens, one of his favorite writers.

His early stories were collected in a volume entitled *Tales from Firozsha Baag* (1987), retitled *Swimming Lessons* in its American edition. Like Manil Suri's

The Death of Vishnu, it consists of the stories of various characters living in separate apartments within a single building in the Parsi community of Bombay; but unlike Suri's work, the stories have only slight interconnections with each other. Only one character, a boy named Kersi, runs through several of them, and in a seemingly autobiographical sketch at the end of the collection ("Swimming Lessons"), he looks back on his life in Bombay and his burgeoning writing career. Whereas many authors depict their families as attempting to discourage their literary ambitions, the author here depicts his own parents as sensitive readers who respond intelligently and warmly to his works. Mistry's stories are polished, entertaining, and interesting, marking him as a talented writer, but they did not prepare readers for the major achievements of his novels. He obviously remains fond of Firozsha Baag, for he refers back to characters and stories from his first collection in his later works.

His first novel, *Such a Long Journey,* appeared in 1991 and earned a number of prestigious awards including the Commonwealth Writers Prize for best book that year. It is set in 1971, during the fierce conflict between East and West Pakistan that was to lead ultimately to the formation of Bangladesh out of the East Wing, with the support of Indira Gandhi's Indian government. But this is not a grim political tract; rather it concentrates on the misadventures of a well-meaning but hapless bank clerk named Gustad Noble, who is sucked into the murky world of India's secret service by his old friend Jimmy, who asks him to pick up and deal with a mysterious package for him, which turns out to contain huge amounts of illicit cash.

Mistry widens his portrait of Bombay society beyond the Parsi Noble family to include Hindu and Muslim characters, and he develops a wonderful subplot in which a community wall is preserved by having a wide variety of sacred pictures from all kinds of religions painted on it. As members of a tiny minority in India, it has always been in the interest of Parsis to encourage tolerance, and Mistry frequently creates incidents that deal with such themes. The plot lines, although easy to follow, are tangled, depicting the governmental corruption that led eventually to Prime Minister Indira Gandhi being formally charged in 1975. Some readers have found the sensational espionage plot implausible, but the degree of corruption depicted in the novel is quite realistic.

Such a Long Journey is a favorite with many readers, and it is a good beginning point for those just getting acquainted with Mistry's fiction. It was made in 1998 into a beautiful, entertaining, and remarkably faithful English-language film by Icelandic director Sturla Gunnarsson with a script by Sooni Taraporevala, who had earlier written the scripts for the well-known films *Mississippi Masala* and *Salaam Bombay.* Almost every line of dialogue in the movie comes directly from Mistry's novel, and most of his significant incidents and characters are presented except for the wife of Gustad's joking co-worker, Dishawnji—a change that makes the latter somewhat more sympathetic. Also omitted from the movie is the sensational hint

at the end of the novel that one of the characters might have been responsible for the death of Indira's son Sanjay in a 1980 airplane crash. Most
observers in fact believe Sanjay's death to have been caused by his own reck-
lessness or ineptitude in piloting his plane.

Mistry's next novel, *A Fine Balance* (1996), achieved enormous fame and
a vastly enlarged readership by being the final book selected by Oprah
Winfrey for her television book club in 2001. The fact that so many readers
have been drawn to it and that it deals with an otherwise often neglected
phenomenon, India's urban poor, make it an appropriate work to focus on
in this chapter.

Mistry's most recent work is *Family Matters* (2002), the story of feuding
step-siblings trying to shift onto each other the responsibility of caring for
their dying father. The story of the old man's deterioration and the family's
infighting is relentlessly realistic and often grim, with Mistry's characteristic
humor not as prominent as in his other works. His characters, however, are
as vivid and memorable as ever. This novel also depicts the rise in power of
Shiv Sena, the often violent Hindu extremist group that has influenced the
transformation of the political life of contemporary Bombay (now renamed
"Mumbai") and was also the target of satire in Salman Rushdie's *The Moor's
Last Sigh.*

A Fine Balance begins with an epigraph from Honoré de Balzac's *Le Père
Goriot,* warning that comfortable, well-fed readers may find his story incredible, although it is founded in truth. Indeed, many readers have found the
plot of *A Fine Balance* more than a little incredible, resting as it does on
improbably contrived Dickensian coincidences. But the reader simply has to
accept these contrivances to penetrate to the more important level of realism within the novel: the depiction of the lives of impoverished workers
struggling for existence in Bombay at the time of the 1975 martial law
period called the Emergency, decreed by Prime Minister Indira Gandhi in an
attempt to prevent her removal from office by India's high court. Although
the precise ways in which characters get swept up in the various harsh government initiatives depicted in the novel may seem far fetched, the abuses
depicted are in fact well documented.

It is important to keep in mind that *A Fine Balance* is a historical novel.
The Emergency ended and Indira Gandhi was thrown out of office by the
voters in 1984. Although isolated incidents of violence against untouchables
still occur, generally they have made great strides in proving their status in
the past two decades. The Dickensian picture of urban poverty that Mistry
sketches is to a large degree still valid, but the reader should remember that
the novel's narrow focus excludes more prosperous and stable levels of society. This is not a comprehensive portrait of India, but a narrow study of certain groups within it. The Dickens novel that it most resembles is *Our
Mutual Friend,* even to the extent of including incidentally a vendor of
human bones. Like Dickens, Mistry explores the complexities of the social

relations of people at the bottom of urban society. Individuals are pitted against each other in a desperate struggle for existence that leads them to exploit each other mercilessly, reminding us that small employers can treat their workers even more poorly than large ones. In one incident, a small-time pharmacist pays an assistant to sleep in his shop at night, ready to fill after-hours prescriptions. The assistant—eager to maximize his rest—hires a guard to stand out front and screen customers. The guard in turn rents the bit of sidewalk in front of the shop to homeless men looking for a place to sleep.

Mistry's poor are not passive sufferers; they scrabble incessantly for existence, eking out an income and creating a place to sleep with great determination and ingenuity. The reader slowly grows to appreciate what can be accomplished against overwhelming odds with tiny resources. On one level, the book is profoundly pessimistic, for most of the characters are destroyed, maimed, or damaged in other ways in the course of the plot. But on another level, it is a warm portrait of human courage and compassion as four individuals who initially distrust each other find themselves gradually knitted together into a sort of improvised family, compared in the novel to a patchwork quilt. Mistry avoids Dickensian simplification: his most sympathetic characters often behave badly, and even villains like the monstrous Beggarmaster are given some sympathetic traits.

Although mostly set in a cramped Bombay apartment, this is a vast novel, with many characters and plot lines running through it. Despite its length, this is an easy book to read and follow, so a detailed plot summary is unnecessary. The following notes instead highlight some of the more interesting aspects of the work and provide useful background information.

It begins as two young tailors and a college student find themselves arriving together on a train to Bombay to discover they are headed for the same address, the apartment of Dina Dalal, a young widow struggling to maintain a small sewing business, because she is losing her sight, by hiring the tailors—Ishvar Darji and his nephew Omprakash Darji—to work for her, and supplementing her income by renting her own bedroom out to Maneck Kolah, the son of an old school friend. Their arrival has been delayed by a death on the train tracks, and the novel will end with one of them dying just such a death as well. After these characters have been briefly introduced, a series of flashbacks tells each of their stories and explains how they came to find themselves sharing life in a Bombay apartment (the city is never specifically named, but it is clearly meant to be Bombay). These flashbacks make up much of the first half of the novel, with their subsequent adventures making up the rest.

Chapter 1, "City by the Sea," is the story of Dina. Denied because of her gender her wish to follow her father's profession of medicine, she insists on carving out an independent existence even after her father's death leaves her under the supervision of her overbearing older brother. She rejects his pressure to accept an arranged marriage and finds love for herself. The happy early years of her marriage are the high point of her life, ruined when her husband is abruptly killed in an accident. The rest of her story consists of her struggle to create an independent existence for herself. Unlike the poorer characters in the novel, she could retreat to the security of a middle-class life if she were willing to sacrifice her independence. But she is portrayed so sympathetically that we cannot help cheering her on in her struggles even as she sometimes behaves unjustly toward the two tailors. The novel is in large part the story of the education of her heart, as she learns to overcome her prejudices against these two men who on the one hand give her an income and on the other threaten it, for they are illegal workers (and eventually dwellers) in her rent-controlled apartment. If the landlord can document her employment of them, he can evict her. She is a sophisticated middle-class urban Parsi, and they are ill-educated untouchable Hindu villagers. But despite the resentment of young Omprakash and Dina's own wariness, the three manage eventually to knit together a sort of substitute family.

At forty-two, Dina is still an attractive woman who has engaged in a love affair with an older man even after her husband's death, and both the young men in the novel are drawn to her. Throughout much of the work it seems as if a conventional love story might evolve, but it never does. Mistry wisely keeps his focus on other kinds of relationships to reveal the complex strands that make up this society.

Chapter 2 pursues the story of the early stages of the development of Dina's sewing business and introduces a number of other characters, including Ibrahim, the threatening rent collector. Although it is tempting to see him as a villain, he will turn out to have a softer heart than we suspect at first. This Muslim hired to enforce the landlord's will turns out to be kinder to the odd Parsi-Hindu household than other members of their own communities. Throughout the novel there is a subtle emphasis on the way in which Indians with different religious backgrounds can care for each other, creating a theme of resistance to the Hindu supremacist movement that has blighted modern Bombay, as well as much of the rest of India.

Chapter 3 makes this point especially clear, for we learn that the two tailors were born into a caste of cobblers: a trade traditionally considered ritually unclean by Hindus because it involves handling the dead carcasses of animals—cows in particular. Rumors that leather workers have killed cattle for their hides rather than waiting for them to die a natural death can lead to their own murder by mobs, and their father decides to break with caste tradition by apprenticing them to a Muslim tailor, who eventually comes to consider them almost as members of his own family. This is a daring move, for in their conservative village untouchables like the cobblers are expected not only to subject themselves to all manner of humiliating discriminatory customs, but to pursue only their assigned occupation. The incidents in which untouchables are beaten or killed for violating caste law may seem extreme, but such incidents occur occasionally in some villages even today, although caste plays little role in a sophisticated urban environment like Bombay's. Mistry reinforces his antibigotry theme by having the two boys eventually save the life of the Muslim tailor and his wife from a threatening Hindu mob during the violence accompanying Partition, which has been so often depicted in the novels discussed earlier in this volume.

It is important to note the sarcasm that infuses Dukhi's comments on the Pandit Lalluram, who urges him to accept his sons' traditional caste role. A good deal of dry wit runs through the speeches of the two tailors as well, which may be missed if the reader is not alert for it.

The scene of the corrupt election following independence not only shows how small have been the gains made by the poor under the new government, but introduces the local political boss Thakur Dharamsi, who returns in Chapter 15 to take his final vengeance on the rebellious tailors, using as an excuse the notoriously ruthless and abusive sterilization campaign carried out under the leadership of Sanjay Gandhi during the Emergency. This is the same campaign depicted in Salman Rushdie's story, "The Free Radio."

Chapter 4, ironically titled "Small Obstacles," acquaints us with what life is like for the tailors in Bombay, outside of Dina's apartment, as they undergo a series of injustices that she remains blind to until Maneck educates her about the true nature of the lives they must lead. The grotesque lack of sanitation depicted in these scenes is still typical of the lives of the poor in India, where public rest rooms are rare and private ones unavailable below a certain income level. All of Mistry's fiction contains a fair amount of vivid depiction of excrement in it, justified here by realism more than in some instances. The incident of the stolen hair referred to in this chapter is the same as the incident that forms the setting for Rushdie's story, "The Prophet's Hair," discussed earlier.

Chapter 5 is largely devoted to Maneck's story, as we learn how this son of a small shopkeeper came to be studying refrigeration at a trade school in Bombay. His father made his fortune by creating a popular local soft drink during the period that Coke and other international brands were banned from India by governmental trade restrictions. Of all the major characters, he comes from the most secure background, but is the most easily discouraged, and in the end, he is the most easily destroyed. Maneck has a good heart, but little sense of direction or discipline. We see how economic decline has driven not only the tailors but this middle-class boy to the city in search of a living. This is a story replicated over and over, as Bombay has become a vast metropolis jammed with impoverished fortune seekers whose sufferings in the city are marginally better than the fate they have fled back home in their villages. We also meet Avinash, the outspoken and courageous student activist who will eventually fall victim to government repression in a way that is all too realistic. The appalling scenes of hazing at the college residence hall explain clearly why Maneck has taken refuge in Dina's apartment.

Chapter 6 finally catches us up to the point where the novel began. We learn more about Indira Gandhi's tyrannical regime in the farcical scene where a malfunctioning bundle of rose petals kills a man and the gigantic image of the prime minister is blown over by her own helicopter. Although most Westerners remain ignorant of the details of Gandhi's second term in office, they are vividly remembered by most Indians who lived through them, and Mistry is far from being alone in depicting her as a monster. Rushdie notably went far enough in *Midnight's Children* to cause his novel to be temporarily (if ineffectively) banned by the government.

The scene in which Shiv Sena thugs force moviegoers to sit through the national anthem foreshadows many such abuses by this and other such groups, especially in Bombay. Similar Hindu supremacist gangsters play a significant role in Mistry's *Family Matters* as well. Chapters 7 and 8 depict various aspects of Sanjay Gandhi's ruthless urban renewal schemes that benefited corrupt politicians and businessmen while worsening the lives of the people the Gandhis claimed to be fighting for.

More grotesque details about the systematic mutilation of children to create sympathetic beggars reflect well-known patterns. In a culture where all the major religions make charity toward the poor a spiritual duty, begging can be the best option for desperately poor parents, but the apparently most deserving victims are often the tools of criminals like the Beggarmaster, reminiscent of Mr. Peachum in the eighteenth-century British *Beggars' Opera* (and in the Bertolt Brecht adaptation, *The Threepenny Opera*). The dark humor with which Mistry depicts this trade in human wretchedness does not obscure its horror.

In Chapter 9 Dina's negative reaction to Mrs. Gupta's approval of the Emergency and the even more extreme comments made later in the chapter by her brother Nusswan show us just how much she has changed by becoming better acquainted with the tailors and the plight of people like them. The two tailors, meanwhile, have fallen into the clutches of a corrupt businessman who essentially pays the government to supply him with slaves. These scenes are among the grimmest in the book.

Chapter 10 marks a contrasting high point, with the significant title "Sailing under One Flag." The members of the little household face plenty of problems, but they are doing so united. Mistry's characters are not just passive victims; he emphasizes that people can improve their condition best not by scrambling to outwit and exploit each other, but by cooperating for their mutual benefit. Ominous stories about the excesses of the sterilization campaign foreshadow the disasters that culminate in Chapter 15.

Chapter 12 brings a bizarre Dickensian parallel to the theme of family formation that has preceded it as Beggarmaster discovers the true identity of Shankar and eventually enacts his grotesque version of charity. The nurturing of the kittens is also a related theme. Neither of these subplots is destined to turn out perfectly, but they both underline the mutual aid theme running through this part of the novel.

The urgency with which Om's uncle urges his marriage in the chapters that follow may seem rash, given their situation, but it reflects accurately the traditional Hindu stress on the importance of marriage and the begetting of children. The government sterilization campaign largely disregarded the religious and social customs and beliefs that had helped drive India's population explosion. It was doomed to fail for that reason. The population continued to expand until more recent times in which voluntary decision making and not government-imposed policies began to slow its growth. How much Sanjay Gandhi was himself responsible for some of the brutal practices that were carried out in his name is uncertain, but he displayed a callous indifference to the rumors circulating of excesses committed by greedy local officials eager to make unreasonable quotas. In Chapter 16 we learn that a friendly gangster can do more for the downtrodden than the government ever does.

The epilogue gives us a double ending. Maneck, the most fragile of the main characters, cannot bear the isolation and meaninglessness of his life as a foreign technician in Dubai while the still-impoverished and horribly mutilated tailors cheerfully visit with Dina. The three survivors have lost as much as Maneck had gained, materially, yet they remain true to each other, and they manage to boost their spirits by dining together in secret, behind Nusswan's back. Although this is a dark novel, it is not a hopeless one. Mistry wants us to see that even the seemingly powerless can help each other to a certain extent, if they will.

But it would take more than such kindly gestures to heal the broken society he depicts in *A Fine Balance*. The book's cover image of a girl balanced on a long pole, which is in turn balanced on a man's thumb, depicts the horrific "act" presented by Monkey Man in Chapter 9. When your best hope for supporting your children involves deliberately risking their lives, something is seriously wrong that individual action cannot fix. Avinash may have been defeated by the government, but his example provides more hope than that of the self-defeating Maneck. It will take effective democratic action to fix what is creating the misery these characters suffer from, but the novel offers no views on whether such action is likely. At best, it leaves us feeling there are decent human beings in the world, even among—perhaps especially among—the most downtrodden, and that change, although sometimes extremely difficult, is always possible.

SELECTED BIBLIOGRAPHY

Allen, Brooke. "Triumphant Vision." *The Atlantic Monthly* 17 Sept. 2002: 165–66.
     <http://www.theatlantic.com/issues/2002/09/allen_b.htm>.
     Review of *Family Matters*, which also discusses *A Fine Balance*.

Bennett, Dirk. "Rohinton Mistry, by Chance." *Artsworld.* <http://www.artsworld. com/books-film/news/rohinton-mistry-interview.html>. Accessed 9 Sept. 2003.
  Interview focusing on *Family Matters,* but with useful biographical background information.

Gibson, Stacey. "Such a Long Journey." *U of T: University of Toronto Magazine* Summer 2002. <http://www.magazine.utoronto.ca/02summer/f01.htm>.
  Overview of the author's career, with biographical details and material from an interview.

James, Jamie. "The Toronto Circle." *The Atlantic Monthly* Apr. 2000: 126–30. <http://www.theatlantic.com/issues/2000/04/james.htm>.
  Discussion of Mistry's career, with focus on *A Fine Balance.*

Mazzocco, Mary. "India Rich Resource for Author." *Contra Costa Times* 22 June 1997: 9. "Rohinton Mistry Became an Author Almost by Chance" at <http://lubbockonline.com/news/062697/rohinton.htm>.
  Brief article including material from an interview with Mistry following publication of *A Fine Balance.*

Mistry, Rohinton. *Family Matters.* New York: Knopf, 2002.
———. *A Fine Balance.* New York: Knopf, 1996.
———. *Such a Long Journey.* New York: Knopf, 1991.
———. *Tales from Firozsha Baag.* Markham, ON: Penguin Books Canada, 1987. Rpt as *Swimming Lessons and Other Stories from Firozsha Baag.* Boston: Houghton Mifflin, 1989.

Postcolonial Literature and Culture Web. "Rohinton Mistry: An Overview." <http://www.thecore.nus.edu.sg/landow/post/canada/literature/ mistry/mistryov.html>. Accessed 9 Sept. 2003.
  This site also contains other useful materials, including Jennifer Takhar's: "Rohinton Mistry's Indian Neorealism: The Voice of the People" at <http://www.thecore.nus.edu.sg/landow/post/canada/literature/mistry/ takhar3.html>.

Ruddy, Martin. "Rohinton Mistry." National Library of Canada Web site, <http:// www.nlc-bnc.ca/3/8/t8-2006-e.html>. 13 Nov. 1995.
  Brief introduction with biographical background and a detailed bibliography as of 1995.

Such a Long Journey. Dir. Sturla Gunnarson. Perf. Naseeruddin Shah, Om Puri. Shooting Gallery, 1998. Videocassette: ID0614SL; DVD: ID0600SLDVD. Image Entertainment.
  Faithful film adaptation of Mistry's novel by the same title. For further information, see <http://www.image-entertainment.com/>.

Vintage Books. "A Fine Balance." <http://www.randomhouse.com/vintage/ catalog/display.pperl?isbn=140003065X&view=rg>. Accessed 1 Sept. 2003.
  A brief study guide with background and study questions.

Chapter 12

Arundhati Roy: The God of Small Things *(1997)*

If Salman Rushdie revolutionized the image of South Asian fiction with *Midnight's Children,* it was truly popularized by Arundhati Roy in 1997 when her first (and thus far, only) novel, *The God of Small Things,* became an international sensation. Rushdie seemed clearly to be an influence on the younger writer. The verbal tricks of pushingtogether words and capitalizing other Important Words had both been used by him earlier. The combination of irony and tragedy that runs through Rushdie's major works is also present in Roy's. Finally, both *Midnight's Children* and *The God of Small Things* feature pickle factories, with Roy even slyly alluding to Rushdie's in her own novel.

But Roy insisted from the beginning that she was no mere Rushdie imitator, pointing out that her own uncle indeed owns a pickle factory, so she had better title to use one in her novel than had Rushdie. As time passed, readers began to notice the significant differences between the two. The most obvious difference is that Roy's novel is much easier to read than most of Rushdie's works, which explains why she was able to attract a wider public. Although her prose is intricate and rich, it is seldom obscure. She uses many words and phrases of Malayalam, the principal language of Kerala, but not so the reader with no knowledge of that language has difficulty following the story. The narrative switches back and forth between a "present time" in 1993 and a "past time" in 1969, but in a fairly straightforward way.

Her language strives for charm and beauty more than for cleverness and complexity. Roy makes extensive use of alliteration (an example from the first page: "The nights are clear, but suffused with sloth and sullen expectation").

Her characters, unlike Rushdie's, spring vividly to life as individuals. Her strongest point is the depiction of children and their views of the world. Women generally dominate the novel's foreground, with men relegated to supporting roles. Several of the male characters are abusive, and Estha and Velutha are ineffectual victims. Emotions are more important than events in this work, and the emotions are vividly conveyed.

Less pleasant physical realities are also vividly portrayed. There is a good deal of excrement in this novel and repeated references to genitalia. Roy is a modern Indian writer, artfully indirect at times, but not discreet or polite. The prominent theme of child sexual abuse in the book reflects intense interest in that subject during the very period it first appeared, when it was read by some as a South Asian contribution to an ongoing international discussion of keen interest to many readers.

Roy's book was rich and complex enough to beat out Rushdie himself for the 1997 Booker Prize, but it was also captivating and simple enough to become a favorite with a host of enthusiastic readers unwilling to work their way through Rushdie's more challenging prose. Having become a multimillionaire and international celebrity overnight, Roy also inspired not a few other young South Asian women to try their hand at writing in a trend that continues to this day.

Since the novel first appeared she has expressed no interest in writing another and has concentrated instead on crafting a series of powerful and controversial essays on various issues ranging from the South Asian nuclear arms race to economic globalization. Not everyone admires her writing. From the beginning many dismissed her prose as overly precious and somewhat repetitive. Some South Asian critics claimed she was exoticizing their country, but most seemed to feel that for North Indians, at least, Kerala is indeed a foreign culture with more than a little exotic to it. The huge advance and international fame this young writer achieved on the book's first appearance aroused a great deal of controversy within India, where many seem to have felt that anyone so admired by ignorant outsiders must be lacking in authenticity. Yet many Indians also enjoyed and praised the work.

The various controversies involving Roy's essays have somewhat displaced discussion of her novel, which has received relatively little sustained academic attention; yet it remains popular and sells well in several languages, whereas most of Rushdie's books are out of print. For many readers, *The God of Small Things* served as their introduction to South Asian fiction, and if only for that reason no survey of recent novels from the region can ignore it.

Arundhati Roy was born on November 24, 1961, in the South Indian state of Kerala. Her mother was of Christian descent, as are about 20 percent of the people in Kerala, belonging to the Syrian Christian Church, which traditionally traces its origins back to St. Thomas, the disciple of Jesus, and certainly predates the first contact of Kerala during the Renaissance with the Roman Catholic tradition via Portuguese warships bent on acquiring the rich trade in spices for themselves. Her father was a Hindu whose family came from Bengal, and her relationship with him was evidently a troubled one. She refuses to discuss him in public. She remains close to her nearest sibling, her brother Lalith.

Her mother Mary ran a small school in the village of Aymanam on the Meenachil River near the town of Kottayam in central Kerala where Arundhati spent her childhood years. Mary achieved some fame by bringing a court case to establish the inheritance rights of Christian women in Kerala, so Arundhati would seem to have inherited her tendency toward social activism. Her uncle, George Isaac, founded and runs Palat Pickles, whose motto is "Emperor in the Realm of Taste."

Muslims, Hindus, and Christians live side by side in Kerala, but one of the most important influences during the era of Roy's childhood was Marxism. local Communists were very active during that whole period and finally achieved state power. Roy critiques their sincerity and efficacy in her novel, but those who took her to be a conservative or apolitical author were startled at the outspoken essays she began writing after the novel was published. Her criticisms of Marxism come from a radical perspective rather than a conservative one. It is the failure of Marxists to remain true to their own ideals that she objects to, not the ideals themselves.

Kerala is not only one of the most varied states in India, it is the most literate, and women from the region are generally regarded as having greater freedom and power than women elsewhere. This may not be immediately apparent to the foreign reader, who may view them as thoroughly subjugated to tyrannical men, but in fact they have strong wills and often exercise them.

When Roy was a teenager, her parents divorced; and at age sixteen, for reasons she has never discussed in detail, she left home to live on her own, winding up far to the north in a squatter's colony in the city of Delhi, surviving by selling empty beer bottles. Very little is known about this period of her life, but somehow she was able to enter the Delhi School of Architecture, and although she never practiced architecture as a trade, she has credited her architectural training with influencing the way she went about creating her novel, building the general framework first and then filling in the details.

She had a four-year marriage with a fellow student, Gerard da Cunha, and before marriage tried living a bohemian life with him in Goa, selling cake. Back in Delhi, she was spotted by film director Pradeep Krishen, who admired her beauty enough to start her on a short acting career with a small part in his film *Massey Sahib* (1985), and who was eventually to become her second husband. After writing for films and a television series that came to little, she became fairly widely known for a controversial essay about "bandit queen" Phoolan Devi, and then she devoted herself for the next five years to writing *The God of Small Things*. Roy also worked at one time as an aerobics instructor. Clearly there is nothing submissive or traditional about her, and her fearlessness is reflected in everything she writes.

The first challenge to the reader is keeping the main characters straight. The following list should help:

Rahel (girl) and **Esthappen Yako (Estha):** fraternal ("two-egg") twins, nine
   years old at the beginning of the story.
Ammu: their mother, born 1942. "Ammu" is a conventional name derived
   from the word for "mother": "Amma." We don't know her real name.
   Married to "Baba" ("father").
Baby Kochamma (born **Navomi Ipe**): Rahel and Estha's grandfather's sis-
   ter, their grand-aunt.
Sophie Mol ("Sophie girl"): the twins' cousin, daughter of their Uncle
   Chacko and Margaret Kochamma. Throughout the novel, "mol" is "girl"
   and "mon" is "boy."
Margaret Kochamma: daughter of English parents, former wife of Chacko,
   then of Joe; mother of Sophie Mol.
Mammachi (Shoshamma Ipe): blind grandmother of Rahel, Estha, and
   Sophie Mol; founder of the family pickle factory. "Mammachi" simply
   means "grandmother."
Pappachi (Benaan John Ipe): late abusive husband of Mammachi.
   ("Pappachi, of course, means "grandfather.")
Chacko: son of Mammachi; divorced first husband of Margaret.
Joe: second husband of Margaret; died 1969.
Kochu Maria: "Little Maria": the tiny cook of the household.
Larry McCaslin: Rahel's American husband.
Velutha Paapen: Paravan untouchable around whom much of the action
   revolves.
Vellya Paapen: his father.

The novel begins in 1992, as Rahel returns to her childhood home as an adult in a passage that establishes her as a survivor and as the character from whose viewpoint the story will be told. Early on are hints of death and other traumas. The work is structured as a spiral, moving repeatedly back and forth between "past" and "present" to fill in more and more details, finally revealing in its closing pages the central tragedy that blighted the twins' childhood and still haunts them. From time to time, Roy adds a detail or two, slowly creating a clearer image of this tragedy.

Estha is introduced as damaged, Ammu and Sophie Mol as dead—the first scene involving the latter is her funeral. As for Ammu, the fact that the Church refused her a Christian burial suggests she must have committed suicide in the hotel room to which she retreated at the end. Velutha's fate is alluded to in Rahel's vision of him falling from heaven. It is a tribute to the evocative power of Roy's prose that we can still become so involved with these doomed characters.

Although he appears only at intervals throughout the novel, Velutha is a crucial character. His story is told in reverse: first his death, then his punishment, and finally his "crime." But meanwhile we learn to see him through the twins' eyes, as a loving and talented young man—the only person to love them unconditionally. He is a Paravan, an "untouchable." Untouchability has been the subject of much discussion surrounding India, where the caste system relegated those born into "unclean" occupations such as butcher and latrine cleaner to a special status. In earlier days they often wore special outfits and were forced to observe a host of restrictions including avoiding the casting of defiling shadows on upper-caste people, calling out to warn of their coming, and drinking from special wells reserved for them. Their name comes from the belief that the touch of such a person ritually defiles the person touched, who has to undergo rituals of purification in consequence. The classic novel of the life of an untouchable "sweeper" (latrine cleaner) is Mulk Raj Anand's realistic and harsh *Untouchable* (1935), and a more recent realistic depiction of the sufferings of untouchables is contained in Rohinton Mistry's *A Fine Balance* (1995).

During the struggle for independence, Mahatma Gandhi stressed the achievement of equality for untouchables (also known as "pariahs") as a central part of his program, and progressive Indians regarded their mistreatment as a major obstacle to modernization. Gandhi called them *harijans,* or "children of God," and later they were referred to in law by the technical term "scheduled castes." The term *dalit* ("trampled upon" or "oppressed") is preferred by many untouchables themselves. After independence, untouchability was banned by the Constitution and affirmative action programs were created to promote their welfare. Many have risen to prominence, including Kocheril Raman Narayanan, who held the ceremonial post of president in the 1990s.

Yet, as Roy's novel suggests, prejudice against untouchables remains. One still hears from time to time of untouchables in remote villages beaten to death by infuriated mobs because they have dared to use the community well. Westerners are prone to feel somewhat smug about this particular blot on India's culture, but it is important to realize that every culture has its shunned groups. Velthua's story is like that of any number of people discriminated against in U.S. culture. He represents the outsider in general. He doesn't even follow his hereditary occupation, but works as a skilled woodcarver and mechanic.

As noted in the introduction to this chapter, Communists have played a prominent role in the history of Kerala, and they play a prominent role in the novel as well. Roy has stated that it was the image of a car with children in it surrounded by Marxist protesters that first came into her mind and formed the kernel of the novel. The Communist demonstrators obviously frighten the children, but it is important to note that they have valid complaints. Chacko exploits the workers at the pickle factory both by underpaying them and by seducing the women. This is not a novel in which children always see things more clearly than their elders; often they understand little of the significance of what is going on around them.

The story is told through Rahel. Estha has slowly retreated into an impenetrable silence that we at first attribute to the trauma of his encounter with the orangedrink lemondrink man, but we later learn was compounded by events that made him feel even more shocked and guilty.

In introducing Comrade Pillai, the local Communist leader, Roy mentions "the old omelette and eggs thing," an allusion to the notorious justification for the murderous brutality of the Terror during the French Revolution uttered by Robespierre: "One can't expect to make an omelet without breaking eggs." Roy returns to this expression more than once in the novel to indicate the heartlessness of certain adults and their willingness to inflict damage on others for their own ends.

Rahel is generally viewed by readers as a self-portrait of the author. She was born the same year as Roy, studied but did not practice architecture like Roy, and has a diamond in her nose like Roy. But so far as anyone has been able to determine, although the setting is definitely the same as that of Roy's childhood, and her brother has claimed the emotions expressed in the novel as true to their experience, the actual events of the plot do not seem to be based on reality. There was no real-life Sophie Mol, Roy's mother is still alive, she has never lived in the United States or married an American, and she has no twin. Although it is natural to be curious, the reader would do better to accept this tale as an affecting and meaningful fiction rather than try to decode it as a covert autobiography.

Note that as in *Jasmine* and several other South Asian novels, the United States is depicted as a violent, threatening place, but Rahel has left for home not so much to flee its violence as to be reunited with Estha, who has come back home after being exiled for two and a half decades following the tragic events of their ninth year. The outside world is rarely glimpsed in the novel except for the references to popular culture, which had penetrated India like Elvis Presley and *The Sound of Music*. Otherwise the West is featured as the source of harmful farming practices and idiotic television shows.

The passage about Keralese history at the end of the first chapter stresses events that resulted in discrimination and oppression. Marxists fight non-Marxists, the Dutch and Portuguese conquer and exploit the people of the region, and bigoted Catholics murder Syrian Christian bishops. All these "communal" conflicts are compared with the forces that separate the characters in the novel by forbidding their love for each other.

Several literary and mythological references are made to sources both Eastern and Western, an understanding of which will enrich the reading of the work. One probably little known to non-Indian readers is the story of Kunti and Karna, from the great Indian epic the *Mahabharata*. Kunti reveals to Karna that he is her eldest son, and thus the older brother of his sworn enemies, the Pandavas. She tries in vain to convince Karna that he should not fight them. However, he rejects her advice and eventually becomes the commander of the Kaurava army arrayed against his brothers. Because she had abandoned Karna in infancy and he had been brought up as a commoner in ignorance of his noble heritage, he suffered many indignities that might be compared to those of Velutha in *The God of Small Things.* The full story is told in Chapter 12 of Roy's novel. Karna is eventually slain in battle by his brother Arjuna.

The story of Poothana and Krishna is a famous episode from the infancy of the great savior god. Poothana was a demon who tried in vain to kill the infant Krishna by giving him her poisonous breast. Although his astounding powers allowed him to thrive despite her attempts on his life, her poison turned his skin dark blue or black.

The story of Bhima, Dushasana, and Draupadi is another tale from the *Mahabharata,* in which an apocalyptic world-spanning war is triggered when the five Pandavas foolishly wager their joint wife, Draupadi, in a rigged game of chance against their enemies, the Kauravas. Dushasana, one of the most important Kauravas, is responsible for dragging Draupadi forward just after their side has won her and attempting to strip her naked (although this attempt is foiled by a miracle). Bhima, the second of the Pandava brothers married to Draupadi, and especially noted for his strength (he was the rival of Dushasana in wrestling prowess), swears to take vengeance on Dushasana by drinking his blood. Draupadi, however, says she wants to bathe her hair in Dushasana's blood, and she does not fasten up or wash her hair until she can do so. Toward the end of the climactic battle, Bhima exacts the revenge described in the passage retold here in Chapter 12, in the process killing a man who, like all the Kauravas, is his cousin. This is another instance of causing the death of those closest to you, a theme central to the novel.

The lines from Sir Walter Scott's "Young Lochinvar," which are mangled by Latha, are as follows in the original:

> O, young Lochinvar is come out of the west,
> Through all the wide Border his steed was the best;
> And, save his good broadsword, he weapons had none,
> He rode all unarmed, and he rode all alone.
> He swam the Eske River where ford there was none,
> But, ere he alighted at Netherby gate,
> The bride had consented, the gallant came late

It is probably not a coincidence that this poem concerns a fatal tryst involving a water crossing. Velthua is Lochinvar. Lenin's contribution is the famous funeral oration of Antony over the body of his slain friend from Shakespeare's *Julius Caesar,* which had earlier been more than once alluded to by quoting the dying words put in Caesar's mouth by Shakespeare as the dying emperor realizes that one of his assassins is someone he cares deeply for and admires: "Et tu, Brute?" ("You too, Brutus?") The twins will stumble into playing the role of Brutus themselves.

On a lighter note, there is the little rhyme that begins *koo-koo koodum theevandi*. Schoolchildren of Roy's generation encountered it in a popular Malayalam reader:

> The train screams koo-koo-koo
> The train sings and screams
> The train runs day and night
> The train stops, exhausted.

The phrase "Spring-thunder" at the end of Chapter 14 is a particularly obscure allusion. "Spring Thunder over India" was the title of a Chinese editorial hailing the Indian Naxalite (Maoist-influenced) Communist rebellion in the *People's Daily,* organ of the Central Committee of the Communist Party of China, July 5, 1967. (It was reproduced in *Liberation* 1.1, Nov. 1967.) Since then the phrase has come to stand for Keralite communism generally.

Finally, the song remembered by Rahel at the end of the novel is "Ruby Tuesday," an early hit by the Rolling Stones. The song concerns parting from a loved one, but this particular stanza emphasizes the urgency of acting on love in the present.

Ammu is depicted as a romantic. She would seem to be basically a decent person, but she is extremely self-centered. She wreaks havoc by pursuing her passions without regard for how she may harm others. She responds to her son's enthusiastic account of her birthday by critiquing his spelling. Her fatal flaw as a mother is to make her love for her children conditional on their pleasing her. They are starved for her affection and terrified of losing her. Their status in the family is precarious, expressed in the phrase "No locusts stand I," which is their childish misunderstanding of the legal phrase *locus standi* (legal standing) and in the course of the novel comes to mean something like "homelessness," or "abandonment." Unlike Velutha, Ammu cannot enter the twins' childhood world, although she behaves with the impulsiveness of a child herself.

Roy often combines sophisticated irony with heartfelt pathos—a combination that prevents her novel from sinking into simple sentimentality—and this is nowhere more apparent than in the scene of Estha's molestation by the orangedrink lemondrink man. The man's actions are horrible and absurd at the same time. Estha's reaction is uncomprehending revulsion compounded by terror that the man will track him down at home and make him suffer terribly if he tells. Although we see glimpses of Estha's state of mind, he is young and inarticulate, and it is only through his increasing numbness and silence that we realize the depth of the damage done him.

This is a crucial scene in the history of Ammu's betrayals of her children, for she sees his abuser as a "nice man" and rebukes the boy for his reaction. Rahel's sarcastic comment that her mother might as well marry him naturally strikes horror into Estha. Of course Ammu doesn't know what has happened, but a more sensitive parent might have noticed that something was seriously wrong. She responds to their sulkiness with this unforgivable phrase that devastates the insecure twins: "When you hurt people, they begin to love you less." Rahel would welcome any punishment other than the diminishment of her mother's love. For the rest of the novel the children are anxiously clinging to her, to Velutha, to each other, starved for affection and envious of their spoiled cousin Sophie Mol, loved from the beginning, without question or possibility of challenge. She is emotionally secure in a way they will never be.

She enters their lives at the moment of their greatest vulnerability, and Roy depicts their typically childish moody, unruly behavior in the airport brilliantly. Their failure to be nice to their cousin is based less on inherent naughtiness than on profound insecurity. She signifies a change for the worse in their lives. The dead elephant they encounter on the way out of the airport is an ominous portent of the disasters that will follow in the wake of Sophie Mol.

Roy may empathize with children, but she does not idealize them. Rahel takes out her fears and frustrations on the column of ants she systematically squashes. Powerless in real life, she has the power of a wrathful god over these helpless creatures, these small things. Like Velutha, the more kindly "god of small things" of the book's title, the power she has is fragile, illusory.

The erotic attraction that is going on over the children's heads is reflected in a pair of passages: at the end of Chapter 10, Velutha is thinking yearningly of Ammu, and at the beginning of Chapter 11, Ammu is dreaming of him. She shrugs off the yearning affection of her children, more and more seeing herself as a lover, not as a mother. It is no coincidence that the story portrayed by the Kathakali dancers in the immediately succeeding scene is one in which a mother abandons her child.

The story of Margaret Kochamma's disastrous love for Chacko is told just before the story of Ammu's even more disastrous love for Velutha. All of the adults damage those they love and marry, even the Kathakali dancer who portrays a delicate woman on the stage and goes home to beat his wife. Only the twins love each other unconditionally, and they are traumatically separated at the very moment when they need each other most.

Chacko had at first admired Margaret for her independence and helped her to accept herself in a way no one had previously done. In addition, Chacko is not only a victimizer; he is also a victim, hurt by Margaret's insensitivity as she happily informs him of what a good father her new husband Joe is. When Joe dies, she turns again to Chacko, not because she really responds to his continued love for her, but because she needs the familiar sense of security he provides—ironically, because her return to him is what makes possible her daughter's death.

Chacko benefits from the pro-male bias of his family: his mother and Baby Kochamma tolerate his constant philandering but are outraged at Ammu's love affair. Although Roy emphasizes they are especially outraged by the fact that her lover is an untouchable, Chacko had certainly slept with untouchable women while they turned a blind eye. What makes Ammu's sin unforgivable in their eyes is that she is a woman.

The yearning for love is a major theme throughout the novel, affecting several characters young and old, as we have seen. But the surprising one is Sophie Mol, who, after scorning Estha and Rahel, decides she would like to befriend them. Most children crave membership in peer groups, and Sophie Mol's sense of superiority does not satisfy that craving. But we already know she will never really belong. Her very need will doom her.

The passage in Chapter 14 in which Comrade Pillai betrays Velutha aroused intense criticism and resentment among Marxists in India, but others have argued that he is not untypical of many radicals who are incapable of seeing how they exploit and oppress others. A particularly vivid instance of this is the moment in which Pillai wipes his sweaty armpits with his shirt and hands it to his wife, who holds it "as though it was a gift." Her role in this relationship is clearly defined. Pillai is not building the sort of revolution that will truly benefit the women around him. Pillai dismisses Velutha as a "Comprador capitalist," a Marxist insult suggesting that the untouchable is a sellout, one who collaborates with the exploiters of the working class. But Roy suggests it is not the fact that Velutha has crossed class lines that so offends Comrade Pillai, but that he has crossed caste lines.

The most tragic betrayal of all is committed by Estha and Rahel, without really comprehending what they are doing. They sacrifice the only adult who truly cares for them for a mother who will abandon them—because of what they did in trying to rescue her. The irony is underlined in the title of the chapter, "Saving Ammu." The guilt is overwhelming, silencing Estha. Having on this occasion spoken disastrously, he will speak less and less until he lapses into complete muteness. This, we realize, is the key to all the ominous riddles planted earlier in the novel. When we are told the twins think they are saving Ammu, we remember with a pang that we have already read of her death. Nothing is more devastating for a child than to be made to feel responsible for a tragedy. The fact that they have been manipulated into what they do by adults is of course not understood by the children, nor have they understood in the slightest the relationship between Ammu and Velutha.

The short scene toward the end of the novel in which Rahel makes love with Estha has naturally aroused intense interest; but Roy provides few clues as to how it should be interpreted. Some readers assume this must be just the final cataclysmic act in a series of disasters, but others see it as a healing embrace between the only two characters in the novel who have selflessly loved each other. It seems likely that Roy was not holding them up as role models, but instead underlining the extreme nature of the anguish they have experienced as children and whose aftermath they have endured as adults. So close as to make almost one person during their childhood, they were abruptly ripped apart and have lived in painful isolation from each other ever since. But this act of incestuous love is such an extreme gesture that many readers are troubled by the way in which it is so fleetingly presented, without any hint of consequences to follow.

One of the novel's most ingenious architectural details is the postponement of the climactic, very explicit, and passionate lovemaking scene between Ammu and Velutha to the very end of the novel. We already know the fatal consequences of this affair, in great detail. But now Roy wants us to experience their mutual passion directly. Instead of blaming the lovers, she presents them as victims. It is jealousy, bigotry, ignorance, and lust for power that causes the calamities that destroy them—it would be wrong to blame love itself. This is a variation on the old Romeo-and-Juliet theme of lovers doomed by a society that refuses to make room for a romance that transcends the petty conflicts and prejudices swirling around them.

Ironically, her attempt to bridge the gap between castes resulted in charges being brought against Roy in 1997 by a lawyer who accused her of obscenity. He was widely suspected of having been offended not so much by the explicitness of the sex in the novel as that it positively portrayed an affair between an upper-caste woman and an untouchable.

That the book ends with the word "tomorrow" is not a bit of cheap irony. Roy is hinting that perhaps the world can change. Velutha and Ammu did not get their tomorrow, but if the people around them can learn from their story and open their hearts, a better tomorrow is possible.

SELECTED BIBLIOGRAPHY

Baneth-Nouailhetas, Émilienne. *The God of Small Things: Arundhati Roy.* Paris: Armand Colin, 2002.
   An excellent analysis of the major themes in the novel. Worth struggling through its academic language.

Brians, Paul. "Arundhati Roy: *The God of Small Things* Study Guide." <http://www.wsu.edu/~brians/anglophone/roy.html>.
   Detailed annotations to various allusions and images in the novel, including several too numerous to discuss here.

Dhawan, R. K., ed. *Arundhati Roy: The Novelist Extraordinary.* New Delhi: Prestige Books, 1999.

An uneven but comprehensive collection of short pieces on Roy from various points of view; especially interesting for its emphasis on South Asian critics and reviewers.

Jana, Reena. "Winds, Rivers, & Rain." *Salon* 30 Sept. 1997. <http://www.salon.com/sept97/00roy.html>.
One of the more interesting and accessible of Roy's many interviews.

Roy, Arundhati. *The Cost of Living*. New York: Random House, 1999.
Essays on various public issues.

———. *The God of Small Things*. New York: Random House, 1997.
Thus far, Roy's only published work of fiction.

———. *Power Politics*. Cambridge, MA: South End Press, 2001.
More essays, mostly on globalization.

Sharma, R. S. *Arundhati Roy's* The God of Small Things: *Critique and Commentary*. New Delhi: Creative Books, 1998.
A detailed discussion of various aspects of the novel.

Simmons, Jon. "Arundhati Roy." <http://website.lineone.net/~jon.simmons/roy/index.htm>. Accessed 1 Sept. 2003.
A very helpful Web site that provided most of the biographical details for this chapter.

Chapter 13
Michael Ondaatje: Anil's Ghost (2000)

Michael Ondaatje was born on September 12, 1943, to well-to-do parents in the Sri Lankan capital city of Colombo. Although his life was at first relatively luxurious, his father's alcoholism led to the collapse of the family finances and the breakup of his parents' marriage in 1948 while he was still a small child. His mother worked in local hotels to support her children for four years, sending Michael to St. Thomas College in Colombo, then moved with them to London where she worked in a boarding house. Michael continued his schooling in England at Dulwich College until 1962, when he emigrated to Canada to join his elder brother Christopher in Montreal.

In Canada he studied for a BA in English and history at Bishop's University, Quebec, and the University of Toronto from 1962 to 1965. In 1964 Ondaatje married artist Kim Jones, with whom he had two children (the couple separated in 1980 and he married again, this time to novelist Kim Spaulding). He went on to get an MA at Queen's University, Kingston, Ontario, in 1967. While doing graduate work, he began to publish his poetry and won a prize for his writing. He taught English at the University of Western Ontario and later at Glendon College, York University, as well as holding visiting positions in Hawaii, Rome, Turin, and at Brown University in Providence, Rhode Island.

During the early part of his career, Ondaatje was known primarily as a poet, publishing several well-reviewed volumes of poetry, including the lengthy verse narrative, *The Collected Works of Billy the Kid* (1970), the first of several books in which he takes historical characters and settings and reshapes them into new fictional creations. The combination of serious research and playful invention in his various books has some of the same qualities as the well-known writing of E. L. Doctorow, notably *Ragtime* (1975). His first extended piece of prose fiction was *Coming through Slaughter* (1976), a series of imaginary scenes from the life of the pioneer New Orleans jazz trumpeter Buddy Bolden, the real facts of whose life are almost entirely unknown. From this point on, music was destined to be a continuing theme in his fiction.

In 1976 he visited India for the first time, to attend a conference on Commonwealth literature. In 1978 he returned to Sri Lanka for the first time since childhood and spent five months visiting with family and exploring his roots, returning for another extended visit in 1980, resulting in the slightly fictionalized family memoir *Running in the Family* (1982), which focuses on the colorful figures of his maternal grandmother and his father and depicts in a comic way the catastrophic collapse of the family. This work, like *Coming through Slaughter,* is more a series of sketches than a novel.

Throughout this period Ondaatje continued to produce poetry, increasingly including poems with Sri Lankan themes. But his next book had an entirely Canadian setting. *In the Skin of the Lion* (1987) is more recognizably a novel than anything he had produced so far. Set in the 1920s, its characters and incidents are freely invented, although placed against a background of historical events.

But Ondaatje was to achieve worldwide fame when he won the Booker Prize for his next novel, *The English Patient* (1992), in which two of the characters from *In the Skin of the Lion* reappear, now in Italy during the waning days of World War II. Ondaatje's language—always rich and polished—achieved an intensity in this work that captivated both critics and ordinary readers. The novel is an intricate mystery in which people slowly reveal themselves and their histories as their lives become increasingly entangled with each other. One of the main characters is Kripal Singh ("Kip"), an Indian Sikh who is an expert in defusing unexploded bombs and mines. He is Ondaatje's first fully developed South Asian fictional character, and the irony of his devotion to his work for the British while they are ruling his homeland is made clear. He is also a romantic figure, a more successful lover than Caravaggio, one of the characters carried over from the earlier novel.

The 1996 film version of *The English Patient* brought Ondaatje to the attention of a much wider audience, although at the cost of deemphasizing his South Asian roots, for it reduces Kip to a relatively minor role and brings to the foreground the English married couple around whom much of the plot pivots. The political aspects of Ondaatje's work are muted to emphasize romance. Whether in reaction or not, in his next novel he was to plunge fully into the world of politics.

Anil's Ghost appeared in 2000 to generally enthusiastic reviews, although it remains far less popular than *The English Patient*. It is the first of his prose works thus far that can be squarely placed in the framework of South Asian fiction. Its background is the ongoing civil war in Sri Lanka during the late

1980s and early 1990s. For general background to this struggle, see Chapter 10 on Shyam Selvadurai's *Funny Boy.* But it may be useful to add some historical details relevant to this particular work.

In the author's note with which the book begins, Ondaatje comments that the conflict in Sri Lanka had three sides: "the government, the antigovernment insurgents in the south and the separatist guerillas in the north." Other than that, he avoids identifying the various groups that are so ferociously fighting each other. The long-standing conflict between the Tamil minority (the north) and the Sinhalese majority (the government) was complicated when radical Sinhalese students launched their own rebellion (the south). The leading southern rebel group was the Janatha Vimukthi Perumuna ("People's Liberation Front"), normally referred to as the JVP. Its founder, Rohana Wijeweera, had studied at a Soviet university and brought a rural, lower-class revolutionary attitude to his rebellion, both anti-Tamil and antigovernment. This is the main group the government is fighting in *Anil's Ghost,* although it is never mentioned by name.

On November 13, 1971, Wijeweera was killed under circumstances that are still unclear. JVP members accused the government of having murdered him while he was in their custody. In 1989 one Lionel Ranasinghe was arrested, with the government claiming he had been responsible for Wijeweera's death, to widespread public skepticism. Ranasinghe operated under the alias "Gamini," and Ondaatje's use of this name for one of the main characters in his novel may be a subtle allusion to this incident.

Meanwhile the Tamil Tigers were continuing their campaign for a separate Tamil state, engaging in a wide variety of terrorist acts, including a number of suicide bombings, the most politically significant of which was the assassination of President Ranasinghe Premadasa on May 1, 1993. This is the event that is fictionalized as the assassination of President Katagula in *Anil's Ghost.* Just a year before the novel was published, the new prime minister, Chandrika Kumaratunga, was injured by another suicide bomber. And the violence was not limited to Sri Lanka. On May 21, 1991, the prime minister of India, Rajiv Gandhi, was assassinated by Tamil separatists. His mother Indira had initially supported their cause, but both mother and son earned the enmity of the Tigers when they eventually came to oppose a separate state for Tamils.

All three sides engaged in a wide variety of acts of terror. Mobs of government police and soldiers would descend on villages suspected of disloyalty and slaughter the residents indiscriminately; torture, kidnapping, and secret murders were routine government policy. The JVP did not limit its own acts of terror to opposing the government; they often used violence to intimidate other ordinary citizens who disagreed with them. The Tamil Tigers for their part became notorious for kidnapping children and forcing them to become soldiers for their cause and for committing many atrocities against other Tamils as well as against their Sinhalese foes.

After decades of escalating conflict, which produced an estimated death toll of some sixty thousand victims, a degree of exhaustion began to set in. Many Sri Lankans simply wanted the violence to end. All sides had discredited themselves in many people's eyes and seemed often to be fighting more out of a desire for vengeance than for any rational political cause. A turning point seems to have been reached when the Tigers announced a cease-fire in 2001, and the next year they publicly renounced their goal of a separate Tamil state during negotiations with the government.

This conflict is the backdrop for Ondaatje's novel, which takes a stand against the violence on all sides. Naturally, Sri Lankans who still feel committed to one group or another in this bloody struggle are liable to feel that a novel which refuses to take sides—or to even identify them—is irresponsible and escapist. Some have argued that Ondaatje has no right as an outsider—living in Canada throughout most of the conflict—to lecture Sri Lankan citizens on their misdeeds. But for others, Ondaatje articulates a widespread feeling that the combatants had lost all sense of humanity. As an emigré writer living abroad, he has the freedom to voice a protest that many sympathize with, against the madness that has terrorized Sri Lankans on all sides for so long.

Ondaatje has sometimes been considered even more of an outsider because of his family's European origins, although they emigrated to Sri Lanka some four centuries ago. It's worth noting that his father always insisted he was himself part Tamil. Unless a strict racial litmus test is applied, Ondaatje would seem to be as authentic a South Asian writer as many others who receive that label with even less justification. He is acutely aware of his ambiguous status. Reinforcing his connection with the island, he used the money from the Booker Prize to establish the Gratiaen literary award for Sri Lankan writers resident in the country.

Readers' political biases are thus liable to have a powerful effect on how they view *Anil's Ghost*. Readers also differ on the literary merits of the work. Some find its plot confusing or its central character unconvincing. Others hail it as a worthy successor to *The English Patient*. Clearly, like that novel, it is to some degree a mystery written in a complex way. Characters are introduced whose connection with the plot becomes clear only gradually. The obvious mystery—assigning responsibility for a political killing—is surrounded by the many secrets of the various characters who are trying to solve the murder.

This is a novel for readers who like puzzles, who enjoy using their wits to decipher a book, although ultimately it is far more straightforward and easy to follow than *The English Patient*. And of course it is for readers who are willing to follow a brilliant writer in exploring the horrors of a nightmarish war whose effects on particular individuals are vividly depicted. Despite its sometimes grim themes, *The English Patient* was in the end a charming work—essentially a love story. In contrast, *Anil's Ghost* powerfully depicts human moral courage in the face of overwhelming evil.

The novel opens with the title character's arrival, as she experiences the noisy eruption of the day in Sri Lanka, reminding her of the old Rudyard Kipling poem "By the old Moulmein Pagoda lookin' eastward to the sea" in which the Burmese dawn is said to come up "like thunder out of China 'crost the bay." (The poem was also turned into a once-popular song called "The Road to Mandalay.") That she views her surroundings through such an image marks her as now an outsider who is welcomed back with some suspicion to the land of her birth fifteen years after leaving. Anil Tissera is a forensic pathologist. (Is it possible that Ondaatje was influenced by the popularity of that other attractive female forensic pathologist, Scully of television's *The X-Files?*) Anil works for a human rights organization within the United Nations.

Her attitude toward war and its victims causes her to think of the caustic satire of the seventh-century Greek poet Archilochus, who attributed the havoc wreaked by soldiers in his own time to the same motives as those she associates with modern terrorists, both leaving mutilated bodies behind as a warning to those who would oppose them. It is Anil's job to dig past the shield of terror to the truth about political murder. The use of these very different literary allusions in the space of the novel's first ten pages tells us we are dealing with a sophisticated and cultured woman.

On page 13 comes the first of several italicized passages that will occur regularly in the novel, taking us away from the immediate scene of the action but often providing important bits of imagery or information. Here we get a glimpse of Palipana, a character Anil meets much later in the novel. The scene is the ruin of a Buddhist shrine, vandalized by greedy and careless early Japanese archeologists. The mutilated figures stand for the sufferings of Sri Lanka itself; and this scene will at the end of the novel be balanced by another, more hopeful one in a similar setting in which vandalism is repaired.

The meeting with the students in Kynsey Road Hospital tells us something about her methods of working, but it is more important for establishing the atmosphere of terror in which these students live, who have to imagine a young man being beaten while praying. That the second victim was probably dropped from a helicopter establishes that he is probably a victim of the government—the same government officially sponsoring her investigation. Anil is caught from the beginning in a perilous situation, summoned by officials steeped in murder to investigate murders. Foreign human rights organizations and trading partners have caused the government to essentially call for an investigation that it is in their interest to frustrate. Anil is in danger of playing the classic crime-novel role of the person who "knows too much."

Her consciousness of this danger will be reflected later when she muses on a relevant quotation from Alexandre Dumas's famous novel *The Man in the Iron Mask,* which she evidently read in a Spanish translation while working in Latin America because she also alludes to it by its Spanish title: "We are often criminals in the eyes of the earth, not only for having committed crimes, but because we know that crimes have been committed" (54). She pairs this work with another French novel about an innocent man unjustly and tyrannically imprisoned for years: Victor Hugo's *Les Miserables* (fans of the musical version may remember Enjolras as the student leader of the uprising).

Anil's brief memory of her parents in the rain is one of the few in the book that links her back to Sri Lanka. Their death while she was young can be presumed to have helped move her toward a career in which she wrestles daily with death, trying to comprehend what seems incomprehensible. Her curiosity about her father later in the book resembles Ondaatje's curiosity about his own father, whom he barely knew. Her rootlessness has been criticized by some readers; but the novel wants to show her as initially distant, only gradually becoming enmeshed with the people she meets in Sri Lanka. She strives to shrug off her old identity as a swimmer and be treated only as a professional. The insistence of Sarath in asking whether she is married and has children within minutes of meeting her is not a sign he is interested in dating her; it is absolutely typical of most South Asians that they will put these questions to any apparently unattached young professional woman upon first meeting her, for such a woman is an anomaly. It is to Sarath's credit that he quickly begins to treat her as the expert investigator she is.

Sarath Diyasena, as an archeologist, is the historical counterpart to Anil. He also studies bones to discover their secrets; but the secrets he uncovers are not normally as loaded with contemporary meaning—and danger. He seems reluctant at first to trust a stranger who risks bringing the wrath of the government down on both their heads and cultivates a studied political neutrality. When Anil sums up the situation in Sri Lanka by sarcastically toasting "every political opinion supported by its own army," he refuses to be drawn into a political discussion and accuses her of sounding like a visiting journalist. But as he becomes more and more enmeshed in her investigation, he gradually shifts away from this neutral posture.

The joking Anil engages in while at work may seem shocking, but those who work constantly with the remains of the dead often develop a macabre sense of humor to deal with the terrors of their subject matter. By the end of her first examination she learns what Sarath has already suspected: the dead man was probably killed by government forces and his corpse transported to another location to make it look like an ancient burial. Because she must prove her suspicions to hostile authorities, she needs to trace the story of this murder in more detail, by establishing first of all the victim's identity, a task that will take most of the rest of the novel.

Anil's visit to her old nanny reinforces her sense of separation from her roots and reminds us of the Tamil side of the conflict, because Lalitha mentions that she works in the refugee camps up north. Anil is Sinhalese, although she seems like many upper-class Sri Lankans to have been raised mainly speaking English. The relationship between the two women underlines the tangled history of these two groups in Sri Lanka.

The italicized passage about the assassination of a government official on a train, probably by a JVP member, serves to remind us of the brutality on both sides. Neither side is pure villain or pure victim.

In the immediately following section we are introduced to Anil's lover Cullis. It is typical of Ondaatje's technique that at first we know nothing of this relationship and read only some pages later how they met, and at the very end of the section we realize that he is married to someone else. No sooner do we learn that she has someone to love than we learn there are problems. We see Anil more and more as an isolated loner, an orphan, a loser in love.

Readers may wonder at the repeated references to Anil's sexuality throughout the novel. Many of her memories of the United States involve sexual relationships, and she is repeatedly shown undressing or otherwise behaving in an erotic fashion in the novel.

Some are quick to suspect that authors throw this emphasis into their writing for commercial reasons; but in fact modern fiction so routinely incorporates sex scenes that Ondaatje can hardly be accused of unusual sensationalism. In fact, all his other books deal more heavily and explicitly with sex than this one. One way to view Anil's sexuality is to liken it to her love of music—an intense source of pleasure that connects her with life and helps stave off the chaos of torture and death that makes up her working environment. It is not uncommon when people feel threatened for them to think of the people they love, and throughout this novel Anil is threatened with the gravest danger. In this context, eros means life and symbolizes everything Anil is risking by standing up for human rights. Thinking about sex is a way of reminding herself, "Yes, despite everything, I'm still alive."

The conversation between the two lovers involves a few pop-culture allusions. James Bigglesworth ("Biggles"), the fictional hero of a long series of stories about a British Royal Flying Corps pilot, was created by W. E. Johns and is of special interest to South Asians because Biggles was depicted as having been born and spent his childhood in India. When Anil reveals she is a rabid Prince fan, it is the first step in unveiling her passion for popular music.

The next italicized passage about the atlas muses on the absence of human beings from its geography. Sri Lanka used to be known for its products, its beauty, its climate; now it is known abroad almost entirely for its political geography, defined by the mutual hostility of the people who inhabit it. This is why the atlas seems to come from another time.

This passage is followed by a list of the "disappeared" being studied by Anil, which underlines the way that violence descends abruptly into everyday life, among the most mundane activities. As the book goes on, we learn together with Anil more and more about the conflict into which she has been plunged, which is precisely Ondaatje's purpose. The final words in this passage reflect the novelist's view that the Sri Lankan conflict has become emptied of meaning and degenerated into a self-perpetuating catastrophe.

Finally, as Sarath takes Anil into the hills, we learn who Palipana is: his former teacher, a brilliant archeologist who ultimately lost his reputation and wound up isolated and blind in the wilderness for reasons explained in the book. He is just one of a series of experts who are recruited to work on the mystery of the relocated corpse. On one level this seems like a typical fantasy quest plot device, assembling a team of experts with varied skills to complete a challenging task: but in fact their task is to demonstrate to us the many-sided reality that is modern Sri Lanka. It is not what they tell Anil about the body that is most important, but what they reveal about themselves. Once this is understood it becomes clearer why Anil herself is not more fully fleshed out. She is here as a witness, a vehicle through which we learn about the conflict in her homeland. This is not primarily her story, but Sri Lanka's.

The corpse is irreverently dubbed "Sailor," according to the old children's counting rhyme that begins "Tinker, tailor, / Soldier, sailor, / Rich man, poor man, / Beggar-man, thief." Little girls used to recite it to determine what sort of man they would marry. The name is part of the grim humor hinted at throughout the text.

As Anil works more and more with Sarath, she begins to think of herself as a modern archeologist—uncovering traces of a contemporary catastrophe similar to famous historic ones like the volcanic eruption that buried Pompeii and created casts of dead bodies caught in the ash; or like Laetoli, where footprints of fleeing hominids and other animals were left behind in African volcanic ash; or like Hiroshima, where the flash of the nuclear bomb that destroyed the city burned the silhouettes of people caught by it into walls and roadsides. The victims of these disasters are nameless, but she feels she can somehow redeem a bit of the past by assigning an identity to at least this one victim.

In the following section we learn that Sarath did not tell Anil the whole truth about his wife. This is important because it helps explain why he is so estranged from his brother, who will grow in importance in the latter part of the novel. Their tangled relationship will be slowly revealed in passages scattered throughout the remainder of the book.

The writers whose books Anil finds in the rest house are all popular British authors of the sort a reader would enjoy who identified more with England than with South Asia. The Anglo-Indian John Masters wrote sensational novels about India like *Bhowani Junction,* and he often comes in for criticism when South Asians take the English to task for distorting their reality.

Anil's consciousness of her vulnerability is conveyed in a symbolically vivid form when she falls sick with a fever and dreams that her naked body is being traced on the floor beside the skeletons they have been working on, resembling the way that police detectives outline the position of a murder victim on the ground. It seems only too possible that she might join Sailor as one of the government's victims.

When in her feverish stupor she has an incoherent phone conversation with Leaf, the Cherry Valance she refers to is neither the rock band by that name nor the character in S. E. Hinton's *The Outsiders,* but a gunslinger in *Red River,* the famous 1948 Western directed by Howard Hawks. This is an early hint of Anil and Leaf's shared obsession with trivia from classic Hollywood Westerns, and all will be made clear in a passage toward the end of the book. There may also be another, more subtle allusion here. Note that Ondaatje reveals Leaf's gender for the first time in this passage, leaving unclear for the moment the nature of their relationship. Valance has been treated by gay film critics as a covert homoerotic character, which may explain why Leaf and Anil might have discussed him. It is also another reminder of how much Anil fears for her life.

The quotation by the chief medical officer's door in Kynsey Road Hospital is often posted—usually in Latin—at the entrance to human anatomy labs where students and specialists like Anil work on corpses. Its admonition to awed silence conflicts with the irreverent, noisy habits of the pathologists depicted in the novel, and it is balanced by the bawdy song Anil has running through her head a couple of pages later. Note that she likes the song not so much for its obscenity but because she loves "songs of anger and judgement" (70).

This is also the passage in which we learn how Anil got her first name. Some South Asian readers find it implausible that a Sri Lankan girl would have claimed and borne a boy's name, and Ondaatje's claim that she did suggests to them his lack of understanding of the culture. But for other readers the incident works well enough to single her out as a strong individualist who follows her own instincts regardless of what others think of her, and it also demonstrates her desire to link with the past, for the name was her grandfather's. The central characters of novels are rarely supposed to be merely typical of the cultures they come from; almost by definition, they are exceptional.

In the passage that follows, Anil adds Chitra, the expert on insect pupae, to her investigative team. She will contribute useful information, but she is also a reminder that Anil is not unique as a Sri Lankan woman in carving out a career for herself in a male-dominated scientific field.

When Sarath photographs the skeleton and prepares to mail the resulting Polaroids, we become aware that he fears the evidence he is uncovering may be destroyed and he is trying to preserve it. It is no surprise that this section ends with Sarath acknowledging that he and Anil need help.

That help at first takes the form of the blind epigraphist Palipana in the next section, entitled "The Grove of Ascetics" after the ruins of a Buddhist monastic forest retreat where he now lives. His specialty, Pali, is the language in which the sacred texts of Theravada Buddhism were first written down in Sri Lanka and later spread all over Buddhist Asia. Palipana's name obviously connects him with the language. He is presented here as possibly deluded but not fraudulent, despite the beliefs of his fellow anthropologists who follow the pattern laid down by the French Napoleonic Code in considering the accused to be guilty until he can prove himself innocent. In the novel, he plays the role of the retired gunslinger or samurai warrior summoned back for one last battle combined with an all-wise Yoda figure.

The hostility of early Buddhist monks to idols ("graven images" is the equivalent biblical phrase from the Ten Commandments) is treated colorfully here, appropriately because the author is telling the story of someone whose expertise is text, not pictures. Early Theravada Buddhism abhorred images of the Buddha and preferred to depict only symbols at one remove from him, like his footprints or his begging bowl. As the novel makes clear, later Buddhists slid back into the Hindu practice of carving and painting images for worship.

The story jumps abruptly from the scene with the blind epigraphist to another—seemingly unrelated—passage in italics that we will eventually realize is our introduction to the next member of the research team, a young gem miner named Ananda. The reader has to mentally tuck away these little scenes and fit them into the puzzle as their place later becomes apparent. The last sentence of the passage is ominous in underlining his vulnerability.

The passage in which Palipana explains to them the tradition of *Netra Mangala* is often referred to in discussions of the novel, and it is clear enough to need no further explanation; but notice that this fascinating tradition centered on sight is being explained by a blind man. Seeing leads to understanding, but the seeing need not be literal. Sailor will leap into life when he is sufficiently understood, although his face will never be clearly *seen*.

It is while trying to sleep in this peaceful setting that Anil's mind wanders back to her parting scene with Cullis. We realize first, how very alone she really is in the world and, second, that she understands from personal experience the human potential for violence.

Despite being one of the most vividly depicted characters in the novel, Palipana really does not move the solution of the mystery along very much. What he does instead is convey to us the story of his niece Lakma, yet another victim of the pervasive violence. Like Anil, she has great reserves of inner strength. She is a survivor, obviously destined to become a highly skilled scholar, yet another example of a Sri Lankan woman with ambition. It's worth remembering that Sri Lanka elected the world's first woman head of state and later put her daughter in the same office. It is not safe to assume that we know the limits of women's lives in cultures like this.

On the way back to Colombo, their encounter with the man whose hands have been pierced reminds us naturally of Anil having similarly stabbed Cullis. Then she expressed her fury in violence; now she will use her expertise to fight violence.

The section titled "A Brother" marks a major shift in the focus of the novel. Before now, we have been mainly following Sarath as he assists Anil's research. Now we turn to Gamini, a character who has been shadowy up to this point. Emotionally exhausted by the suffering of the endless numbers of victims he must treat, he has ended by turning against the idea that war is ever just. No matter how noble its supposed purpose, every war, he believes, becomes warped by the carelessness—literally, the lack of caring—of those with the power to wage it. But unlike his brother, he cannot retreat from the conflict into his professional interests; his job has become dealing with the horrible results of war.

We get the story of the kidnapping of Dr. Linus Corea, forced to work for the insurgents, an account that paints a not unsympathetic portrait of them; but this is immediately followed by an account of how insurgents killed other medical personnel trying to save the lives of their victims. Some readers have seen in Ondaatje's work a bias toward one side or the other; but he seems to have gone to considerable trouble to balance his narrative in this way.

It is typical of Ondaatje's cinematic technique that we have these scenes of Gamini at work before we switch point of view to see Sarath and Anil going to visit him and learn that the two men are brothers. Their alienation, caused by the love of both men for the same woman, is profound, but Anil brings them together briefly on an errand of mercy. Gamini is worried about the investigation Anil has gotten his brother involved in because he fears the government's backlash, with good reason, as it turns out.

In the middle of discussing the horrors he has to deal with daily, he falls asleep, exhausted. Anil thinks of a line from the James Taylor song "Sleep Come Free Me," which is sung in the voice of a young man serving a long sentence for murder whose only escape from his wretched Alabama prison cell comes in sleep.

The passages that follow are a mosaic of brief sketches filling in bits of information about Sarath, about Sri Lanka, and about Anil, including an early marriage that has not previously been hinted at. We learn how she developed her controlled exterior partly in reaction to her overemotional husband, an adaptation that will serve her well in her new profession. The flaw that finally does in the relationship, however, is his irrational jealousy, which conflicts acutely with Anil's independent spirit.

During this period her father, shocked at her anatomical studies, asks, "Is there nothing you won't do?" She replies by alluding to a line from the classic Richard Rodgers and Lorenz Hart song "That's Why the Lady Is a Tramp," which lists typical activities engaged in by pretentious socially respectable people and scorns them: "I don't like crap [dice] games with barons and earls." She's probably showing off, aiming her answer over his head. Not only this line but the entire song represents the sort of headstrong individualism characteristic of Anil.

From this point on, allusions to songs occur more and more frequently. Standing in the Archaeological Offices in Colombo she amusingly sings to herself a variation on Sam Cooke's song "Wonderful World," which begins by listing the various school subjects the singer doesn't know much about. We are already aware, of course, that she has had to consult Chitra, an entomologist, for her research. This allusion to the old rock-and-roll classic leads to a whole passage on the playing of music in the morgues. The scene of Vernon Jenkins listening to rock while studying lung tissue slides makes her imagine the slaughter resulting from a civil war scattered about the famous Fillmore auditoriums, West (in San Francisco—the original) and East (in New York), where all the biggest groups played in the late 1960s and early 1970s.

The song Anil sings on page 150 while working in Borrego waiting for Cullis would seem to be a variant on Bessie Smith's "Jailhouse Blues," in which the imprisoned woman sings about having her back to the wall for thirty days and asks the guard to put another woman in the cell with her. Because Smith is known to have been bisexual, she may have been looking for more than company.

Anil's mind flashes back once more to her meeting with Cullis in Borrego Springs, looking for clues to what led to the explosion that ended their relationship. The paragraph that begins this section on page 150 seems to say no great general truth can be extracted from the story of a love affair. Perhaps that is what frustrates Anil about her relationship: unlike the crimes she works on professionally, the crimes of the heart cannot be definitively "solved" and settled. They remain "unordered and private"—and painful.

The scene of kidnapping by insurgents using a bicycle is often referred to in discussions of the novel because it is, as Ondaatje claims, unforgettably bizarre. It is also significant for what it tells us about Sarath's fearfulness. His earlier inaction makes it all the more impressive that he is willing to work with Anil now. In the passage that follows, he thinks about the contrast between the tender gesture of a mother toward her child painted on a cave wall and the random acts of violence going on outside and muses on how the foreign press's misuse of crucial bits of information can lead to new rounds of slaughter. Finally he worries that he may be making a mistake in trying to uncover the truth. Ondaatje is trying to show us that he is aware of the complexities involved in exposing the crimes of terrorists and cruel governments.

The next section is named for Ananda Udugama, the expert at reconstructing faces from skulls. His attempts to give Sailor a face will reveal more about himself than about the owner of the skull he is trying to flesh out.

One of Ondaatje's most striking images occurs here, as a small yellow leaf floats down into Sailor's rib cage and for a moment seems to give him a sort of life. At the end of the novel, a different and more important object will lodge in the same location.

Anil mischievously wakes Ananda up with the bizarre Tom Waits performance of a song about other gem miners—the Seven Dwarfs—from the album *Stay Awake: Various Interpretations of Music from Vintage Disney Films.* He prefers less hip old 78 RPM records of the Portuguese-influenced Sri Lankan popular music known as *baila.* Then Anil listens to Steve Earle's "Reckless Heart," a plea for love after intense suffering, to buck up her spirits while her mind circles back again to Cullis.

The next italicized passage gives us a detailed and moving portrait of a woman who will turn out to be Ananda's wife Sirissa. Ondaatje gives us her thoughts and feelings before he gives her a name, and—finally—a face, as he often does in this novel. Her story makes clear why Ananda might have become so obsessed with skulls. It's not his expertise that leads to the next discovery about Sailor, but his example, as Anil realizes that the victim must have been a miner too.

Her brief phone conversation with Dr. Perera is yet another reminder of Anil's peril; she dares not tell the government doctor her exact location. But, exhilarated by her progress, she defies the danger and expresses her energy by dancing as she listens to Bob Marley's reggae song, "Coming In from the Cold," which urges the listener to shrug off the deadly coercion of "the system" and embrace the possibilities of life; but the context suggests she is thinking especially of a passage that says when one door closes, another opens. It is a song not only about hope, but about the possibility of love despite everything, and the life the song breathes back into her is compared to the leaf that seemed to give life to Sailor a few pages back.

In a dramatic gesture, Ananda tries to bring some of the same sense of peace to Anil's face that he had earlier molded into Sailor's. His greatest skill is not in the objective, meticulous science of detection but in the expression of compassion and love, for which there is perhaps an even greater need. Unfortunately, his compassion is directed outward, and his pain is so great that he tries to kill himself in a way that will unite him with his wife. While Sarath takes the gravely injured man to the hospital, Anil remains behind and hears the sounds of the tea pluckers, which give her a flashback—a rare moment of memory from her childhood—when she had expected something very different from her life than her present reality. This is quickly followed by her statement to Sarath that she has come back to Sri Lanka not just to do a job, but because she wanted to come home again. She is struggling to make a connection with her past that has seemed very distant for the last fifteen years. By having saved a life, she has put her mark on the place.

In the description of the abandoned *walawwa* that follows, there is a rather misleading reference to it as a "grand meulne," seemingly based on

Ondaatje's faulty memory of Alain Fournier's 1913 novel, *Le grand Meaulnes*, which depicts a man's search for a wonderful, almost magical mansion he had stumbled into in childhood and then lost. The allusion is poignant, but "Meaulnes" (not "meulne") is the name of the character, not the name of the building, and the final "s" is part of his name, not an indication of a plural. At any rate, the abandoned mansion moves Anil to meditate on the common fate of all humans in a way she avoids when she is working directly with the dead.

There follows the second of two sections named after Gamini. Because in the first we were being introduced to him through Sarath, it was called "The Brother," but now we learn to know him more intimately by his family nickname, "The Mouse" (because of his large ears). We learn that, like Anil, he takes refuge from the pain of lost love in work, plunging into the sufferings of others to flee his own. He has lost not only his wife, but his home, as we soon discover. He had always wanted to be his brother; Anil wanted her brother's name. It becomes easy to understand why he and the similarly rootless Anil would be drawn to each other. Ondaatje builds up a detailed sketch of the doctor to make us care about him, to understand why he cares so deeply about his work. This portrait also reveals that Gamini has worked with Tamils despite his own Sinhalese identity.

Ondaatje now turns to the final section of the novel, "Between Heartbeats." The section title, taken together with the title of the novel, is ominous. It is often said that a person can die suddenly, unexpectedly, between one heartbeat and the next. The central characters have been moving closer and closer to tying Sailor's death to government forces, and we have been given more and more reasons to fear for their safety.

But the section begins with what at first appears a comforting memory, happier days for Anil with Leaf. Leaves seem to be a symbol of life in this novel: the leaf hall where Palipana lives, the fluttering leaf in Sailor's chest, and this close friend's name, but we will learn not much later that she has lost her. It is not clear who exactly shouts to whom, "Watch out for the armadillos, Señorita" (translated later, in the last passage about Leaf for those who don't know Spanish), but the exhilaration of their friendship is clear. We don't need to follow in detail a lot of movie trivia in this passage to understand they share many enthusiasms as well as a profession. Anil probably suggests doing a forensic study of Stanley Kubrick's 1960 film *Spartacus* because it features many nearly naked gladiators and slaves, notably Kirk Douglas in the title role.

We move from exploring Anil's past to exploring more of Gamini's past. The two are obviously being knit together. His heroic courage and devotion to his patients, no matter what their ethnic origin, becomes clearer. He tells Anil about how he had to be faced with the suicide of the only woman he truly loved, his brother's wife. Anil suspects at first he is speaking of this lost love as a way of trying to seduce her, but he seems to be sincerely approaching her as a friend, opening his heart to her. In response Anil tells him about her loss of Leaf, which is ongoing.

Ondaatje calls the two women best friends and says they love each other like sisters; but he also says they would wake up entangled in each other's arms, and lets us know that Leaf was fascinated with Westerns not because she liked cowboys so much but because she wanted to *be* a cowboy. In their last conversation Leaf surprises Anil by calling her "my darling." Are we meant to think of them as lovers or of Leaf at least as lesbian? It probably doesn't matter, for the important fact is not their sexuality but the fact that they cared so deeply for each other and have been so cruelly separated. Anil's letter to John Boorman following up on their old question about *Point Blank* is a way of trying to maintain a sort of connection with a friend who can no longer even remember asking the question for which the letter seeks an answer.

We return to the Sri Lankan context with Sarath's account of the ancient murdered Chinese women's orchestra, which he uses to illustrate the bizarre reasons for which people will agree to die, comparing it to the fanaticism of the terrorists he lives among. This is followed by Anil's account of how she became involved with Cullis. Presumably she wanted him to remember the words of "Brazil," a popular 1939 ballad (melody by Ary Barroso) because S. K. Russell's lyrics speak of the determination of lovers to be reunited although they are widely separated from each other. But we then jump from the beginning of the relationship to its end, and Anil thinks of one last ballad, Kate McGarrigle's "Talk to Me of Mendocino," another song of separation and yearning.

A conventional writer of thrillers would be feverishly following up leads to the central mystery at this point, keeping the narrative momentum going, but instead Ondaatje chooses to delve deeper and deeper into the characters of his "detectives." He does at last provide a solution of sorts in the next section, "The Life Wheel." But instead of teasing out the question of Sailor's identity, he simply announces that it has been established: he was a former toddy tapper named Ruwan Kumara. Toddy tappers have to climb tall palm trees to harvest the sap that becomes palm wine, or toddy; so this explains why he would have been athletic and have shown signs of working with his arms stretched upward. More important, they have a date for his disappearance that will allow them to pin the responsibility for his death more precisely on the authorities.

When she cannot reach Sarath, Anil has to turn to Perera, and he is clearly aligned with the government and more inclined to hinder than to help her. The scene in which the officials, pretending to cooperate with the UN, do everything they can to make her mission fail, is all too familiar from recent history in other parts of the world. Anil is secretly recording the proceedings so their interference can be revealed to the world outside. But Sarath seems to have turned against her, trying to shift the blame for

Sailor's disappearance from Perera, the probable culprit, to Anil herself and ridiculing her research, finally dismissing her from the room, separating her from everything she needs to prove her case—most especially her tape recorder. What has happened to him? This about-face is so abrupt and unexpected that many readers seem to lose track completely of what is going on. Because so many seem to misunderstand the end of the novel, it will be explained in the passage that follows, although first-time readers should give themselves the pleasure of following the ending on their own first, if they can.

It turns out that Sarath has been rescuing her by posing as her enemy. In making a public display of her ejection from the building without any supporting evidence, he is rendering her not worth killing. As he wheels the trolley along through the hallway, we get glimpses of his past (incidentally revealing his wife's name, "Ravina"), which convey to us his familiarity with death, his readiness to accept it. He knows that when it is revealed how he has deceived the authorities, they will not forgive him. When he sends Gunesena off for water, he switches the unimportant skeleton she had been told to examine in public for Sailor's skeleton, which he—and not Perera—had sequestered, to preserve it. Because he has not dared to explain his plan to Anil, he has to force her to take the body, even going to the extent of slapping her in public, which again helps make her for the moment appear harmless and shifts suspicion away from what he is doing. So far as anyone watching can tell, Anil has been both frustrated in her investigation and humiliated to boot.

Only when Anil is safely on the boat does she discover the truth: Sarath has delivered into her hands exactly the evidence she needs to prove the government's guilt: Sailor's skeleton and the precious tape recorder, to which Sarath has added a farewell and instructions for escaping early the next morning on a flight he has arranged for her. He implies that he expects to be arrested or to disappear before then. He could well be in jail, or dead.

In the passage that follows, Gamini talks about how Western stories always view conflicts in far-off lands through the eyes of Western observers. Such stories invariably turn on the response of these outside observers to the situation they are plunged into, and the sufferings of the people involved become mere background. Ondaatje is determined that his novel will be different. Instead of ending his story from the perspective of the departing investigator soaring through the clouds for home, he has shifted back to Gamini as he continues his work with the civil rights organization investigating the atrocities. It is not pretended that because one crucial piece of evidence has been secured, the crisis is over.

The murders have continued, and the latest body to find its way onto Gamini's table is his brother's. For all their alienation from each other in life, they are united in death, not as would be the case in a Hollywood movie because they have both fallen in love with Anil—nothing like that has happened—but because they have both fallen in love with truth. As Gamini holds Sarath's mutilated corpse, his pose is compared to the classic image of Mary holding her son, the crucified Jesus, dead across her lap: the *Pietà*. We understand that not only is this novel not Anil's story, we realize that "Anil's ghost" is not the ghost of Anil, but the ghost of Sarath. As explained in the closing pages of the book, his courage and his sacrifice, and all it represents, will haunt her for the rest of her life.

The blow that strikes next is not governmental retribution, but a terrorist bombing, the assassination of the president of the country. The conflict goes on, and the wheel of life—and death—continues to turn.

But Ondaatje is not content to leave it there. He didn't want us to climb on that plane with Anil and fly safely off; nor does he now want us to sink into despair as the death toll mounts. Instead he adds a sort of postscript, a short section titled "Distance" with Ananda restoring the vandalized Buddhas, bringing them back to life. Some of his countrymen have chosen to impersonate demons; he has chosen instead to resurrect gods, to send them back to the serene heavens overhead.

As he finishes his work, he looks from his vantage point high on the sculpture over the landscape and reaches out to capture all its detail. It is not his connection with the spiritual world the novel ends with, but his connection with the earth, with the hand of a boy who, concerned, reaches out to him as Ananda thinks of his dead wife. Such small gestures of compassion are all the book offers as counterbalance to the grotesque cruelty all around; but in the long run the concern of one human being for another is the only hope we have.

SELECTED BIBLIOGRAPHY

Barbour, Douglas. *Michael Ondaatje.* New York: Twayne, 1993.
> This survey of Ondaatje's career was written before the appearance of *Anil's Ghost*, but it provides useful background information.

Bayley, John. "A Passage to Colombo." *New York Review of Books* 2 Nov. 2000: 44–46.
> An unusually long and thoughtful review of *Anil's Ghost*.

Fernando, Dinali. "Anil's Ghost: Contrived Exotica." *The Sunday Leader* 18 Mar. 2001. <http://www.lanka.net/sundayleader/2001/Mar/18/review.html>.
> A nitpicking review in a Colombo newspaper that catches Ondaatje in a few errors of local detail. Interesting, but not a substantial critique of the novel.

Jaggi, Maya. "The Soul of a Migrant." *The Guardian* 29 Apr. 2000: 26. <http://www.guardian.co.uk/Print/0,3858,4012797,00.html>.
> A survey of the writer's career based on an interview with Ondaatje, exploring among other issues his identity as a Sri Lankan writer.

Ondaatje, Michael. *Anil's Ghost.* New York: Knopf, 2000.

————. *The English Patient.* New York: Knopf, 1992.

Vintage Books. "'Anil's Ghost' by Michael Ondaatje." <http://www.randomhouse. com/vintage/catalog/display.pperl?isbn=0375724370&view=rg>. Accessed 1 Sept. 2003.

    A reading group guide including discussion questions and brief review excerpts.

Chapter 14
Jhumpa Lahiri:
Interpreter of Maladies
(2000)

In recent times the literary world has become used to brilliant new writers emerging from South Asia. But when a book by a previously little-known woman author won the prestigious Pulitzer Prize for best American work of fiction in 2000, it was sensational news, partly because Jhumpa Lahiri's *Interpreter of Maladies* was a collection of short stories in an age when the novel is dominant. Two of the stories had appeared previously in the premier American outlet for short fiction, *The New Yorker,* and six others in less widely read periodicals; but to most reviewers and readers her brilliant writing came as a complete surprise. The book earned other major honors as well, including the PEN/Hemingway Award and an award from the American Academy of Arts and Letters.

Lahiri was born in London in 1967 to Bengali immigrant parents from Calcutta. Her father is a librarian at the University of Rhode Island, and her mother a teacher who earned an MA in Bengali literature. The family had moved to the little town of South Kingston, Rhode Island, when she was three, so she has spent most of her life as an American and became a U.S. citizen at age eighteen, although from childhood on she has made many long visits to India. Some Indian critics have criticized Lahiri as an "outsider," but considerable praise for her work has also appeared in the South Asian press. So strong has the interest in her writing been in India that translations have been commissioned into Bengali, Hindi, and Marathi.

She studied English literature at Barnard College in New York City, and then at Boston University earned three master's degrees (in English, creative writing, and comparative literature and the arts), capping her academic career with a Ph.D. in Renaissance studies. Such a course of study would normally be a prelude to a career of teaching about literature, but Lahiri realized that her true love was creating literature. Indeed, she had been writing fiction steadily since the age of seven; her most influential educational experience was a two-year fellowship in writing at the Fine Arts Work Center in Provincetown, Massachusetts; and her only academic appointments have been in creative writing, at Boston University and the Rhode Island School of Design. In January 2001 Lahiri married Alberto Vourvoulias-Bush, deputy editor of *Time Latin America,* in a traditional Bengali ceremony in Calcutta. They now reside in New York City. She published a novel, *The Namesake,* to general acclaim in 2003, too late for inclusion here.

Lahiri has been hailed as an outstanding member of a post-Rushdie generation of Indian writers who have turned their backs on magical realism and other experiments to write well-crafted traditional realist fiction. Her stories belong to the long tradition of delicate character sketches, avoiding sensational effects and overly clever endings. Although her work has often been described as focusing on the problems of immigrants—and it is true that such characters dominate her writing—her real subject is miscommunication. The relationships in her stories are a series of missed connections.

The first story in the collection, "A Temporary Matter" (originally published Apr. 20, 1998, in *The New Yorker* as "A Temporary Prayer: What Happens When the Lights Go Out"), is a fine example. A husband and wife who have drifted apart in the wake of the death of their child seem to find intimacy during a series of planned power outages, but the conclusion reveals that the wife is experiencing their relationship very differently from her husband.

Women sometimes criticize men for being so emotionally insensitive as to be unaware that their wives are drifting away until the eve of their departure. It is true that Shukumar, the husband, has not made much of an effort to penetrate his wife Shoba's grief. Like many married male students, he is supported by his wife's work, and it was his academic conference that prevented him from being with her when the stillbirth occurred.

But this is no anti-male tract. He hadn't wanted to go to the conference: she had insisted. He clearly cares for her and worries about her. Since she has become depressed, he has taken over the cooking, and enjoys it. Earlier in their marriage, she was the organized, disciplined one while he drifted. Now he keeps the household running. Shoba is a very private person, and at the very least may be said to send mixed signals to her husband. Lahiri doesn't seek to assess blame, merely to portray the way in which a marriage stricken by the death of a child may collapse as grief drives the couple apart.

As the narrator explains, power outages (called "load sheddings") are commonplace in India. It perhaps strains credibility that an American power company would shut off electricity for five nights running to repair local line damage, but if the reader accepts this premise, it is easy to be moved by the intimacy that blooms in the dark as the two begin to tell each other their secrets. These exchanges are full of subtle details, like the fact that he notes her fading beauty just before he tells her how he first realized they would marry.

From Shoba's perspective she is delicately, even affectionately, disentangling herself from Shukumar, but we experience the process from his point of view, which is very different. When he is stunned by her final declaration, he flings out the most hurtful secret he can think of: he had held and seen the infant. It is not clear whether Shoba had also seen him before falling asleep, although that seems likely. It may be that her husband's absence during this crisis marked him irrevocably in her mind as an outsider (her mother certainly seems to regard the incident that way).

Although he means to assert himself and perhaps hurt her by describing the dead child, his confession seems to bring them together in sorrow in a way that does not suggest their marriage can be saved, but that they now understand each other better. Maturity and sensitivity cannot necessarily heal all wounds. As another couple walks arm in arm past their window, they sit together for the last time, weeping. Like the power outage, both their intimacy and the marriage are "temporary matters." The distinguished Indian director Mira Nair (*Monsoon Wedding*) announced a plan to make this story into a film for PBS, but it is not clear whether that project is still under development.

"When Mr. Pirzada Came to Dine" (first published in 1999 in *The Louisville Review*) is set in 1971, at the height of the crisis that resulted in the secession of Bangladesh from Pakistan, with support from India. The British and American news was full of stories of starving refugees from the brutal assaults of the Pakistani forces ordered by General Yahyah Khan on the Bengalis in Pakistan's Eastern Wing. Although Lilia, the narrator of this story, is a little older than Lahiri herself would have been at the time, she may well have experienced the news in the same distanced, confused way.

The first sentence of the story underlines the irony of Mr. Pirzada coming to feast on Indian food at the home of fellow Bengalis and handing out sweets while agonizing over the dangers his wife and seven daughters are facing at home. He can express his parental affection only for this substitute child. Lilia is old enough to understand something of what is going on, but to her Mr. Pirzada is principally a source of candy. For the adults, his visits are a mirror of the growing alliance between Bengali Indians and Pakistanis in their homeland. In another ironic contrast, Lilia is studying the American Revolution in a typically celebratory way while she witnesses the all too vivid tragedy of another nation being born on the news that is not being studied at school—indeed, her teacher rebukes her for reading about Pakistan.

At first, this is another story of misunderstandings and miscommunications, as Lilia reveals her ignorance of the matters that most concern Mr. Pirzada and her parents. But it is also a very subtle coming of age story, in which her growing understanding of the tragedy in South Asia finally makes her reluctant to eat their guest's sweets. She is no longer the innocent, pampered object of affection, but an aware participant in the ongoing history of her parents' homeland.

The book's title story, "Interpreter of Maladies" (first published 1998 in *Agni Review*), resembles in plot the episode in Narayan's *Guide* in which a tour guide is drawn to the Westernized wife of an Indian traveler; but the encounter here is much more ambiguous, and the outcome far more unexpected. Lahiri has said that the phrase "interpreter of maladies" came to her when she encountered a man who made a living translating Russian for immigrants trying to explain their ailments to a non-Russian-speaking doctor.

She tried for years to work it into a story, and finally succeeded by transplanting the interpreter to India and giving the phrase a metaphorical twist. Mrs. Das chooses Mr. Kapasi to hear her confession because she thinks of him as a professional listener-to-troubles; but he is startled to find himself in this unwelcome role because he has been dreaming instead of himself as her potential lover. Like "A Temporary Matter," this is a story of two people crossing at an angle through each other's lives, neither satisfied with the response of the other.

The fact that Mr. and Mrs. Das were born and raised in America, where women are used to a good deal of independence and privacy, makes her affair more credible than if she had been a native-born resident of India. But this story is not ultimately about South Asians living abroad or in exile. Lahiri skillfully builds the tension as we gradually realize how much Mr. Kapasi desires Mrs. Das, and how much he has let his fantasies carry him away in dreams of a romantic future. Shocked at her heartless confession, he somewhat hypocritically rebukes her, considering that he has just been dreaming of seducing her himself. Yet he is clearly also aware of her suffering, realizing that she has "fallen out of love with life."

The final scene is typical of Lahiri's subtle ambiguity: Mr. Kapasi, who has lost his own child, watches the unloving mother brushing her rescued son's hair while the slip of paper that once promised him so much flutters away in the wind. No one is simple in this story, which is a mark of Lahiri's mastery.

"A Real Durwan" is the first story in this volume entirely about Indians living in India. A *durwan* is someone who watches over a building, a caretaker who guards the entrance against intruders and keeps track of the residents' comings and goings. Some Indian readers have criticized this story as distorting Indian reality. Lahiri tells amusingly of having been sternly rebuked by an Indian for suggesting that Calcutta apartment buildings ever lack sinks, when in her own grandparents' building where she had just been before writing the story in 1992, there were only plastic buckets on each landing.

The story is not really about the inadequacies of Calcutta plumbing, but more about the casual cruelty the poor can be subjected to in any culture.

Even more important, it is a character sketch of the destitute old woman called "Boori Ma," reportedly based on a old woman who lived in the house of Lahiri's uncle and aunt in Calcutta. Although she is welcome at first, the kindliness of the apartment dwellers in her building evaporates when their new sink is stolen, and they blame her for not being "a real durwan," even though she has suffered a theft of her own far more disastrous, considering her poverty. Boori Ma is not portrayed as a particularly sympathetic victim; it is never quite clear whether she is lying about having come from a wealthy *zamindar* (landowning) family. Clearly she greatly resents her fall in the world to the point that she cannot qualify even as a durwan. Lacking wealth and power, she also lacks the humility and submissiveness that might appeal to well-off people in a poor woman, and that is her downfall.

"Sexy" (originally published in *The New Yorker,* Dec. 28, 1999) is another story of three different perspectives: that of Miranda, a twenty-two-year-old woman having an affair with a married Indian man; that of the wife of such a man (via her cousin Laxmi); and that of an innocent young boy (Laxmi's son). Like most of Lahiri's stories, the presentation is complex and subtle. We learn little of Miranda's inner thoughts; in fact, we may suspect that she avoids thinking clearly about the implications of the affair she has fallen into. Lahiri introduces the topic of infidelity by telling us first how badly Laxmi's cousin and son have been hurt by the husband's affair. The narrative implies that this story leads Miranda to think about her own affair with Dev, but that she resists thinking about it as harmful. She is still enjoying the bliss of a budding relationship. She is young enough to find it difficult to identify with a married woman's problems; she belongs to the generation from which mistresses are commonly chosen.

Her name suggests wonderment at the discovery of the new, which is associated with Shakespeare's Miranda in *The Tempest,* but Dev seeks to make her a naturalized Indian by associating her name with "Mira." She is charmed by her older lover's romantic gestures, so unlike the clumsiness of previous younger boyfriends. This is her first true love affair. In contrast, for Dev she is simply "the first woman I've known with legs this long," which implies he's had the opportunity to study the anatomy of a substantial number of women. His whispered message in the mapparium that gives the story its title thrills her, but it also clearly demonstrates the limits of his interest in her: she's sexy.

The story of their continuing affair is counterpointed against the unfolding disaster of the cousin's marriage. Gradually Dev seems to take her more for granted, make fewer romantic gestures, especially after his wife has returned to town. This behavior makes the reader wonder whether he has just been seeking some diversion in his wife's absence rather than seeking a substitute for her.

But more threatening is the fact that Dev says his wife looks like the famously beautiful Bollywood actress Madhuri Dixit (b. 1967), famous in part, incidentally, for her long legs. The story does not explicitly articulate the worry and jealousy Miranda feels, but her quest for a picture of the actress in the Indian grocery store reveals that she cannot take it for granted Dev will ultimately choose her over his wife. The fact that she can't even correctly spell the name of this wildly popular Indian star underlines the fact that she's only playing on the fringes of a world she knows little of.

The fact that Miranda's only other association with Indian people involves the fearsome goddess Kali may be meant to suggest potential vengefulness: Kali is a fierce warrior, slayer of demons, bedecked with the heads and limbs of her victims. Another threatening image is the "too spicy" Hot Mix, which implies that she may not have what it takes to hang on to Dev.

Thus far Miranda has been able to cling to her attachment to Dev successfully, despite the discouraging stories she is hearing from Laxmi. But her encounter with Rohin finally causes her to face the harm she is doing by continuing her affair. A simpler story would simply present Rohin as a brokenhearted damaged child, but Lahiri does something considerably more complex. When the boy says to Miranda "you're sexy," he draws a clear connection between his father's behavior and Dev's that is powerful precisely because is so young and naïve that he doesn't even realize she will feel stung by his words. He has arrived at his childish definition of "sexy" by deducing its meaning based on his father's case: "sexy means loving someone you don't know." Without meaning to, he has revealed to Miranda what she should have known all along: Dev doesn't love her, he just finds her sexy.

Lahiri again avoids the obvious by choosing not to end the story with a tumultuous confrontation between the two lovers or with Miranda experiencing a dramatic change of heart. Even now, she yearns for Dev and would like to prolong the affair. This is much truer to most people's lived experience than a sudden and dramatic conversion. It is not so easy to disentangle oneself from a love affair, even when the basis of that love affair is purely sexual. It is too easy to speak dismissively of "mere" sex; Miranda shows us how powerful it can be, and she is not even shown as repentant. But the driving force of the relationship, the belief that she was something truly special for Dev, has been drained away. Yes, Miranda is sexy, but so is Dev's wife, and the mistress of Rohin's father—and in the end that's not enough to sustain the relationship. She's left with her memories—and with the emptiness of the sky over Boston.

"Mrs. Sen's" (first published 1999 in *Salamander*) is the story of an unhappy immigrant. Mrs. Sen is not just constitutionally timid; she is terribly homesick. The United States is famously a country dominated by individualists, people eager to break out of the shackles of identity forged in small hometowns and create new identities in the anonymity of the big city. Sons and daughters who remain at home after they have turned adult are frowned on as failures. In countries like India, the successful family tends to be regarded as one that stays together, in which everyone knows what everyone else is up to, and in which the rewards of individualism are sacrificed for the rewards of *belonging*. Mrs. Sen yearns for a culture in which she would be cared for simply because of who she is.

She isn't comfortable in a country where it's routine for a mother to hire someone to care for her child while she works, even though that pattern provides her with a job she seems genuinely to enjoy. She's depressed to be living in a place where the neighbors call you up only to complain about the noise you're making. She lacks the drive for independence that would motivate her to master the art of driving, content to have her husband pick up the fresh fish she so longs for. Unfortunately, he does not feel the same. He's just the sort of immigrant that has built America: eager to move on, impatient with tradition, bent on change.

What Lahiri accomplishes in this story is to show us that Mrs. Sen's point of view has a good deal to be said for it. Good seafood and the intimacy of family connections are worth having; and it is not clear that the independence Eliot gets by becoming a latchkey child at the age of eleven is superior. But the story is not trying to establish that one pattern is good, the other bad. It simply portrays two characters crossing paths, headed in opposite directions, Eliot becoming more typically American, and Mrs. Sen more typically Indian.

We never learn whether Eliot's mother is a divorcee, a widow, or simply a single mother. A father doesn't feature in his world. Lahiri is particularly good at portraying the point of view of children. Much of what Mrs. Sen says goes over Eliot's head. He has no way of understanding a great deal about India, including the fact that the bald man at a spinning wheel on the stamps Mrs. Sen receives is Mahatma Gandhi, who vigorously promoted the production of homemade cloth to help Indians break free of the dominance of imported English goods. It would be unrealistic to expect him to have arrived at any deep insights about this intercultural encounter, but we can guess that some day he will look back on this experience with deeper understanding and an appreciation for another way of life.

"This Blessed House" (first published in *Epoch,* 1999) is another story of a mismatched couple drifting past each other, but with a comic undertone. We can tell they are not on the same wavelength when Sanjeev reads how Mahler expressed his love for his wife in what must be the fourth movement of his Symphony no. 5 and Twinkle's response is to flush the toilet and pronounce the music boring.

Twinkle is delighted by the array of Christian artifacts she finds in the couple's new home, not because she is particularly religious, but because they amuse her. When her husband repeatedly insists "but we are not Christian," she dismissively waves aside his objections. Lahiri does not draw the parallel, but it is difficult not to be reminded of Westerners who collect Hindu images, buy lunch boxes with images of Kali or Ganesh on them because they find them exotic and entertaining, with no sense of the religious sentiments attached to them by believers.

There is nothing uniquely Indian about this story. True, their marriage was an arranged one, but they had a Western-style courtship as well, in which they might have been expected to learn to know each other better. Yet it is commonplace for couples everywhere to discover after marriage that they have married strangers with tastes and habits that are distinctly not shared. But Sanjeev's conservatism never has a chance against her exuberance.

It would be a mistake to regard Twinkle, despite her frivolous nickname, as merely childish. She is writing a thesis on an obscure Irish poet for a graduate degree at Stanford, likes depressing German films, has sophisticated taste in music, and is capable of inventing a tasty fish dish, although she's a sloppy housekeeper. Her witticism about the "virgin on the half shell" is a clever reference to the traditional image—borrowed from pagan images of Venus rising from the sea—of Mary standing on a scallop shell. "Oysters on the half shell" is a traditional way of serving this seafood raw, and Lahiri probably got the idea for this joke from a Kurt Vonnegut–inspired novel called *Venus on the Half-Shell.*

Her friends appreciate her sense of play and find her charming; it is Sanjeev who is the odd man out in this setting. He is not sure he loves her and not sure she loves him; but by the end of the story it is clear that she is the one whose tastes will prevail in their home. She dances off barefoot at the end of the story while he lumbers reluctantly along under the weight of the silver statue of Christ that delights her, doomed to live under its gaze for the rest of his days—or at least for the rest of their marriage.

"The Treatment of Bibi Halder" (originally published in *Story Quarterly* 30, in 1994) resembles "A Real Durwan" in being the story of an unfortunate woman treated badly by those around her. It should not be assumed that Lahiri means to imply that Indians are particularly heartless: consider how family supportiveness is emphasized in "Mrs. Sen's." But not every family is a loving one, and Bibi's parents' treatment of their epileptic daughter is particularly heartless in ways that can be found in any culture.

Many societies have believed that a woman who lacks a man may fall ill as a result. Shakespeare's generation spoke of "green-sickness" as the malady afflicting young women ripe for marriage, which could be cured by a fulfilling wedding night and ensuing love life. Sigmund Freud argued that unsatisfied suppressed yearnings for sex caused the neuroses of many of his women patients, with little more evidence than the Elizabethans had.

This early story lacks the subtlety and complexity of Lahiri's best work. She seems to share the amusement of the neighbors at the afflicted girl's fantasies of marriage, the unflattering matrimonial ad her father places for her is played for laughs, and her eventual "cure" is almost a joke.

The volume's moving concluding story, "The Third and Final Continent," is more typical of Lahiri at her best and indeed one of her most admired works. Traces of the story of Lahiri's parents appear in this tale. Mukesh, like the author's father, is an immigrant to England from Calcutta who moves on to the United States where he becomes a librarian at a prominent New England university (North America being, of course, the "final continent").

In this story two distant relationships develop warmth: The narrator's growing affection for the senile and irritable Mrs. Croft and his growing affection for his wife. If the latter illustrates an Indian tradition in which the partners in an arranged marriage are expected to gradually fall in love after the wedding rather than before, his relationship with Mrs. Croft reflects much more universal patterns. She does try to assert American supremacy by forcing him to celebrate the American landing on the moon, but she seems otherwise welcoming of her South Asian border. Her prejudices are not racial or nationalistic, but academic: she rents only to "boys" from the prestigious schools of Harvard or the Massachusetts Institute of Technology ("Tech"). Mukesh, with his training at the famous London School of Economics (LSE), fits in nicely.

Their relationship cannot be called an intimate one: she reigns haughtily from her centenarian perch of superiority without the slightest comprehension of her tenant, not even grasping he is married. The antiquated prudery with which she forbids her aged daughter from visiting with Mukesh in his room is comic. Even her pride in asserting that an American flag stands on the moon is rendered somewhat amusing by Sanjeev's awareness that the flag has in fact toppled over.

Yet he grows to care for this irascible old woman, and when his wife arrives to join him, he feels he must present her to his former landlady. She pronounces Mala, who had had difficulty attracting suitors in India because of her dark skin, "a perfect lady." His days with Mrs. Croft become a family legend, and her appreciation of his wife seems to be echoed in Sanjeev's growing affection for her. After so many stories of couples drifting apart, it is comforting to see that the volume, which appeared as the author was planning her own wedding, concludes with a marriage that—after a very unpromising beginning—ends in mutual love and affection.

SELECTED BIBLIOGRAPHY

Aguilar, Arun. "One on One with Jhumpa Lahiri." *PIF* 28 (1 Sept. 1999).
    <http://www.pifmagazine.com/vol28/i_agui.shtml>.
    A particularly interesting interview with Lahiri.

Bushi, R. "Death in the Hills: False Reality and Realisation in 'Interpreter of Maladies.'" (2001). <http://members.lycos.co.uk/thaz/RedGhost/lahiri.htm>.
An interesting essay on the title story in *Interpreter of Maladies.*

Choubey, Asha. "Food Metaphor in Jhumpa Lahiri's 'Interpreter of Maladies.'" *Postcolonial Web: The Literature & Culture of the Indian Subcontinent (South Asia).* <http://www.scholars.nus.edu.sg/landow/post/india/literature/choubey1.html>.
Discusses food in her stories.

Flynn, Sean. "Women We Love: Jhumpa Lahiri." *Esquire* (Oct. 2000): 172–73.
Clearly captivated by Lahiri's beauty, Flynn also has some interesting comments about her writing.

Houghton Mifflin. "A Reader's Guide: *Interpreter of Maladies* by Jhumpa Lahiri." <http://www.houghtonmifflinbooks.com/readers_guides/interpreter_maladies.shtml>.
Study questions, background information, and a brief interview.

Kakutani, Michiko. *The Interpreter of Maladies.* Boston: Houghton Mifflin, 1999.
———. "Liking America, but Longing for India." *New York Times* 6 Aug. 1999: 48.
A follow-up article, more interesting than the *New York Times Book Review*'s original review on July 11, 1999—which is, however, available on the Web at <http://www.nytimes.com/pages/books/review/index.html> for "Interpreter of Maladies."

Lahiri, Jhumpa. "Translato ergo sum." *Himal* (October 2000). <http://www.himalmag.com/oct2000/voices.html>.
Excerpt from an article that originally appeared in *Feed Magazine* as "Jhumpa on Jhumpa." A response to Indian critics and others who find Lahiri's stories inauthentic because she is was born and lives abroad.

———. *The Namesake.* Boston: Houghton Mifflin, 2003.
Lahiri's first novel.

Patel, Vibhuti. "The Maladies of Belonging." *Newsweek* 20 Sept. 1999: 80.
A good, readily accessible review.

SAWNET (South Asian Women's NETwork). "Jhumpa Lahiri." <http://www.umiacs.umd.edu/users/sawweb/sawnet/books/jhumpa_lahiri.html>.
Brief article with links.

Voices from the Gaps: Women Writers of Color. "Jhumpa Lahiri." <http://voices.cla.umn.edu/authors/jhumpalahiri.html>.
Useful overview and bibliography.

Chapter 15
Manil Suri: The Death of Vishnu *(2001)*

Manil Suri was born in Bombay in 1959, raised in that city, and went on to study mathematics at the University of Bombay. At the age of twenty he emigrated to the United States, where he earned an M.S. and Ph.D. in mathematics at Carnegie-Mellon University. He has worked since 1983 as a professor of applied mathematics at the University of Maryland.

Along with his professional interests, however, Suri developed a desire to write fiction, and he began working on short stories in 1985, most of them with fantastic plots and none with Indian settings. His attempts to get them printed failed, with the exception of a story called "The Tyranny of Vegetables," which was published in Bulgarian translation in an obscure literary journal and has never appeared in English. He continued to polish his skills in workshops led by Jane Bradley, by distinguished Indian author Vikram Chandra, and—most significantly—by Michael Cunningham in 1997 at the Fine Arts Work Center in Provincetown, Massachusetts. Cunningham urged him to abandon the short stories he had been working on and develop the beginnings of *The Death of Vishnu* into a novel.

It was Cunningham who persuaded Suri that if he were going to use the name "Vishnu" for his central character, he should explore the religious associations of the god by that name. Because "Vishnu" is a not uncommon name in India, this is not altogether obvious, any more than a Mexican character named Jesús should have to be depicted in Christian terms. However, the suggestion sparked Suri's interest in his childhood religion. His father is a pious Hindu, but Suri considered himself an agnostic who knew little about Hinduism except for its various rituals. He began to read on the subject, being particularly taken by the *Bhagavad Gita,* especially the eleventh chapter, in which Krishna, an avatar of Vishnu, explains to the great hero Arjuna his many-sided reality, rooted both in both various aspects of the physical world and in the realm of the gods. After ignoring or resisting religion for most of his life, Suri began to be intrigued by what he found. The result is a highly ambiguous treatment of Hindu themes in the novel, a mixture of skeptical satire and awe.

Five years after he had begun work on his book, an excerpt was published called "The Seven Circles" in the *The New Yorker,* America's most famous outlet for distinguished short fiction. When the full novel appeared about a year later, it was thus already eagerly anticipated, and received generally very warm reviews as the latest in a long series of distinguished literary works by writers of South Asian origin. The book was quickly translated into numerous languages, including Spanish, Italian, German, French, Danish, Finnish, Swedish, Dutch, Portuguese, Catalan, Hebrew, Polish, and Greek.

Suri has said that *The Death of Vishnu* is the first part of a projected trilogy whose other titles will concern the remaining gods who together make up the rest of the "the Hindu Trinity": *The Life of Shiva* and *The Birth of Brahma.* Among authors who have influenced him, he cites Rabindranath Tagore, whose fame inspired him to think of the possibility of becoming an Indian writer; S. K. Narayan, whose humorous depiction of the frustrated lives of ordinary people in his Malgudi novels is a clear influence on *The Death of Vishnu;* and Trinidad-born V. S. Naipaul, whose *A House for Mr. Biswas* helped him see how to write dialogue for his characters. He also credits his reading of some racy bestsellers with providing him the model for a couple of explicit sex scenes that occur in his novel.

An author's note at the front of the book explains that its ultimate inspiration was a real man named Vishnu who lived on the stairs in the apartment house in Bombay where he grew up and where his parents still live. It struck him as interesting to imagine the life of such a man and use him to knit together the stories of the various other characters who might inhabit such an apartment building. On a visit home in 1995, he learned that this Vishnu was very ill, and later that year heard he had died. Other than that, his Vishnu is entirely invented, and Suri's apartment dwellers are fictional creations, meant to evoke the Bombay of his youth in the 1970s and depict various human foibles and passions.

The Death of Vishnu is a combination short story collection and novel—a structure that has been frequently used by other writers of both fiction and film scripts. His teacher Michael Cunningham's novel *The Hours* (made into a successful film in 2001) has a somewhat similar structure. If the various stretches of narrative were disentangled and arrayed in an orderly fashion the book might be easier to follow, but a good deal would be lost. Most of the characters interact with Vishnu in one way or another, and with others in the building, and their reactions to each other reveal a great deal about them as individuals.

In addition, Suri is attempting something more ambitious than a simple kaleidoscopic portrait of lives lived in parallel. The novel proceeds from the grossly physical concerns of the Pathaks and Asranis on the first floor, to the spiritual quest of Mr. Jalal on the second, to the mournful isolation of Mr. Taneja, who is in permanent mourning for his beloved wife Sheetal on the third. As a mathematician, Suri prided himself on creating a complex, functional structure for his work, which he sketched out in advance. The order in which the characters' stories are told is meant to reflect the traditional Hindu stages of life through which one passes: material gain, spiritual quest, and eventual abandonment of the world. Obviously Suri has given this structure a secular slant, and some Hindu readers have expressed offense at his use of the traditions in an impious way. His novel achieves a satisfying structure with this device, but it hardly becomes a vehicle for spiritual teaching.

In fact, his use of religion throughout the work is highly controversial among South Asians, and not only because some of them feel it is blasphemous. Whereas many Western reviewers found the passages dealing with Hinduism to be the most inspiring and intriguing in the novel, South Asian critics tended to dismiss them as superficial, frivolous, or clichéd. For such readers, making a connection between this character and aspects of the god Vishnu is as unoriginal as a Western novel would be about a modern man named Adam who falls in love with a woman named Eve. Although many readers have commented that they felt they needed to know more about Hinduism to appreciate the book fully, knowing too much may rob the work of some of its intended effect.

This justifies to a certain extent the accusation of some Indian critics that Suri is writing for a Western audience (the standard phrase is "pandering to the West"). This is an accusation that almost every Indian writer in English has had to deal with. Like most of his contemporaries, Suri consciously includes numerous non-English words and phrases in his text, but usually in contexts that make their meaning clear (a fairly complete glossary is printed in the back of the book). Yet while some non-Indian readers complain about such language, at least one Indian interviewer criticized him for not including enough authentically Indian language.

This is probably a battle no author can finally win. Any South Asian writing in English is going to be subjected to accusations of inauthenticity, and it is probably well to begin by acknowledging that Suri is an immigrant mainly aiming his writing at a non-Indian audience and at others like himself who have roots in India but who have for most of their lives resided abroad (NRIs: "nonresident Indians"). He has expressed satisfaction at the number of Indian readers who have welcomed his novel, but he clearly has far more readers outside India. There is nothing illegitimate in such an approach. Writers rarely wish to address themselves solely to their communities of origin. But readers need to be wary of interpreting any writer as having the last word on a particular ethnic group's experience.

The Death of Vishnu is one of those works in which no characters are nearly as intelligent as the author. The one possible exception would be Mr. Jalal, a character somewhat modeled on Suri himself, but he has lost his wits long before the novel begins. This is a satire, not entirely lacking in affection for the characters, but not holding them in high regard either. Like Narayan, Suri enjoys depicting the foolishness, selfishness, heedlessness, and other failings common to ordinary human beings, and only readers who enjoy this sort of satire are likely to admire his novel.

Also like Narayan, he depicts his female characters as immensely more energetic and assertive than his male ones, who tend to be intimidated before women's ferocity or their erotic appeal. Such charity and affection as occurs in this novel is largely confined to the men. Mrs. Pathak and Mrs. Asrani—the two neighbor women on the first floor who fight constantly over their shared kitchen space—are almost indistinguishable from each other. Both have cowed their well-meaning but humble husbands into submission in ways that recall a great deal of older prefeminist fiction.

The first lines of the book establish the satirical tone of the rest: Mrs. Asrani is concerned not for Vishnu's own sake but because his dying is creating an unpleasant mess on the stairs. She leaves tea for him not because it will do him any good—he's incapable of drinking it at this point—but because it is a "propitious" act, one that she believes will earn her religious merit. All the various ostensibly charitable gestures the characters make toward Vishnu are similarly useless or self-centered. Vishnu is in no shape to spend the money Kavita leaves for him, and Mr. Jalal embraces him not to make Vishnu feel better but to absorb some of his supposed divinity for his own benefit, in the process dragging his sheet off the dying man—a sheet provided not so much to comfort as to conceal him. Every single item bestowed on him during the story is taken by someone else: the money, the mango, and the sheet.

In these and other ways, Vishnu helps reveal the basic self-centeredness and isolation of the other inhabitants of the building. Hardly any relationship depicted in the novel is really intimate with the exception of Mr. Taneja's with his late wife, and his continued longing for her has done nothing but blight his existence and turn him away from the world and the possibility of a new marriage.

Vishnu is the most isolated of all, for the high point of his existence seems to have been a one-sided love affair with Padmini, a heartless prostitute who granted him her body just once in return for having stolen his employers' automobile to give her a ride to a popular honeymoon spot. She relentlessly exploited his doglike devotion to her, but his thoughts still circle obsessively back to her mocking beauty. The only real love he has experienced came from his mother, who liked to play the game of asking which of the many avatars (incarnations) of Vishnu he thought he was today. Years of musing on these roles has led his mind to wander in his final hours into speculation that rather than simply dying as an ordinary mortal he may be in the process of becoming the god himself. He imagines himself climbing the stairs, making his spiritual ascent story by story (in both senses of the word "story") until the very end; but in fact he is lying on the first-floor landing from the beginning of the novel until the moment he dies. The passages that seem to suggest otherwise are meant to be understood as his dying fantasies.

Eighteen-year-old Kavita imagines that she has transcended the limitations of her Hindu family by finding true love with the Muslim boy from upstairs, Salim. But her ideas of romance are entirely derived from popular Bollywood movies, many of which are cited by title in the book. Suri's father worked for many years as an assistant director of music in the vast Bollywood (Bombay film) industry, and in the Bombay of his youth there was no television, only the movies, which had a powerful effect on many of the people who eagerly viewed them. In a culture where the ideal is arranged marriage between young people who barely know each other, the wild passions and stories of forbidden love portrayed by Bollywood are eagerly consumed fantasies, but hardly sound guides to real life. Kavita throws away what may in fact be her best chance at happiness simply because eloping with Salim is more romantic, more cinematic.

Their relationship triggers the climactic scene of the novel in which the enraged mob of Hindu residents assaults the deranged Mr. Jalal, whose attempts to pacify them by explaining his conversion experience on the stairs is treated by them as arrogant blasphemy—and plagiarism to boot. More than one critic has pointed out that although Suri may have followed in Narayan's footsteps for much of the time, in this climactic sequence he delves frankly into Indian interreligious conflicts in a way his predecessor never had. His portrayal of formerly peaceful neighbors being transformed into a murderous mob has been reenacted only too many times in modern Bombay, and elsewhere.

Vishnu, although a pathetic failure in life and a drunk, is in some ways treated with more respect by the author than the other characters. His memories and longings are treated sympathetically, and the conclusion of the novel even suggests that his religious visions are perhaps not entirely deluded—although Suri deliberately leaves unclear whether we are to take the final scene literally. In it Vishnu recognizes and becomes reconciled with his most famous avatar, the blue-skinned, flute-playing Krishna, and prepares to be reborn. If this seems unjustified by the otherwise mostly skeptical tone of the work, we should not be too surprised. Suri himself has affirmed that despite becoming intrigued with Hinduism, he still considers himself an agnostic. Yet that is how he chooses to end the novel: with a religious vision.

But before deciding the ending is sincere, consider the earlier scene in which Vishnu imagines his entire preceding life and the events of the novel as a sprawling Bollywood movie he is watching with his beloved Padmini.

Like a typical Bollywood production it has featured romance, melodrama and comedy, feuds, fights, and an elopement, all punctuated by music. Should we read the final scene with Krishna as the true ending of which the movie version was an illusory foreshadowing? Or are both equally products of Vishnu's disordered mind, despite the fact that the narrator tells us Vishnu has died before that final version? Or does the story inhabit some uncertain fictional space, hovering in the realm of the imaginary, neither entirely credible nor flatly impossible? Readers will differ, and Suri means them to.

Once the various characters and their relationships and motivations are sorted out, the novel is not really difficult to follow. Suri's style is polished and assured, not overly ornate or obscure, and vividly evokes the various settings and characters depicted in the novel. Whether or not the reader finds it absorbing will be determined by personal taste. The following notes offer some suggestions for those intrigued enough to keep reading but feel the need of an occasional bit of explanation.

Very little Indian fiction in English except for that written by the Marxist-influenced social realist Mulk Raj Anand deals in any detail with the struggle for existence of India's poorest city dwellers. Starving peasants can be given a certain romantic gloss by writers who do not have to live among them, but urban beggars and outcasts like Vishnu are liable to be treated as rubbish in the background, if their existence is acknowledged at all. Suri stresses that Vishnu's status is a function of class, not caste. In sophisticated urban centers like Bombay, economic and religious divisions are far more important than the largely discarded traditional caste system. The story of Short Ganga conveys vividly the trap in which a poor woman can be caught whose daughters need dowries in order to get married. She has virtually enslaved herself to accomplish this one task, and shows how the very poor can scrape by, extorting pitiful sums from those even more wretched than themselves.

The grinding misery and limited horizons of such people is vividly depicted in the novel as well in the story of Nathuram, the second-floor landing dweller who scraped together the price of his beloved portable radio (called a "transistor" in the old-fashioned slang of the time), although one wonders how he could have afforded to keep it supplied with batteries. There are no Anands or Gandhis crusading for the downtrodden in this novel; the other apartment dwellers take the wretchedness of the poor for granted and judge them by how useful they are for their own purposes. Their verdict on Vishnu is that he has been generally unsatisfactory and his dying agony is now an irritating nuisance.

In his first vision, Vishnu remembers his violent, intoxicated father who turned the usually joyful celebration of Holi into a traumatic incident that will haunt him for the rest of his life. Holi is a favorite holiday for children, who run around throwing colored powders and squirting tubes of colored liquid on other people. It can also, however, involve the consumption of a marijuana-infused drink called *bhang*, which has a bad effect on his father.

The first Bollywood title mentioned, in Chapter 2, *Main Chup Rahungi*, was one of the biggest hits of the very popular Meena Kumari playing a young woman seduced, impregnated, and abandoned by a wealthy industrialist. The film was released in 1962. Readers interested in tracing other movies mentioned in the book can easily find information about them on the Web.

Mr. Asrani's rounds of visits to various places of worship are not so much a spiritual quest like Mr. Jalal's as an attempt to keep his bases covered out of a pervasive sense of guilt. But although his guilt motivates him to perform ceremonies of atonement everywhere, it does not motivate him to acts of charity, and he quickly repents having agreed to cooperate with Mr. Pathak in summoning and paying for the ambulance. Suri has said that when he was working on the book he got stuck at the point where the ambulance arrived, because he couldn't imagine how to continue if Vishnu were carried off; but his eventual solution creates a delicious satire: the neighbors are just charitable enough to create a fuss and furor that disrupts the old man's final hours but not charitable enough to really do him any good.

The passage depicting the developing relationship between Kavita and Vishnu shows her maturing from a fun-loving little girl into a desirable young woman. Like his adoration of Padmini, this is a one-sided relationship. He is infatuated with her, whereas she is at best entertained by the fact that he makes her feel attractive. Kavita is more romantic than Padmini, not mercenary like her, but neither one really cares for Vishnu. Padmini's heartlessness is underlined when she refuses even to have her picture taken with her pathetic suitor. When he asks if he can come into her room, she says it depends on whether he can pay—and of course he cannot.

At the "kitty party" (a card party where the "kitty" is the pot made up of the money of the various women playing), we hear the story of Mrs. Jaiswal, who had a brief career in films. In India a "silver jubilee" film is one that has run for twenty-five weeks, one popular measure of a hit. None of the other characters is as intimately involved in the world of Bollywood film as she, but few of them are entirely untouched by it.

The scene in which Vishnu, obsessed with young Kavita, follows Salim and her up to the roof, must have taken place some time earlier, when he was still mobile. Its place in the sequence of events will become clear as the story of the romance between the two young people unfolds. The hint that this is the past is the phrase in the first paragraph: "It is the night he fell asleep, waiting for her to come." Throughout the novel the past tense is used for present events, as is conventional in fiction, but the present tense is used for his memories of the past. His vivid vision of disposing of Salim and claiming Kavita for himself is a fantasy of the sort that will occupy his mind more and more in the pages that follow. This dream of love is followed by the prolonged farce involving the arrival of the ambulance, which underlines how thoroughly unloved Vishnu really is.

While his neighbors are trying to have him taken out like the garbage with minimal cost to themselves, he is dreaming of his mother's stories of the incarnations of "Jeev" (meaning "individual human spirit"), which are supposed to teach him to transcend the material world. But his instincts are as greedy as his neighbors'—the part of the story he likes best is the stage of Jeev's existence where he lives in self-indulgent luxury.

At the end of Chapter 3 he begins his imaginary ascent of the building. Although actually unable even to move, he fantasizes floating effortlessly up the stairs, and in subsequent scenes he will rise higher and higher—in his mind.

Suri does a masterful job of depicting the marriage of the Jalals from their two very different perspectives. Ahmed sees himself as kindly condescending to liberate and enlighten a humble and neglected girl whom he will transform into a progressive modern woman. She sees herself as tied to a blaspheming, egotistical oaf who doesn't understand the first thing about her, even before he goes mad. Her piety has little depth, however. She exercises her Muslim duty of charity (*zakat*) by writing routine checks, not by improving the lot of the wretches inhabiting the stairwell in her own apartment building.

Mr. Jalal identifies with Akbar, the greatest of the Mughal emperors of India ("Akbar" means "great," so the common designation of him in English as "Akbar the Great" is a bit redundant). He reigned from 1556 to 1605. Enough is suggested in the book to justify this admiration, but Indian readers will also know that he ruled over a golden age in the arts, was a painter, patronized great poets and musicians, and commanded the construction of the palace complex of Fatehpur Sikri, one of the sublime masterpieces of architecture. Born a Muslim, he rejected his father's militant, intolerant version of Islam, inviting representatives of various faiths to debate their beliefs before him, and finally creating a synthetic religion that all could join in. However, he was also a supreme egotist who carved out a prominent role for himself as an object of worship in the new faith.

Mr. Jalal's spiritual quest is similarly depicted as self-centered, as he neglects the simplest acts of kindness toward his wife while indulging himself in painful but pointless ascetic practices. It is normal for pious Muslims to fast during the daylight hours of the month of Ramadan ("Ramzan"), but once the sun sets, feasting is in order. The self-discipline of the day is balanced by the communal celebration of the night. But Mr. Jalal makes fasting into an obsession for its own sake. However, his extreme aversion to pain makes him a poor candidate for martyrdom, and his quest is depicted as a farce.

When Mrs. Asrani accuses Salim of being an "Eve-teaser," she is using a common term in India for a man who sexually harasses women. Note that the women's magazine Kavita reads is called *Eve's Weekly.* Using "Eve" to stand generically for "women" may seem odd in this non-Christian society, but remember that Eve is also the first woman created in Muslim belief.

Having a horoscope calculated is a traditional preliminary to setting up a suitable arranged match, and the reference Mrs. Asrani makes to henna refers to the practice—increasingly popular these days in the United States—of using it to paint elaborate designs on the bride's hands before the wedding. But the reference to "blackening her face" is not literal; she is warning her that her behavior will soon cause her to lose her reputation. But the metaphor is based on a literal strong bias in favor of light skin among most Indians. Note that the worst sort of marriage the astrologer can predict is the sort that will produce girls—dark-skinned girls.

The second scene of Vishnu's ascent, in Chapter 4, makes clear that it is imaginary by depicting the floating Vishnu gazing down at his own body, which is still lying on the landing. Mrs. Jalal's thoughtful offering of the services of the hospicelike Hajrat Society is introduced seemingly to demonstrate the bigotry of her Hindu neighbors, who would rather let Vishnu suffer than let him be cared for by a Muslim institution. It is worth noting that the city Suri grew up in is currently governed by Hindu supremacists who have exacerbated the always difficult relations between themselves and the Muslim minority in the city. Liberal Hindus like Suri might well be inclined to depict bigoted Hindus harshly. (Many such liberals object to the 1995 renaming of Bombay as "Mumbai" after a Hindu deity, and they refuse to use the new name.) Hindus dispose of their dead by cremation; Muslims, by burial.

Vishnu's vision of the ants reminds him that he should regard them as potentially reincarnated human beings, but they also lead him back to the scene with Padmini and the barfi. When Mrs. Asrani stamps on the ants, he imagines them screaming in agony. In the last paragraph of this chapter, Vishnu looks down to see Mr. Jalal crouching next to his own body, which is still resting below on the stairs.

Surdas, whose story is alluded to in Chapter 5, is a famous Hindu saint and poet who was so inflamed with desire for women that he endangered his own life and their honor until he voluntarily blinded himself to end his obsession. He was the subject of a popular movie in 1942. Muharram is a Shi'ite Muslim observance commemorating the martyrdom of Husain ibn Ali, in which some of the more devout worshipers slash or flail themselves. Both these provide impossible role models for Mr. Jalal, whose attempt at self-flagellation is a comical failure. Note that one is Hindu, one Muslim; it's not the specific religion that fascinates him: it's the suffering involved.

When he joins Vishnu on the stairs and compares himself to St. Francis, whom he presumably discovered in his eclectic reading among the world's religions, he is probably referring to Francis's habit of personally caring for lepers, going so far as to lick their open wounds with his tongue. Mother Teresa ran a famous hospice for the poor of Calcutta where she and her nuns cared for the dying. Mr. Jalal has the right idea, but his execution of it makes his supposed good deed worse than useless.

Just when Mr. Jalal is at his most ascetic, Vishnu lying next to him is being his most fleshly, recalling the day when Padmini finally allowed him to have sex with her. The scene is described vividly, in explicit language that some readers have found objectionable, but it is perfectly justified by the vivid hold the experience has on Vishnu's memory, a memory of what may well have been the only satisfying sexual encounter of his life. It makes sense that he would lovingly recall every detail. To have him vividly recollect squashing ants and then be vague about sex would have been highly unrealistic. The scene ends on an ominous note as he drives past Bombay's famous *dakhmas,* the structures the English call the "Towers of Silence" where the Parsis traditionally deposited the corpses of their loved ones to be picked clean by vultures (until a steep decline in the vulture population recently put an end to the practice).

Saraswati Chandra (1968) is a historical romance in which the famous actress Nutan plays Kumud, a young woman who dutifully but sorrowfully saves the family honor by marrying the man her family has picked out for her even though she has lost her true love, so it is not surprising that Kavita should think of her. Note that her first reaction to Pran is not to him as individual, but to his first name, which reminds her of the popular actor Pran Kishen Sikand, who played numerous villains over the years, like many Bollywood stars going under a single name professionally. Later, when she fantasizes about him, it will be as a player in an imaginary movie. Note how this sadly absurd and doomed courtship is juxtaposed with Vishnu's similarly doomed idyll with Padmini.

India is not the only culture where it is considered bad luck to speak well of your children, for fear of attracting the punishing "evil eye" that will punish your pride by afflicting the person who's been praised. The same notion is also common among many ethnic groups around the Mediterranean. Suri reveals Mrs. Jalal's style of parenting by the fact that she is unable to remember the last time she praised her son. When she's told at the shrine that only close relatives of those under treatment inside can be admitted, she lies to get in, although it does her little good.

While Kavita is constructing her imaginary romance as a Bollywood movie, Vishnu is having his own revelation of the power of women, personified by Lakshmi, who, along with the other gods, reveals herself to him through odors, mostly the odors of foods. This is a passage some find one of the most beautiful in the book and others scorn as overly exotic. Most Indian writers incorporate passages on foods in their works, but Suri does so more often than some. He has acknowledged in interviews that one of his favorite activities is cooking.

At the beginning of Chapter 7 Kavita displays her immaturity by giving her opinion that Pran has not turned out to be the Prince Charming of her dreams, but that like Cinderella's magical coach, he has turned out to be "a bit of a pumpkin." But Salim's caution and his greed in snatching the money Kavita leaves for Vishnu are ominous signs. It is becoming clearer and clearer that he is not really the man of her dreams either, but she's not mature enough to acknowledge the fact.

It is typical of Mr. Jalal that in beginning his search for faith he should consider even Buddhism and Jainism, both tiny minorities in modern India. It is typical of Suri's general skepticism that Mr. Jalal's temporary "enlightenment" should turn out to be nothing more than some schoolchildren playing with a mirror, and that his grand vision of Vishnu will turn out to be a bit of ill-remembered reading. Traditionally, Vishnu is regarded as the giver of life, the protector of humanity, so it is ominous that Jalal's first thought on imagining that he may have become the god is to fantasize about the destruction he could wreak by withdrawing his protection. Vishnu is often worshiped through his ten principal avatars, several of which are mentioned somewhere in the novel and annotated in the glossary. So in Chapter 8 it is not surprising that a man who believes he has become a god imagines he is Vishnu. Meanwhile the fictional Vishnu of the novel is imagining his own avatars in a magical scene with his mother, followed by a scene of divine communion with Lakshmi inspired by the mango that has been set down next to him—a mango that Short Ganga will soon devour.

Clearly neither one of these would be gods is going to do anybody any good. A saint who tries to drive reason out of his skull by banging it against the floor is no role model. The eighteenth-century Irish philosopher George Berkeley was indeed a fervent antimaterialist, and like Suri was a mathematician as well, so he is undoubtedly the philosopher Mr. Jalal is trying to think of.

In the middle of Chapter 9 we finally make the acquaintance of the mysterious Mr. Taneja, who stays all day in his room playing Bollywood songs that remind him of his late wife. Readers starved for a character to identify with in this novel are prone to seize on him as sympathetic, but he is far from perfect, as we shall see.

The story of the early days of their marriage is delightfully told, with Sheetal's shifting stand on vegetarianism wonderfully illustrating her humanity. The long-postponed lovemaking depicted is a feature of several accounts of Indian arranged marriages. Although convention dictates the couple should engage in sex on the first night, it is hardly natural that a couple with no sexual experience or education who have barely met each other would easily make love just because they have gone through the marriage rites. In a long tradition of stories, newly married couples slowly fall in love after the ceremony, and this is one of them. He almost loses her when he strikes her, but he has the courage and devotion to defy his mother in sticking by her, a devotion rare in other fictional husbands with carping mothers.

At the beginning of Chapter 11, just after the account of how Vinod lost Sheetal, Vishnu loses the mango that had made him think earlier of sex and he remembers losing Padmini. Clearly the novel has entered the traditional final phase in which the aging Hindu theoretically sheds worldly attachments, including attachments to loved ones.

When Kavita is snuggling with Ahmed on her bed, she keeps having distracting thoughts. It is not reassuring that his nuzzling reminds her of the goat sacrificed for the great feast of Bakr-Eid held to commemorate the end of Ramadan, and for a moment she is tempted to sacrifice him, but unfortunately her romantic bent prevails.

Vishnu's vision of himself as Kalki, the final avatar of Vishnu who will come at the end of the world to punish evildoers, stresses the least loving and merciful side of the god he has identified with. It is interesting to note that like Death in the Christian book of Revelation, he rides on a white horse. His vicious imaginary anti-Muslim acts foreshadow the emotions of the Hindu mob that will in the next chapter surge up the stairs in pursuit of poor Mr. Jalal.

At the end of Chapter 12 we hear the absurd story of the third and final landing dweller, Thanu Lal, whose reputation for holiness blew away with the ash on his forehead. He is not an inspiring example for the would-be god Vishnu. But Suri continues to treat Vishnu's visions with a certain amount of dignity. As the novel approaches its end, his mixture of the absurd and the moving becomes more intense.

In Chapter 13 we get the rest of Vinod's story, which reveals he has abandoned good work on behalf of the poor simply to avoid the threat of another romantic relationship. The swami he follows, rather than preaching self-sacrifice, urges first the satisfaction of desire. He speaks like an acute psychiatrist, however, in diagnosing Vinod's problem as anger—but the grieving man at first rejects this insight. Clearly his devotion to his late wife's memory, even though he may have eventually found a measure of peace personally, is doing the world very little good. This passage is followed by the story of the mob, which brilliantly mixes slapstick with pathos, and with Mr. Jalal achieving enlightenment while hanging from the balcony above while a bird right out of a cartoon pecks at his knuckles: he's been a bad father and husband.

As he makes his final imagined ascent to the top of the apartment house, Vishnu seems to remember the tradition according to which Brahma surrendered the right to be worshiped when he falsely claimed to have had a vision of Shiva's crown, which becomes the symbol of Vishnu's power. In Hinduism, as in many ancient religions, the creator god is not the object of actual worship, his role being relegated to the distant past. Worshipers in these traditions tend to be more engaged with gods whose human qualities they can relate to, like Vishnu, the most popular member of the Hindu Trinity. But at the height of Vishnu's triumph, as he looks for the consorts he loved in his various incarnations, he realizes he is face to face with Yama, the god of death.

In Hinduism, gods can die, as the avatars of Vishnu have, repeatedly; but death is important primarily as a gateway to rebirth. How one understands this final struggle will depend on how seriously one takes the theme of reincarnation. Is Vishnu merely deluded? Or is he undergoing a necessary preparation for rebirth? Given his poor performance of his *dharma* (duty) in this life, it seems unlikely from a conventionally pious point of view that he would experience any very great increase in status in the life to come.

Like Mr. Jalal, he is mistaken in thinking he has entered heaven. The white light that blinds him as darkness gathers is not a vision of God; in his mind it is the glare of a movie projector that has been unspooling the story of his life. Continuously Suri switches back and forth between exalted imagery and farce, never allowing the story to tilt entirely in one direction or the other.

Suri refuses to let his book end in darkness. Kavita for the first time seems to experience an emotion produced from the memory of a real event and not a movie—the encounter with Vishnu recounted at the beginning of the book. And following his death, Vishnu meets Krishna. Maybe.

But clearly Suri is not out to convert anyone. He has wanted to give us a tour of the lives and minds of a number of vividly imagined characters, and in that he has succeeded admirably. We may not have learned what follows life, but we have learned a bit more about what some people experience in life. And that's really all we should expect of a novel.

SELECTED BIBLIOGRAPHY

Birnbaum, Robert. "Interview: Manil Suri." *Identity Theory* (Feb. 2001). <http://www.identitytheory.com/people/birnbaum4.html>.
   A lengthy, very interesting interview.

D'Erasmo, Stacy. "Interview; Solving for X." *New York Times Book Review* 28 Jan. 2001: 9. <http://www.nytimes.com/pages/books/index.html>. Fill in "solving for x" in the "Book Search" blank.
   Interview with the author emphasizing his relationship to his hometown of Bombay.

Gorra, Michael. "The God on the Landing." *New York Times Book Review* 28 Jan. 2001: 8–9. <http://www.nytimes.com/pages/books/index.html>. Fill in "the god on the landing" in the "Book Search" blank.
   Positive review of the novel with comparisons to other writers.

HarperCollins. "Reader's Guide: The Death of Vishnu." <http://www.harper collins.com/catalog/guide_xml.asp?isbn=006000438X>.
   Information about the author, study questions, and other useful materials from the publisher of the paperback edition.

Sattar, Arshia. "The Death of Vishnu." *Persimmon Asian Literature, Arts, and Culture* (Summer 2001). <http://www.persimmon-mag.com/summer2001/bre_sum2001_10.htm>.
    Generally negative review, making points similar to those made by several South Asian critics.

Suri, Manil. *The Death of Vishnu.* 2001. New York: HarperCollins, 2002.

Tharoor, Sashi. "Epitaph of a Small Winner." *Los Angeles Times* 4 Feb. 2001. <http://events.calendarlive.com/top/1,1419,L-LATimes-Books-X!ArticleDetail-20054,00.html>.
    Positive review by a distinguished Indian American writer, setting Suri in the context of other such writers.

W. W. Norton. "The Death of Vishnu by Manil Suri." <http://www.manilsuri.com/>.
    Much more sophisticated and detailed than the HarperCollins site, including a biographical sketch, an explanation by the author of his research sources for the novel, photos of places described in it, and an illuminating interview with Michael Cunningham.

Glossary of Terms

This glossary provides definitions of non-English terms that occur in the novels and stories discussed in this book. Words clearly defined in their original context are not included. Nor are those that may be readily found in an English unabridged dictionary. Not all possible definitions are provided: only those appropriate for the works are discussed. When a plural form is used in the source, the plural is used here rather than the singular form, to make the definition easier to find. When looking for further information on a term, note any alternative spellings given here. Recipes for the many foods discussed are readily available on the Web. Simply type the name of the dish and the word "recipe" into your favorite search engine. For an explanation of many words ending in *-ji,* see the entry for that suffix.

Abba. Father.

achaar. Pickle.

achha. Good; OK.

achhoot. Untouchable.

achkan. Long fitted coat worn by men, buttoning down the front.

adabs. Polite formal greetings.

afargan. Vessel for performing Parsi fire ritual, or the ritual itself.

aga-ni-dahdi. Cotton candy (literally "grandfather's beard").

agarbatti. Incense sticks.

ahimsa. Nonviolence; a term much used by Gandhi and his followers.

Aiyyo. Expression of dismay.

Aiyyo kashtam.   Literally, "Oh, what a pity!" but also used as a reproach: "How could you say that!"

Aiyyo! Mon! Mol!   Aiee! Boy! Girl! (literally, "Son! Daughter!").

Aiyyo paavam.   What a pity!

Ajantha.   Famous Buddhist cave site, more commonly spelled *Ajanta,* and also the brand name of an audio equipment company in Kerala named after it.

Akalis.   Violent dissenting sect of Sikhs.

alayti-palayti.   Spiced chicken livers and gizzards; a Parsi delicacy.

Allah.   Arabic word for "God." Characters uttering this name may usually be presumed Muslims.

Allah-o-Akbar.   God is great. The beginning of the *adhan* (Muslim call to prayer).

Allay edi.   Isn't that so? (rudely).

almari.   An *armoire,* an upright wooden wardrobe.

aloo masala.   Spiced potato stew.

Amhoo.   Moo.

Amma, Ammi.   Mother.

ammoomas.   Grandmothers.

Angarkha.   Old-fashioned full, long-sleeved long coat for men fastened with loops.

Anglo-Indian.   People of mixed British and Indian heritage; often looked down on both by the British in the colonial era and by other Indians, although their knowledge of English gave often gave them access to jobs and privileges. English novelists like Rudyard Kipling who lived in and wrote of India are usually also referred to as "Anglo-Indian." "Indo-Anglian" has been invented to describe authors of completely Indian descent who write in English.

Angrez.   English.

anna.   Old coin introduced by the British and no longer in use; one-sixteenth of a rupee. Each anna can be divided into four *paisa* (see later).

Anthurium andraeanum.   Large waxy flower that originated in Colombia but is now common in Hawaii and other tropical locales. The most popular varieties are red (*rubrum*).

antimony.   See *kohl.*

Apa.   Sister.

Appoi and Ammai.   Mother's brother and mother's brother's wife.

appoopans.   Grandfathers.

arrack.   Distilled liquor made from the same fermented tree sap as palm wine.

array, aray, arré.   Hey!

ashram.   Also asrama. Traditional Hindu religious retreat where people may stay, study, and meditate.

ASP.   Assistant Superintendent of Police.

Aurangzeb . . . Jehangiri. Of the Muslim Mughal emperors, the two most renowned for persecution of Hinduism.

aven. Uncle; mother's brother.

avial. Spicy vegetable stew cooked in coconut milk; a typical Malayali dish.

Ayurvedic. Traditional Indian medicine.

baaj. Parsi prayer for the dead, at funerals, and to commemorate death anniversaries.

baba. Father, or in other contexts, baby.

babu. Originally a title of respect for an educated man, but used sarcastically by the British to label Indian officials who they found comically inept in their attempts at English respectability. It now has some of the connotations of an "Uncle Tom" in India.

Babur. Founder (1483–1530) of the Mughal Dynasty, which ruled much of India until the British arrived.

Bacchan, Amitav. More often Amitabh. Greatest of all Indian film stars; later a successful director of spectacular adventure films.

bachao! Help!

badmash. Thug, criminal, "bad guy."

badmashi. Rascality; bad behavior.

Baghavadgita. Section of the great Hindu epic the *Mahabharata,* in which Krishna explains to the warrior Arjuna his duties (and, by extension, those of all humanity). It is a crucial sermon in Hinduism, much commented on and studied. More commonly rendered as two words in English: *Baghavad Gita.*

Bahen. Sister or cousin.

Baijee. Female head of household.

Bakreid. See *Eid.*

baksheesh. Originally Persian; especially used in the Middle East to refer to tips or bribes to expedite services; also used to refer to alms given beggars.

bandh. General strike used as a political protest.

bania or **banya.** Small shop, or keeper of a small shop.

banian or **banya.** Title of a merchant caste. Often refers to an Indian trader associated with a British firm, used as a way of implying that a person is corrupted by the wealthy imperialists. Banians are often thought of as greedy and scheming.

banyan. Large fig tree (*Ficus benghalensis*), commonly regarded as sacred in South Asia, which spreads by dropping new roots down from its sprawling limbs and establishing new trunks. Banyans can grow to an enormous size, creating a whole grove beginning with one tree.

banyas. See *banian.*

baraat. Groom's family and friends who go together to his wedding.

baradari. Public audience hall.

barey (or **baray**) **mian.**   Respectful term of address to an elder; analogous to "honored sir."

barfi.   Popular fudge-like, milk-based sweet.

bas.   Enough.

bas kar.   Stop it.

batata.   Potato.

bechareh.   Bengali epithet for a pitiful person.

BEST.   Brihanmumbai Electric Supply and Transport, which runs tramways and buses in Bombay.

Beta or **Betay.**   Son.

betel nut.   Technically the areca nut, usually wrapped with a betel leaf smeared with various flavorings; chewed like gum as a mild stimulant that turns the user's lips and saliva bright red. This confection is called *paan*. The cutting up of areca nuts and preparing them for consumption is often featured as a womanly activity in fiction, although they are also often bought from street vendors.

betelwallahs.   Vendors of *paan*, wrapped in betel leaf.

Beti.   Daughter.

Bhagavad puranas.   Ancient Sanskrit narratives, the most famous of which tells the story of Krishna.

bhaghwan.   Honorific term used in addressing a god-filled holy man.

bhai.   Brother or cousin; often used figuratively to mean "friend." The leader of a Sikh temple may also use this title.

bhajan.   Devotional song.

bhakras.   Fried spice cookies.

bhang.   Beverage made with marijuana, often using alcohol.

bhats.   Kind of dish made with rice.

Bhel-puri.   Puffed-rice dish made with spiced potatoes.

bhistee.   Water carrier.

bhung.   See *bhang.*

bibi.   Respectful term used to address a woman.

bidis.   Small hand-rolled cigarettes.

bilkool.   Completely.

billa.   Tomcat.

bindis.   Red dots worn on the foreheads of women.

biryani.   Dishes made of meat or vegetables layered with spiced rice.

Bismillah.   In the name of God (way of swearing honesty).

Bitia.   Daughter.

bolay se nihaal.   "Only those who say it will prosper." Standard phrase that precedes the Sikh greeting, *sat sri akal* (see later). A statement of the superiority of Sikhhism.

bonhomie.   French for "good nature."

bouledogue.   French spelling of "bulldog."

Brahmo Samaj.   Radical reform movement in late-nineteenth-century Hinduism rejecting many traditional beliefs and social practices, comparable in some ways to Unitarianism in Christianity or Ethical Culture in relation to Judaism.

Brindaban.   Village where Krishna loves Radha.

brinjals.   Eggplants.

buckwas.   Nonsense, lies.

budmash, badmash.   Criminal, gangster, ruffian.

budmass.   See *badmash.*

buffalo.   Everywhere except in the United States, this word designates the water buffalo, a common beast of burden in India (the American "buffalo" is properly called a "bison"). Its meat is also eaten on occasion. Unlike the cow, it is not considered sacred.

bulbul.   Bird often mentioned for the beauty of its song in poetry. The South Asian bulbul is actually unrelated to the European nightingale, but nevertheless in literary translations, *bulbul* is often translated as "nightingale" because the two words have similar musical associations.

bund.   Dikes.

bun muska.   Buttered bun, eaten with tea.

burning ghat.   Riverside steps where funeral pyres are burned.

burqa burkha, or **burkah.**   All-enveloping covering worn by a woman observing purdah when she goes out.

bustee.   Slum.

cadju.   Cashew.

cannae Canna indica.   Ornamental plant, originated in tropical America, but has been commonly cultivated in England, under the name "Indian shot."

carrot-ma-gose.   Carrot stew with meat.

caste no bar.   When progressive-minded Indians advertise for a bride or bridegroom, they use this phrase to indicate they are not determined to marry their offspring to someone of their traditional caste.

chacha.   Uncle (father's brother or cousin).

chachen.   Father.

chachi.   Aunt.

chakka velaichathu.   Jackfruit jam.

Chakravartyrajagopalachari.   Chakravarti Rajagopalacharya was the first Indian governor general of independent India and sometimes teased for the length of his name, often spelled as one word.

chappals.   Sandals.

chappatties.   The *chappati* is the best known of the many fried flat breads of India, the most basic of foods.

Chappu Thamburan.   A spider.

chaprassi.   Doorman.

charpoy.   Simple four-legged bed made of a woven support stretched over a wooden frame.

chatta.   Blouse.

chaudhry.   Village headman.

Chemmeen.   A 1965 film directed by Ramu Karia based on a novel by Thakazhy Shivashankar Pillai. The film was made in Malayalam, and its English title was *The Wrath of the Sea.*

chenda.   Drum traditionally used in Keralese temples and to accompany Kathakali dancers.

cheroot.   Cigar.

Chetan and Cheduthi.   Older brother and older brother's wife (Malayalam).

chhee.   Exclamation of surprise, something like "yikes!"

chhi-chhi, chi-chi.   Expression of disgust used as a euphemism for excrement.

chick.   Woven window screen.

chickoo.   Fruit of the sapodilla, or common rubber tree.

chilli.   British/South Asian spelling of "chili," chili peppers.

Chit-Pavan.   High-caste, light-skinned Brahmins, mostly from Maharashtra, often stereotyped as conservative and snobbish. More often spelled as one word: *Chitpavan.*

choli.   Brief form-fitting blouse, worn with a sari.

choorail or churail.   Witch.

choot.   Vagina.

chootia.   Literally, the same as *choot*, but commonly used as an insult describing a stupid person, like French *con*.

chotela.   Long braid into which women traditionally put their hair.

chowk.   Square, or market in such a square. A *police chowki* is the small police outpost.

chuddar or **chador.**   Large head covering and veil, hiding much of the body; worn by conservative Muslim women.

chumpee.   Type of massage, more often spelled *chumpi*.

chunam.   Lime made from oyster shells, used in *paan*.

churidar.   Traditional narrow, tight-fitting trousers with folds near the ankles; worn by both men and women in North India.

communalism.   This word, which implies cooperative sharing in the West, has almost the opposite meaning in South Asia. It refers to prejudices held by the followers of one community against others, and to the resulting violence. Communalism has erupted repeatedly in Indian history, most notably during the vast massacres that accompanied Partition in 1947. Communalism in South Asia is primarily religious, although it can also be based on caste or ethnicity.

coomas. Parsi cake made of semolina, almonds, eggs, and cardamom.

copra. Dried coconut meat.

crèche. UK term for day-care center.

crêpe suzette. Properly *crêpes suzette*; sugared crepes cooked in butter and flamed in an orange liqueur sauce—very European.

curds. Curdled milk product somewhat like cottage cheese, used in many forms in South Asian cooking; usually called *paneer*.

Daab-Chaab. Squeeze-fondle.

Dadi. Paternal grandmother.

dai. Traditional midwife, healer.

dakoo. Bandit.

dal. Various lentils and other grains; a staple of the Indian diet.

danda goli. More often *goli* or *guli danda*. A boys' stick game a bit like cricket. The batter tries to hit the thrown *guli* with the *danda* (stick).

dandy. Sedan chair borne on two poles by bearers. More often spelled *dandi*.

darbar or **durbar.** Royal assembly.

darshan. "Auspicious viewing"; spiritual blessing gained from seeing a sacred image or person.

Dasara. Also called Dussehra or Durga Puja. Ten-day autumn festival dedicated to the powerful goddess Durga. In Tamil Nadu, the holiday also honors Lakshmi and Saraswati.

dervish. Sufi mystic known for whirling meditation in which the worshipers feels filled by the spirit of God. The word literally means "gateway"; the dervish becomes a gateway to the divine.

devi. Goddess.

dhal. See *dal*.

Dhammapada. Collection of sayings attributed to the Buddha.

dharmic. Appropriate for one's *dharma*: the duties and restrictions associated with a particular caste or other group.

dhobi. Also dhobi-wallah. Laundryman.

dholak. Long double-headed hand drum.

dhoti. Loosely draped piece of cloth that functions as traditional trousers for Indian men.

dhurries. Cotton carpets.

dishoom-dishoom. Noises of fighting in movies, like "sock-pow" or "wham-bam."

Divali or **Diwali.** Very popular fall Hindu festival of lights. Also known as *Deepavali*.

djinni. Plural of *djinn*, usually rendered "genie" in English; a magical creature in Islamic tradition capable of performing wonders, featured in many fantastic tales.

dopatta or **dupatta.**   Head-covering scarf worn by women.

duffa ho!   Get lost!

dustoor.   Parsi priest.

Eid al-Fitr (also known as Eid Mubarak, or "Great Eid").   Joyous holiday celebrating the end of the Ramadan fast. Two months and ten days later comes *Eid al-Adha* (also known as *Bakreid*, or "Lesser Eid"), which marks the end of the period of pilgrimage to Mecca.

ekka.   Small horse-drawn cab; more enclosed than a *tonga*.

Emergency.   Period during which Indira Gandhi suspended constitutional law and ruled in a dictatorial fashion (1975–77).

Ende Deivomay! EEE sadhanangal!   My God! What creatures!

faroksy.   Parsi prayer recited on the fourth day after a person's death as part of the funeral ritual.

fez.   Round, tapered, flat-topped felt hat, formerly commonly worn by Muslims.

FIR.   "First Information Report"; the initial report of illegal activity at a local police station.

funtoosh.   Finished, done, over.

gaadi.   Wheeled platform.

gaanth.   Knot.

gaddi man.   A *gaddi* can be any number of wheeled vehicles, but is probably here a wheelbarrow in which the yard man carries his gardening tools.

Gandhi cap.   Simple white cloth hat worn by members of the Indian National Congress to demonstrate their nonsectarian attitudes, because it was not traditional for either Muslims, Hindus, or Sikhs. Worn by India's first prime minister, Jawaharlal Nehru, it became a symbol of independent India.

gandoo.   Insulting term for a gay man.

Ganesh or **Ganesha.**   Popular pot-bellied, elephant-headed God, remover of obstacles.

Ganpati.   Another name for *Ganesh*.

Ghagra Choli.   Festive women's outfit consisting of an ornate blouse and flowing skirt, often decorated with mirrorwork.

gharara.   Loose pajamas.

ghat.   Stairs, especially those leading down to a body of water.

Ghats.   The Eastern and Western Ghats are mountain ranges that run along India's southern tip, outlining the two coasts and meeting in the South. They take their name from their stairlike appearance.

ghazals.   Short poems in Urdu consisting of rhymed couplets, often dealing with love. The form was imported into South Asia from Persia. Often performed as songs.

ghee.   Butter simmered slowly until the milk solids are removed, leaving pure butterfat behind. Ghee, easily preserved without refrigeration, is the classic cooking oil for fine dishes, although too expensive for everyday use.

ghoongat or **ghoonghat.**   Veil covering the hair and the upper half of the bride's face. Traditionally she is supposed to catch her first glimpse of her groom when the ghoongat is lifted during the wedding ceremony, and—ideally—fall in love.

git mit.   Bit of slang referring to English as unintelligible jargon, "jabbering." More often *git pit.*

gobi aloo.   Spicy stewed potato and cauliflower dish.

godown.   Commercial storehouse.

gola.   See *ice gola.*

goonda-giri.   Hooliganism, gangsterism.

Goonda Raj.   Government of thugs, gangsters.

goondas.   Bullies, thugs.

gota.   Delicate, intricate appliqué, usually applied in gold, to hems of fancy garments.

got-pit, sot-pit.   See *git-mit.*

gram.   Grains of various kinds, particularly lentils, that play an important part in the Indian diet. Parched gram are roasted lentils, a common snack food. "Horse gram" (*Dolichos biflorus*) is eaten by humans as well as animals.

Granth.   Sacred book of the Sikhs, often referred to reverently as *Sri Guru Granth Sahib.*

granthi.   Sikh priest.

gulab-jamuns.   Deep-fried balls made from flour and boiled-down milk soaked in rose-flavored sugar syrup; a popular confection.

gulli-danda.   Game in which the player uses a foot-long stick (the *danda*) to scoop a small piece of wood (the *gulli*) over his opponents' heads while they try to catch it.

gurdwara.   Sikh temple.

guru.   Spiritual teacher. There is an enormous variety of such teachers advocating different disciplines and paths, fittingly for the many-sided nature of Hinduism, which does not have one orthodox path that must be followed by the worshiper. Sikhs especially revere ten founding gurus of their own tradition, and "in the name of the guru" is a common greeting among them.

guruji.   See *-ji.*

haandi.   Traditional clay cooking pot.

hai, hai.   Exclamation: "oh oh," "alas," or, depending on context, "yes, yes."

Haider or **Haidar.**   Literally "lion," but a term applied to Ali by Shi'a Muslims.

haikim.   Healer.

Hai Ram.   Religious phrase in praise of Lord Rama, but also often used as a simple expletive of shock or despair: "Oh God!" "Ram" is often used as a generic term for "god" without necessarily specifically referring to Rama. These were reputedly Gandhi's last words as he was shot. Also spelled *He Ram* or *Hey Ram.*

halwa, halva.   Fudgelike candy that can be made of various ingredients. The classic kind is made of ground carrots. Related both as a food and as a word to Turkish/Jewish *halvah.*

hanh.   Yes, right.

hanhji.   Yes, sir.

haram-khor.   Literally "scavenger," but used like "bastard"; also implying "bum" or "parasite."

haramzadi.   Bastard.

Harey Ram.   "O Lord Rama." *Harey* is more often spelled "Haré" in English.

harijans.   Literally "children of God"; a euphemism for "untouchable" promoted by Gandhi.

harmonium.   Small organ consisting of a rectangular box with a bellows attached to the rear that is worked by the left hand while the right plays the keyboard in the front. Brought to India by British missionaries, but adopted as a popular instrument to accompany vocal music and now manufactured and found mainly in South Asia.

Hasan, Husain.   Shi'a Muslims consider that Ali's son Hasan inherited his father's designation by Muhammad as leader of the faithful, although he chose not to claim it. This status then passed on to his son, Husain, who was murdered. His martyrdom is observed each year by Shi'as on the tenth day of the month of Muharram with grieving processions chanting the two men's names.

haseen.   Beautiful.

hashish.   Concentrated marijuana resin.

hathiyar.   Literally weaponry, but used as a euphemism for penis.

havaldar, hawaldar, or **havildar.**   Sergeant; police officer ranking just above a common constable.

Heer and Ranjah.   Traditional Punjabi story of two Muslim lovers separated by their feuding families.

henna.   Dye traditionally applied decoratively to women's hands and feet in much of the Muslim world, especially as a preparation for marriage.

hero-ka-batcha.   Movie star (literally "son of a hero").

hijra.   Transsexual. Because they can make a living dancing and singing at weddings, some poor men castrate themselves to become hijras; but the term can also refer to natural hermaphrodites.

hilsai.   Variety of shad much prized in cooking.

Holi.   Wild and extremely popular Hindu holiday involving people tossing colored powders and squirting colored water on each other.

hookah.   Water pipe in which tobacco smoke is filtered by being bubbled through water and inhaled from an attached hose.

houris.   In traditional Muslim belief, beautiful virgins who will serve the saved in Paradise, particularly martyrs for the faith. Often used as a metaphor for extraordinary female beauty.

hus-mukh.   Smiling or laughing face.

Huzoor Master.   Title of respect used by a servant.

ice gola.   Snow cone.

idi appams.   Steamed rice noodle cakes.

idli.   Steamed rice and lentil patties; often eaten for breakfast.

imam.   Leader of a Muslim mosque, chosen for his learning and piety; in his role as a religious scholar, he may also be referred to as a *mullah.*

imambara.   Muslim building used for prayer, lectures, and community celebrations, including those involving feasting. It is not so specialized or solemn as a mosque.

Inquilab Zindabad!   Long live the Revolution!

Ividay!   Over here!

jackfruits (or jakfruits).   Very large sweet fruit common in South and East Asia.

jaggery.   Palm sugar; often used in the making of sweets.

Jai Hind.   Victory to India.

jalebis.   Made of slightly fermented batter dropped in a swirling ribbon from a pastry bag into hot *ghee,* fried until it is crisp, then briefly soaked in hot syrup flavored with saffron. The result is a very popular sticky bright orange confection.

janab.   Sir.

"Jana Gana Mana."   Indian national anthem, written by Tagore, named after its first line addressing God as the ruler of all human minds.

jaripuranawalla.   Junk collector and dealer.

jati.   Caste or subcaste.

Jay Prakash Naraya.   Former left-leaning leader in the independence movement who helped lead agitation against Indira Gandhi during the Emergency period.

-jee.   See *-ji.*

jhopadpatti.   Shantytown slum.

ji.   Yes. Not to be confused with the suffix *-ji.*

-ji.   Suffix added to names and titles as a sign of respect. Gandhi, for instance, was often referred to affectionately by his colleagues and others as "Gandhiji."

jibba.   Simple shirt worn by men.

jutka.   Simple horse- or bullock-drawn carriage, often used as a taxi.

jyotishis.   Astrologers.

kaaj.   Matchmaking.

kabootur, oodan/dekho, usman.   "Pigeon, fly/Look, sky."

kaccha house.   Simple mud or stone house, distinguished from a more sophisticated *pukka* house.

kaccha roads.   Unpaved roads.

Kailas.   Mythical mountain in the Himalayas; the home of Shiva and other gods; comparable to Mount Olympus in Greek mythology.

kajal.   See *kohl*.

Kalyug.   Also Kali Yuga. Despite its faith in vast repeated cycles of life, death, and rebirth, Hinduism is not immune to the pessimism that marks other faiths in regarding the present age as one of extreme decline from an earlier period of virtue. The current age, comprising all of recorded history, is the Age of Discord (*Kalyug*), in which the universe inclines toward destruction.

Kama Sutra.   Elaborate ancient sex manual by Vatsyayana, not well known in India until it was discovered and publicized by the British, especially through Sir Richard Burton's popular translation. It has given an undeservedly erotic impression of Indian culture to many Westerners.

kameez.   Short dress (or long shirt) worn traditionally by northern Indian and Pakistani women, worn over loose drawstring pants called *salwar*. The ensemble, called a *salwar kameez*, is traditionally topped with a large scarf called a *dupatta*.

kanji.   Rice gruel.

kappa.   Cassava root, cooked in various ways.

karakuli cap.   This simple gray lamb's wool hat became Jinnah's symbol as the not dissimilar Gandhi white cloth cap became Nehru's.

kathakali dancer.   Classical folk dance of Kerala, performed, unlike Bharata Natyam, exclusively by men playing both male and female parts.

kavani.   Top part of a two-piece sari, draped diagonally across the upper body, worn by Christians in Kerala.

karma.   In Hinduism your behavior in this life earns good or bad karma in the next, creating your destiny in reincarnation. Good karma is generally earned by following your *dharma*—the proper behavior associated with your age, gender, and caste.

kebabs.   Spiced, marinated meat, ground or in cubes, usually grilled on a skewer.

keech-keech.   Squawking.

keto.   "Thanks, *keto!*" said. "*Valarey* thanks" means roughly "Thanks a lot, OK?"

khichri.   Porridge, sometimes made of split peas and rice.

khuda hafiz.   May God protect you; a term of farewell.

keto?   Have you heard?

khaddar or **khadi.**   Coarse homespun cloth. Gandhi advocated wearing it to support local industries and to boycott imported English goods. A person who could afford better cloth but is wearing *khaddar* before Partition is supporting the independence movement. Indian politicians later wore it to symbolize their solidarity with the common people.

Khali-pili bom marta.   Making a fuss for no reason.

khas.   Perfume fixative derived from vetivert (*Anatherum zizanioides*). Its roots are also are woven into products, including mats, which, when wet, emit a pleasant odor.

kho or **kho-kho.** Complex sort of tag game played by teams.

kholi. Room.

Khuda Hafiz. May God protect you.

khus fibre. Mats are woven of fragrant *khus-khus root* (vetiver; see *khas*), used to cool and perfume the air.

kirpan. Curved ceremonial sword traditionally worn by Sikh men.

Kishore Kumar. Extremely popular Hindi comic actor and singer (1929–87).

kismet. Arabic term for "fate," used principally by Muslims.

kodam puli tree. Variety of tamarind tree bearing fruit shaped like a *kodam* or round bowl.

Koh-i-noor. Enormous diamond now part of the crown jewels of England, but it originally belonged to the Mughals, Muslim rulers of India.

kohl. It is popular to put black kohl (powdered antimony) around the eyes of both children and women to enhance their appearance.

Konarak. The temple of the sun at Konarak in Orissa is famous for its artwork, including some erotic sculptures mentioned in Lahiri's "Interpreter of Maladies."

koojah. Earthenware water jar.

Koran Sharif. Holy Qur'an, the sacred book of Islam.

korma. Kind of stew made with yogurt.

Koshy Oommen. Typical Syrian Christian name.

Kotha. Former royal district of Lahore became a center for prostitution, so "Queen-of-the-Kotha" means something like "Queen of the whores."

kothmeer-mirchi. Classic chutney made of chopped green chilies and cilantro.

Krishna. This blue-skinned *avatar* of Vishnu is famous as a handsome, charming lover. Often shown with his beloved Radha or others of the many women he loved.

kulah. Tight boat-shaped cap worn by the bridegroom, around which the turban is wrapped.

kum-kum. Bright red powder traditionally used to make the round *tilak* dot on women's forehead and the red streak in the parting of married women's hair.

kunukku earrings. Type of ancient Christian Keralite jewelry, usually gold earrings consisting of a short thin chain with a small ball hanging from it.

kurta. Long shirt worn by men over trousers, reaching well beyond the knee.

Kushumbi. Jealous woman.

kusti. Woolen strand wrapped around the waist three times over an inner garment, worn by Parsis; made of seventy-two threads.

kuthambalam. Inner part of the Hindu temple, just outside of the inner sanctum.

kutt-kutt. Chatter.

Kya karta hai? Chalo, jao! What are you doing? Get out of here!

laddoo. Common sort of confection made of lentil flour, ghee, raisins, nuts, and spices.

lakh. 100,000

lala. Man who cares for children, or a clerk. In Rushdie's story "Good Advice Is Rarer Than Rubies," the lala is a gatekeeper.

laltain. Tallow stick: a stick daubed with fat that can serve as a feeble sort of torch.

lambardar. Village headman.

lamprais. Complex spiced meat and rice dish stuffed into banana leaf packets and baked. A dish invented by the Dutch immigrants to Sri Lanka.

Lanka. The island where the demon Ravana dwelt, to which Hanaman, the monkey-king, built a miraculous bridge in *Ramayana*. Usually identified with Sri Lanka.

lathi. Long wooden pole used as a weapon, most often wielded in fiction by police beating demonstrators.

loata. See *lota*.

Locusts Stand I. Derived from a misunderstanding of a Latin phrase [*locus standi*] meaning "[legal] standing," but "no locusts stand I" comes to signify something like "homeless" or "unloved" in Roy's *The God of Small Things*.

lohar. Iron smith.

lota. Metal water pot.

Love-in-Tokyo. A 1964 hit movie directed by Pramod Chakravorty featuring a young woman whose ponytail was held by two beads on a rubber band. Like Estha's puff, her "fountain in a Love-in-Tokyo" becomes Rahel's symbol in *The God of Small Things*.

lund. Penis.

lungi. Sarong-like leg covering tied around a man's waist.

maaderchod. "MF-er."

Madiyo? Is it enough?

ma-gose. Suffix to various names of dishes meaning "with meat included."

Mahabharat or **Mahabharata.** Classic Sanskrit epic, telling the story of a great world-spanning war; a sacred text of Hinduism.

maharaja. Sanskrit for "great king," but used generally to denote any royal prince in India.

maharani. Queen, wife of a maharaja.

Maharishi. Great seer, spiritual teacher.

Mahatma. "Great Soul"; title especially associated with Indian independence leader Mohandas K. Gandhi.

maidaan. Large open field, often used for playing games.

Ma-ji. Literally, Honored Mother, but when used to a stranger, means "Lady."

malai. Cream sauce, often made of coconut milk.

Malayalam.   Principal language of Kerala.

malida.   Traditional Parsi sweet made with nuts and dried fruits.

mallung.   Mixture of spiced shredded ingredients, usually greens. In *Running in the Family*, Ondaatje lists it as one of the dishes in his favorite meal.

Mamoon.   Mother's brother or cousin (female form: *Mumani*)

mangosteen (*Garcinia mangosiana L.*).   Tropical fruit with a thick dark red skin.

Manu.   Author to whom the traditional Hindu rules on caste and gender are ascribed.

Marnikarnika-ghat.   One of several sets of stairs leading down to the sacred river Ganges where cremations are performed. Devout Hindus consider cremation in this spot to be especially propitious.

masala.   Mixture of spices and other flavorings used in a recipe.

masala wada.   Spicy pancake made with *chana dal* flour batter and ground coconut.

Mashah Allah.   God be praised (expression of admiration).

matar panir.   Curry made with homemade farmer's cheese and peas.

Matka.   Illegal but popular lottery in Bombay, named after the earthen vessel from which cards are supposedly drawn to produce winning numbers.

meen.   Fish.

meeshas.   Moustaches.

mela.   Fair.

"Meri Dosti, Mera Pyar."   "My Friendship, My Love"; hit song from the 1964 movie *Dosti*.

meri kasam.   Literally, "my oath," but used as an affectionate term of address to woo a woman, swearing one's devotion.

mirasin.   Female folk performer.

mittam.   Courtyard.

mochi.   Shoemaker.

Modalali Mariakutty.   Landlord Mariakutty.

mohalla.   Community, neighborhood.

mombatti.   Candle.

moulvis.   Islamic religious teachers. More commonly spelled *maulvis*.

morcha.   Political demonstration.

Mr. T.   Nickname of a physically huge black character in the popular 1980s television series *The A-Team*.

mubarak.   Arabic word meaning "blessings." Used as congratulations.

Muezzin.   One who calls the worshipers to prayer at a Muslim mosque.

Muharrami.   Shia Muslims in Pakistan hold a large number of colorful processions to holy sites early in the month of Muharram, particularly on the ninth and tenth.

mui.   Rotten (as an insult).

mullah.   Muslim religious scholar, respected as an authority because of his learning.

mundu.   Single piece of cloth arranged as a sort of loose pair of trousers, tied at the waist, worn by both men and women (although women add upper garments to it). Longer than the *dhoti*.

Musslas.   Muslims.

Mussulman.   Old-fashioned term for Muslim.

Naga spear.   Spectacularly barbed weapon created by the formerly fierce members of the Naga people of the Himalayas in the northeast of India.

nah.   Isn't that so? Often rendered in English by Indians as "isn't it?"

namaskar or **namaste.**   Traditional Indian gesture of greeting, bowing slightly, palms together and upright, a little like traditional "prayer" posture in the Christian West. The person performing the gesture accompanies it by saying one of these words, meaning literally "I bow to you," indicating respect for the other person.

nar admi.   Powerful man.

nasbandi.   Sterilization; more generally, birth control.

naswar.   Kind of flavored chewing tobacco product made of powdered leaf, lime, and other ingredients.

Nataraja or **Natarajah.**   "Lord of the dance"; an incarnation (*avatar*) of the creator/destroyer god Vishnu, who danced the world into existence and dances it to destruction. The most famous images of him are derived from the tenth-century Chola Dynasty bronzes depicting him as a four-armed dancer in a ring of fire.

Natya Shastra of Bharat Muni.   Classical treatise on Indian classical dance, including *Bharata Natyam* (*Natyam* means "dance"). Bharat Muni may have lived as long ago as 500 BC, although estimates of his period range as far forward as AD 200.

nautch.   Dance. A "nautch-girl" is a dancing girl.

nawab.   Noble title; source of the English word "nabob." Sometimes used sarcastically of pretentious persons.

Naxalite.   Radical and sometimes violent Maoist groups, including notably the Communist Party of India (Marxist-Leninist), commonly referred to after the locus of their origin in Bengal.

Neem tree.   Popular in India for its medicinal properties. People often use a neem twig as a toothbrush. Botanical name: *Azadirachta indica*.

nikah.   Muslim wedding ceremony.

nimak-haram.   Traitor; treacherous.

Nonvegetarian.   So common is vegetarianism in India that the meat sections of menus are routinely labeled "non-veg."

nullah. Rivulet.

nuss. Testicle.

nussbandhi. See *nasbandi*.

O baap! baapu-ré! baap-ré-baap-ré-baap! Oh God! (expression of dismay).

O babu, ek paisa day-ray! Loosely: Spare change, Mister? (Literally, Oh sir, give me a *paisa*.)

Odissi. Famous classical dance form from the eastern Indian state of Orissa.

O, me-kiya! I say! (expression of astonishment).

Om Jai Jagdish Hare. O Lord of the whole universe; first line of a hymn known as the "Universal Aarti," most commonly addressed to Vishnu.

Onner Runder Moonner. One, two, three.

Orkunnilley. Don't you remember?

Orkunnundo. Do you remember?

Ooty cupboards. Ooty is the popular name of Udhagamandalam, a luxurious "hill station" in the Nilgiri Mountains of Tamil Nadu, just across the border from Kerala in the northeast. Furniture from there would have belonged to wealthy visitors.

Oru kaaryam parayettey? Shall I tell you something?

O vay! Oh, you!

paagal. Crazy.

paagal-ka-bacha. Crazy kid (literally, "son of a crazy person").

paakit. Wallet.

padayas. Gangsters; criminals.

paisa. The smallest of coins, less than a penny. Plural *paise*. Also formerly spelled *pice*.

pakispetti box. Delicate wooden box.

pakora. Vegetable fritters made with chickpea flour batter.

palkhi. Elaborate palanquin.

pallavi. Final section of a traditional Carnatic (South Indian) classical musical work, set to various *talas,* or time schemes, which can be quite complex.

pallu, palloo. Loose end of a sari that is draped over the shoulder.

pan or **paan.** See *betel nut*.

paneer. Indian cottage cheese; used in many dishes.

pao-bhaji. Spicy potato stew. The *pao* is the bun traditionally eaten with this dish.

papadum. Thin wafer made out of lentil flour and quickly fried in oil. Also spelled *pappadum*.

paratha. Fried flatbread, often stuffed with spiced vegetables (and generally an unsuitable companion to chocolate sauce).

Paravan.   Untouchable; the Malayali equivalent of *pariah.*

pariah.   Traditional term for the "untouchables" of India. Stray dogs are sometimes referred to as "pariah dogs."

parippu vadas.   Also vadai. Spicy fried patties made of ground lentils. A common street food.

Parsis.   Zoroastrians, called "Farsis" in Persia (Iran). They have only small communities in India, necessarily somewhat inbred.

Parvathi.   Consort of Shiva. Also spelled *Parvati.* According to one story about a previous incarnation of this goddess, she was so insulted by her father's discourtesy to her husband and herself that she leaped into a fire in protest and became *Sati* ("the chaste one").

peepul, pipal, or **pipul.**   Majestic fig tee, also called the "bo tree," particularly associated with religion (in fact, its scientific name is *Ficus religiosa*). Gautama Buddha is said to have sat under a peepul tree meditating before achieving enlightenment in its shelter.

philosopher's stone.   Material believed by alchemists to have the miraculous property of turning baser metals, like lead, into gold. Often used as a metaphor for any magically transformative force.

piaray.   Darling.

pirith.   Buddhist ceremony involving the chanting of sutras.

plantain.   Large firm banana, less sweet than the kind Americans eat on cereal; usually served fried. The peels are tough and very unpalatable.

Poda Patti!   Get lost, you dog!

pokuna.   Pond.

pol sambol.   Sri Lankan equivalent of salsa, made with shredded coconut, chilies, and lime.

prawn patia.   Sour-flavored shrimp dish; traditional Parsi recipe.

Prem Chand.   Distinguished early writer of modern fiction in Hindi and Urdu (1880–1936). Also commonly spelled as one word: *Premchand.*

puggaree.   Turban.

pugree.   Rental security deposit.

puja.   Worship, or act of worship.

pujari.   Priest who performs *puja.*

pukka.   Proper, traditional.

pukka Sahib.   Proper gentleman.

pulao, pulau.   Dishes based on rice, often including spiced vegetables or meat. Derived from the Persian-Turkish word *pilaf,* which traveled to the West.

pundit.   Also pandit. Master of some art or discipline, regarded as a teacher. The word has been adopted into American English with the rather different meaning "political commentator."

punkah.   Fan. Often a large fan used to cool the rich in the tropical heat, traditionally worked by an impoverished *punkah-wallah.*

purdah. Seclusion of pious upper-class women, especially in Muslim families. Women in purdah are traditionally not allowed to go out except to weddings and to visit close relatives, and they may not socialize with unrelated males in their own homes. Now rare except among the most conservative South Asians, although more common in Pakistan than in India.

puri-bhaji. Spicy fried potato dish (*bhaji*) eaten with deep-fried whole wheat flat breads (*puri*).

pyol. Broad front porch of a house, right on the street. A place for doing business, socializing, or even learning lessons.

rabri. Sweet milk pudding.

raga. Traditional pattern in classical Indian music, analogous to a Western musical scale or mode.

Raga Shahana. Raga traditionally performed at weddings.

Rahim. The Merciful (title of God in Islam).

Raj karega Khalsa, aki rahi na koi. Roughly "Sikhs rule, unchallenged." Litany attributed to Guru Gobind Singh and recited daily in Sikh places of worship, but also a slogan associated with Sikh nationalism.

raksha bandhana. Red thread tied around the arm. This is the Indian term for a similar tradition. The Sri Lankan word is *pirith noola*. Such threads are donned on various occasions, including weddings.

rakshasa. Demon.

Ramayana. Also Ramayan. Popular Hindu epic of the kidnapping of Rama's wife Sita by the demon Ravana and her eventual rescue. The story is known by every Indian and endlessly retold in every conceivable art form, including comic books. The most popular version is by Valmiki and was written some seventeen hundred years ago. A Tamil version by Kamban from the eleventh century was the basis of Narayan's retelling of the tale.

rani. Queen; wife of a *rajah*.

ras-malai. Balls of sweetened, flavored *paneer*, boiled in milk and served cold. More often spelled as one word: *rasmallai*.

Ravan or **Ravana.** Ten-headed demon; villain of the *Ramayana*.

rickshaw. Simple two-wheeled carriage pulled by hand in the old days, but more commonly by a pedaling bike rider today.

rogan josh. Classic stew made with tomatoes and spices, usually with lamb.

roti. Thin flatbread something like a flour tortilla, commonly eaten with all sorts of foods.

RSS. Rashtriya Swayamsevak Sangh, a Hindu supremacist organization agitating against tolerance for Muslims.

rulang. Rulang is usually a nut-based candy, but Ondaatje seems to be confusing the name with Ogu Ruolong, a Dutch Sri Lankan egg dish.

rupee. National currency of India. If a rupee seems to be worth much in a story, it is probably very old, or the person involved is desperately poor.

rusticated. Kicked out of school (literally "sent to the country").

rutputty. Rundown but interesting.

saala. Bastard. *Saali* is the feminine form.

Saar vannu. *Saar* is a phonetic spelling of an Indian pronunciation of the English word "sir." "Chacko Saar vannu" means "Mr. Chacko has arrived."

sabaash. Great; congratulations.

sadhu. Holy man.

saffron. Precious spice used in festive dishes and also to dye holy robes yellow.

sahab or (more often) **sahib.** Title of respect claimed routinely by the British in India (their wives were called *memsahibs*), but often used to address socially exalted Indians in South Asian fiction. Sometimes used sarcastically by Indians addressing other Indians who are acting pretentiously, like English people.

sait. Merchant, more commonly spelled "seth."

saithan. Demon; related to the word "Satan."

salaam. Short for *assalamu alaikum* in Arabic; the common greeting among Muslims, meaning "may peace be upon you."

salwar. Loose drawstring pants. See *kameez*.

samosas. Deep-fried pockets of dough stuffed with various spiced fillings.

sandal. Fragrant sandalwood is traditionally burned in funeral pyres.

Sanjay Dutt. Popular Hindi film star who rose to prominence in the mid-1980s.

sanyas. Ideal fourth stage in life for a pious Brahmin: isolated meditation.

sarangi. North Indian bowed string instrument; traditionally used to accompany singers.

Saraswathi. Also *Saraswati*. Goddess of education and learning generally.

sari. Dominant traditional costume of Indian women, consisting of an elaborately wound and draped single length of cloth.

Sardar. Literally "chieftain," but now used generally as a title of respect for all Sikh men.

sarkar. Government.

saros-nu-paatru. Parsi prayer repeated for the first three days after a person has died (according to Parsi belief, the soul remains attached to the earth during that period).

sati. Ritual in which a widow would be burned alive on her husband's funeral pyre. The woman herself could also be referred to as a sati. Now illegal and rare in India; spelled *suttee* in older English sources.

Sat Sri (or Siri) Akal. "The Great Timeless Lord." Sikhs normally greet each other with this phrase praising God's greatness, similar to how Muslims say "Salaam" upon meeting.

Scheherazade. Brilliant princess who narrates the tales in *A Thousand and One Nights*. Because she keeps her husband awake night after night with her storytelling, perhaps Rushdie had in mind the wakeful nature of the baby girl in "The Courter" when he gave her this name.

sehrai. Veil of flowers worn by the groom as he approaches the bride.

sepahi. Soldier.

Sepoy. British spelling of *sepahi,* referring to a private soldier in the Indian army.

Shahenshahi. The most common Parsi calendar.

shaitan. Devil.

shak bhaji. Spicy vegetable dish.

Shalimar. Famous garden built by the Mughal emperor Shah Jehan for his beloved wife Nur Jahan, the same woman for whose tomb he had erected the Taj Mahal.

shalwar. See *salwar.*

Shankaracharya's *Mohamudgar.* Also called **Shankara.** The ninth-century theologian Shankaracharya was one of the most influential thinkers in Hinduism, expositor of the Advaita school of Vedanta, which stresses that all we see is ultimately Brahman. Founders of the *Brahmo Samaj* such as Tagore's father were inspired by this tradition, but Tagore uses him as an example of a thinker who rejects the reality of the physical world. He is also briefly referred to in Desai's story "Studies in the Park."

Shatrughan Sinha. Bollywood star famed for playing villains in various films beginning in the 1970s.

shaven Sikh. Sikh men are supposed to leave their hair and beards untrimmed, but some do shave, and they are considered apostates, often called "cut-sird Sikhs."

sheesham. Tree grown for its dense wood, suitable for making furniture and carving (*L. Dalbergia sisso*).

Sherpa. Tibetan mountain guide.

sherwani. Long collarless coat with flared skirt worn over narrow pants by men.

shikara. Small boats that serve as water taxis on the lakes around Srinigar.

shikari. Hunter.

shlokas. Verses from Sanskrit sacred texts.

Shubrat Shab-e-Baraat. Festive Muslim holiday held fifteen nights before the beginning of Ramadan.

sitar. Stringed instrument most typical of North Indian classical music.

Sivaji and Aurangzeb. The Marathi chieftain Sivaji led an uprising against the notoriously fanatical Muslim Mughal emperor Aurangzeb in the seventeenth century.

slokas. See *shlokas.*

sola topee or **solar topee.** Originating in Africa, the traditional round "pith helmet" worn by British explorers and administrators to shield them from the tropical sun, but also by Indian officials who identified with the British.

soo-soos. Urine; also a childish euphemism for penises.

soosoti.   Same as *soo-soo*.

string hoppers.   Fine spaghettilike material used in Sri Lankan cooking.

sudra.   Besides designating a member of a laboring caste, this word can designate a soft muslin undershirt worn by Parsis; more often spelled *sadra*.

sundaas.   Toilet.

Sundari kutty.   Little girl named Sundari.

swami.   Holy man; religious teacher.

swaraj.   Self-rule; independence.

sweeper.   Polite term for the traditionally untouchable cleaners who not only sweep streets and houses, but—most defiling—deal with human waste. "Sweeper" is often used in fiction as a synonym for "untouchable."

tabala or **tabla.**   Traditional two-drum set used in classical North Indian music performances.

takht.   Wooden divan; bed platform.

takth.   Throne.

tamasha.   Literally a kind of folk theater, but often used figuratively of any great commotion or splashy display, in much the same way English speakers refer to something being turned into a "circus."

tandoori pomfret.   Fish baked in a traditional clay oven (tandoori)—very Indian.

tasbih.   Traditional string of Islamic prayer beads, something like a rosary, but treated much more casually.

Tata-Bata.   *Tata* is a brand of Indian-made vehicles. *Bata* is probably added playfully to it.

tazias.   Replicas of the tombs of the Prophet Muhammad's grandsons.

tea.   As in England, often refers to a meal featuring tea and food rather than the drink alone.

teapoy.   Small, usually three-legged table for serving tea.

teelo or **tilak.**   Decorative red dot between the eyebrows on the forehead.

tiffin.   Lunch or between-meal snack.

tika.   Decorative forehead dot, sometimes jeweled; fancier than the traditional red paste *tilak* mark.

ting-ting! Baba, ak-koo!   Loosely, "Cootchie-coo, baby!"

toba!   Shame!

toddy tapper.   Toddy is the sweet fermented sap of various palm trees, tapped to provide a cheap alcoholic drink.

tonga.   Small horse-drawn vehicle.

transistor.   When transistors were first used to replace tubes in portable radios, the miniature sets that resulted were popularly referred to as "transistors."

transmigration.   Short for "transmigration of souls": reincarnation.

trunk road.   Highway connecting towns, which turns into the main street inside them.

ullu-kay-pathay. Fool (literally "offspring of an owl"; owls are considered foolish in South Asia).

Upanishads. Sacred Hindu texts.

Urdu. National language of Pakistan and of many Muslims in India.

vallom. Small boat.

vanaspati. Vegetable-based oil used as a substitute for ghee in cooking.

vasanu. Hot, spicy fudgelike candy; a Parsi specialty.

vazir, more often **wazir** or **vizier.** Adviser to a Muslim ruler.

Vedanta. Mystical philosophical branch of Hinduism.

veshya. Prostitute.

vevichatu. Cooked.

Vijayanthimala. Popular Bollywood star of the 1950s and 1960s, trained in the *Bharata Natyam* classical dance tradition. Her name is usually spelled *Vyjayanthimala.*

wada. Savory pancake; in South India spelled *vadai.*

wah, wah. Exclamation of approval, sometimes translatable as "bravo!"

walla. Also wallah. Person. A *bidi* vendor is a *bidi-walla.* The man who washes your laundry (*dhobi*) is a *dhobi-walla.* The operator of a rickshaw is a *rickshaw-walla.* The word linked with *walla* indicates one's job.

wheatish. "Wheatish" means "wheat colored," a golden brown. This adjective is commonly used in matrimonial advertisements in India to indicate the person being described is not dark skinned.

wog. General term of abuse used by prejudiced English speakers to designate people of other races they consider inferior, especially South Asians. Probably derived from "golliwog," an old term for a cartoonish black doll.

Yaa Ali. Oh Ali. An invocation of the name of Muhammad's cousin and son-in-law, greatly honored in Shia Islam.

yaksa, yakka, or **yaka.** Demon.

Yé Akashvani hai. This is All-India Radio.

zamindar. A landlord. During the colonial period, zamindars exercised considerable local authority, and in fiction can be assumed to be influential persons.

Zamzama. Famous 14-foot eighteenth-century cannon now on display in Lahore. Small replicas of it are still popular souvenirs for tourists.

zemindar. See *zamindar.*

zenana. Women's quarters in which the female members of the household are sequestered from unrelated males. Victoria Zenana Hospital is a hospital for Muslim women.

zhumzhum. Slang word expressing a nice tingly feeling.

zindabad. Long live.

zulum. Persecution.

Index

About the Author

PAUL BRIANS is Professor of English and Coordinator of Humanities at Washington State University. He has published extensively on nuclear war fiction, and has written numerous study guides on the literature of Africa, India, and the Caribbean. He is editor-in-chief of *Reading about the World*.